# Dancing with the Devil
*as you channel in the light!*

David Ashworth

## Survival For Healers & Therapists

CRUCIBLE

First published by
Crucible Publishers,
Norton St Philip, Bath BA2 7LN, UK
e-mail: sales@cruciblepublishers.com
www.cruciblepublishers.com


© David Ashworth 2001
First published 2001
Reprinted July 2002
Reprinted August 2004
Reprinted February 2007

ISBN-10 1-902733-03-7
ISBN-13 978-1-902733-03-6

Set in 10 on 12pt Goudy Old Style & Frutiger

Typeset by Christian Brett

Cover Illustration by Nick Clarke

Printed in Finland by WS Bookwell

# DEDICATION

When I was a younger man, my Father, many times told me he wasn't afraid to die. This was his opening line, usually while we were in the car on the way to work, where I had no chance of escape. Not wishing to be drawn in, and somewhat embarrassed and dismissive of his attempts to engage me in a serious conversation, on matters which I knew to be of the nature of eternal life, knowing as I did that he was a deep soul and felt 'connected', I would respond with a none committal "hmmm". His Fatherly patience outweighed his urgent desire to have his son communicate with him, as I now desire that same communication with my own son, which is yet to be forthcoming.

Dad had been brought up in the New Jerusalem Church Religion which celebrates the enlightenment of the scientist and spiritual visionary Emanuel Swedenborg. As a small boy, I remember he was actively involved in his church, playing the organ on occasion and acting in their amateur dramatic productions. I also discovered very recently, that he was also a popular lay preacher, even at the tender age of 16. Although I attended a Church of England School myself and always felt there was more to this thing called life than met the eye, I never found any answers in religion, even though I have on many occasions, especially in my late teens and early twenties, considered the ministry as a career. Religion has never really played a part in my life, although there has always been a recurring calling to something which I could not describe, but which I know religion would not fulfil. As I have aged, I can see now that the calling was of a spiritual nature. However, as my spiritual aspect has opened up, I have begun to read the various teachings of many religions. Also, I have been able to see the hidden messages therein, which I fear are not visible to the many, due to their inability to experience those things which are outside the immediate physical realm. In short, many people have yet to experience the unfolding of their spiritual dimension or connection in order to see that light which Jesus told us was the living God, who was in all human beings.

Dad often quoted one of his favourite poems of which the subtleties are mostly lost on younger and more flippant souls, such as I was then, and so I would like to leave these lines within these pages in remembrance of the great meaning they had to him and his love of mankind, both of which I am now beginning to understand and appreciate.

## Abou Ben Adhem

Abou Ben Adhem (may his tribe increase!)
Awoke one night from a deep dream of peace,
And saw, within the moonlight in his room,
Making it rich, and like a lily bloom,
An Angel writing in a book of gold:
Exceeding peace had made Ben Adhem bold,
And to the presence in the room he said,
'What writest thou?' The vision raised it's head,
And with a look made of all sweet accord,
Answered, 'the names of those who love the Lord',
'And mine is one?' said Abou. 'Nay, not so',
Replied the Angel. Abou spoke more low,
But cheerly still; and said, 'I pray thee, then,
Write me as one that loves his fellow men'.
The Angel wrote, and vanished. The next night
It came again with a great wakening light,
And showed the names who love of God had blest,
And lo! Ben Adhem's name led all the rest.

I managed to evade Father's desired discussion of his fearlessness of death, for the rest of his life. As a result, and no doubt to my loss, he never had the opportunity to tell me what he knew or had seen.

"I would just like you to know Dad, I have now been there too! See you later".

David Ashworth
Prestwich, December 2000

# PREFACE TO THIS EDITION

*Dancing with the Devil* has been a huge success since its original publication in 2001. It is a book whose core content remains as relevant today as it was when it was first written and it has helped thousands of people to work at a higher level in healing and lightwork.

Barely a few days go by without letters or emails of thanks arriving. The most common comments are 'I just couldn't put the book down' or, 'It's confirmed so much of what I thought.'

Of course, with a bit of luck, people evolve and David and his work have continually and dramatically evolved since the book was first published. His gifts and ability have soared to new heights and his perception has transcended boundary after boundary as his Guides have brought him into amazing realms of understanding about life on Earth and the process of attaining true spiritual evolution.

David is a very down-to-earth person, but when working with The Guides he can see beyond energy structures and into very deep consciousness. He can show you what blocks your pathway into true spiritual evolution.

Using the transformational Essence Programs driven by The Emerald Heart Light and the Wheel of Light energies, he can show you how to move beyond what limits your evolution in this life. The power of The Guides and the Light provides for the ascendance into ever higher states of perfection, allowing the opening of your hidden gifts and talents which in turn enable you to achieve so much more with your clients.

You can keep up to date with David,
his work and teaching by viewing these websites:

www.davidashworth.com        www.emerald-heart.co.uk

# THANKS

I would like to thank many people who have inspired me and unknowingly seeded to me gems of wisdom. Alas, they are too numerous to mention, but they all know who they are.

To Denise, my partner, my lover and my friend, who helps me more than she knows in many different ways, and for reading the first proofs and making me rewrite several parts where she thought normal, intelligent people wouldn't understand my ravings. To those who shall remain nameless for the use of their case histories. To Ivan Fraser of *The Truth Campaign* Magazine, being the first person to read the complete text and give me such glowing and encouraging feedback when I was about to abandon the work. To Malcolm Cawley for help with the reprint. To my editor and publisher Robin Campbell of Crucible Publishers, who's editing taught me that I don't speak the Queen's English as well as wot I thought I did. Apparently, I write without verbs!

Finally to Christian Brett, my former apprentice in an incarnation when he was a mal-adjusted school-leaver and I ran a typesetting business. He came out alright in the end and sweated long and hard at the behest of his erstwhile taskmaster to produce this fine typographical work you now see before you.

*David Ashworth*

# ACKNOWLEDGEMENTS

I would like to give grateful acknowledgement to the following individuals, authors and publishers for allowing me to use extracts from or reproduce their copyright work.

**Nick Clarke** for the front cover design and illustration, the illustration of the Chakras reproduced in the colour section, and the line illustrations.

**Dinah Arnette** for permission to use her copyright photograph of the entity, reproduced in the colour section.

**Dr. Tim Duerden** for permission to use his copyright illustration of *The Subtle Bodies*, reproduced in black and white and in the colour section.

**Norma (Mrs. Edmond) Bordeaux Szekely** and the International Biogenic Society. I.B.S. Internacional, P.O Box 849, Nelson, British Columbia, Canada V1L 6A5, for extracts from *The Essene Gospel of Peace, Book One*. Translated from ancient Aramaic texts by the late Dr. Edmond Bordeaux Szekely.

**The Theosophical Publishing House** and Quest Books of Wheaton, Illinois, for extracts from *The Chakras* by C.W. Leadbeater.

**Finbarr International**, Folkestone, Kent CT20 2QQ, England, for extracts from *Mystic Wisdom for Richer Living* by Dr. Lori M. Poe.

**Society of Inner Light**, 38 Steeles Road, London, NW3 4RG, for extracts from *Psychic Self Defence* by Dion Fortune.

**Gabriel Cousens** M.D., M.D.(H) of the Tree of Life Rejuvenation Center, Patagonia, Arizona, AZ 85624, USA, for permission to quote from his book *Spiritual Nutrition and the Rainbow Diet*.

**Schneelowe Verlagsberatung & Verlag**, D-87648 Aitrang/Germany, with friendly permission from **Lotus Light/Shangri-La**, Box 325, Twin Lakes, WI 53181, USA, for an extract from page 11 of *Reiki The Legacy of Dr. Usui* by Frank Arjava Petter.

**Harper Collins Publishers**, 77-85 Fulham Palace Road, Hammersmith, London, W6 8JB, for extracts from *Jonathan Livingstone Seagull* by Richard Bach.

As one treads the unfolding path of life, one picks up many small treasures, the origin of which can sometimes be lost to one's memory. If I have included any in this book which deserve acknowledgement, I would apologise and be pleased to recognise authorship in future editions. Please let me know.

# CONTENTS

# INTRODUCTION

⌐
He spoke of very simple things - that it is right for a gull to fly,
that freedom is the very nature of his being, that whatever
stands against that freedom must be set aside, be it ritual,
superstition or limitation in any form.

Jonathan Livingstone Seagull

Conversations, encouragement for my observations and a great wealth of
experiences over the past few years have prompted me to write this book. It
could be seen as another book about Reiki, but it goes much deeper than
that. It should be seen as, and in fact is, a first aid manual to surviving all
forms of healing and subtle energy work, but in particular Reiki!

Why should anyone say such a thing … surviving Reiki? Surely Reiki is meant
for healing and saving us — transforming us — how could that be something
which presents any dangers or problems needing survival skills? Well dear
reader, you would be surprised. There are many aspects which remain untold
about working with energy and many unsuspecting students and healers get
into trouble, without the knowledge of how to get out of it again, or where
they can go to for help.

I am a subtle energy worker, my day to day activities are centred around
Geopathic Stress Investigation, Geomancy, Earth Acupuncture, working with
Nature Spirits, Psychic Rescue, Spirit Clearance, Dowsing Healing, Spiritually
Guided Vibrational Healing, Vibrational Spiritual Evolution, Chakra and Aura
Balancing and Repair, Priority Life Issue Diagnosis within the Chakras, Guided
Energy Adjustment at a Vibrational Level to address change, Nutritional
Dowsing and Complementary Health Counselling based around Intuitive
Vibrational Healing. I work with subtle energy almost every single day and
have amassed a wealth of experience in all kinds of subtle energy work.

Subtle energy work is healing work. Healing is my life's work, whether it is
home or office healing using crystals and earth acupuncture; or earth current
and landscape healing, working in co-creation with nature spirits; or clearing
of psychic forces, entities or spirits from a house; or the rescue of healers and
therapists from psychic attack by unknown dark forces; or even dealing with
serious demonic energies and beings. Healing is what I do every day of the

week. Channelling the Reiki energies is an integral part of many of the aspects of the subtle energy work which I engage in, whether straightforward hands-on healing or deep and complex earth acupuncture.

I have been engaged for some time in writing a book on many aspects of subtle energy of which *Dancing with the Devil* began life as a mere chapter. However, my concerns have grown recently, as we celebrated the millennium, (a year too soon) about the quality of teaching and support in some Reiki circles. The lack of knowledge and ability I have observed has lead to, and continues to lead to serious energy system and health problems for Reiki students and healers alike. As I continued to write this particular chapter, it became so long it eventually ended up as this book, of which my editor and publisher, Robin Campbell commented that it was at least the length of two books!

However, there were other aspects which prompted me to pull this out into a book of its own at this time. One of them was when a highly skilled and talented man in many areas of subtle energy work and a Master in more ways than one resigned from the Reiki Association in October 1999. He is a first class Reiki Master, teacher and practitioner with a worldwide reputation, a man who would command the greatest of respect from anyone who had any knowledge at all of healing and subtle energy work. His resignation is important, certainly because of the way he was treated by the Reiki Association, but more than that, because of what is going on in the so called Reiki hierarchy.

In my opinion, politics has no place in healing and therefore no place in Reiki. Some well known Reiki Masters worldwide have found difficulties coming to terms with some of the politics of Reiki and as somebody who values autonomy and freedom of expression, I would be one of them. Reiki is power and, unfortunately, where there is power there is politics. In my time I have also distanced myself from other healing organisations because of their politics, to stand alone and ultimately be judged by the only power which should pass judgement on these matters. I shall have to wait to find out if I have broken any rules or incurred any karmic work to undertake in a later incarnation.

There are those amongst us who would seek to dominate in our position and apply unreasonable rules and regulations to their fellow healers and the practice of their art. There are those whose ego and greed far outweigh their consideration to their fellow man. With subtle energy work, or healing work or light work, whichever you wish to call it, there are no rules except respect for the energy and respect for the freedom of your fellow man or woman. Certainly there should be guidelines to help a student attain skills which will lead them to mastery of their art, but rules have no place in intuitive work. The only other aspect we need to consider is common sense, which most of us have in abundance if only we will allow it to come through. Governments throughout the world dominate and control their subjects with rules, regulations and fear. The healing energies are supposed to be transformational, in as much as their use can reveal to us the truth of our situation on this planet, where control issues dominate our every move, even in what we call the civilised western world or free world. Healers should be leaders in spiritual education, teaching how to transcend the base position of humanity and achieve a higher understanding of spiritual truths. They should help those who are ready to evolve thereby assisting them to receive a glimpse of higher consciousness, guiding and sharing in the freedom of exploration into the esoteric mysteries, which have been denied to so many for so long. Expanding the brotherhood of like minded souls.

There are Reiki Masters who have worked hard to bring forth and share helpful and truthful information for our use and thus have subsequently acquired a high profile for their trouble. Some of these Reiki Masters are now the target of undeserved attention of a legal nature. What is Reiki coming to?

Western Reiki can be traced back through Mrs. Hawayo Takata in Hawaii and Mr. Tujiro Hyashi in Japan to Dr. Mikao Usui, the founder and most recent igniter of the Reiki torch. We have all blossomed from this first seed Usui nurtured during our training, but many of us were told that Mrs.Takata was the last surviving carrier of the Reiki Light and that all other Reiki practitioners in Japan did not survive the second world war.

With the advent of Frank Arjava Petter's work, we now know that Reiki did not die out in Japan, but is thriving, with very many practitioners. Western Reiki practitioners are not recognised by our Japanese counterparts at present, and probably for good reason, but it says something for Frank Arjava Petter's standing that he has been approached by the Japanese Reiki community and allowed to glean some truths for us with the express wish that he pass these on to the west.

In this time of planetary and spiritual evolution, Reiki energy should be the birthright of any man, woman or child who is ready to take that step. However, there has been much controversy and argument over the cost of Reiki training. In terms of energy exchange, an investment of a reasonable sum of money or any item of perceived and agreed value, in return for training is fair. Anyone wishing to further their education in any walk of life would not expect to attend a course without paying a fee. The course tutors have to earn a living just the same as anybody else.  But serious matters concerning the control and domination of the practice of Reiki, by the legal imposition of financial and practical constraints is the work of those who would limit the progression of humanity's spiritual evolution and well-being for personal gain.

When a good friend of mine asked the self styled Grand Master of Reiki, (a title which Dr. Usui never used,) Phyllis Furumoto if she had paid her Grandmother, Mrs. Takata, for her Reiki attunement, she irritatedly replied, "why does everyone want to know that?". Well, I think everyone wants to know because, ALLEGEDLY, Ms. Furumoto is trying to brand name Reiki and charge every Reiki Master in the western world $10,000 for the privilege of using the title Reiki Master. I could be wrong!?

I would like to quote Frank Arjava Petter in his book *Reiki The Legacy of Dr. Usui,* where Dr. Usui says in the introduction of his hand book entitled *Reiki Ryoho Hikkei*, which has recently been presented to Mr. Petter by the Japanese Reiki community… *"Reiki can never and will never belong to just one person or one organisation. Reiki is the spiritual heritage of all of humanity"*.

I would echo Dr. Usui's sentiment, as I am sure will be apparent as you read the text of this book. We have had over two thousand years of organisational repression from world governments, like China's domination of Tibet where monastries have been burned, and where western religious teachings have been changed and esoteric knowledge which would help all of mankind has been hidden from the masses. Enough is enough!

I would also like to reiterate that the main purpose of my book is to introduce the many aspects of energy work which are often unforeseen or misunderstood and guide the reader to understand the necessary precautions to take in order to survive energy work with a powerful and intact energy system. Also, with politics becoming ever more involved in the 'Power Game' I would at the same time like to acknowledge and thank all those who work to keep Reiki free of constraint for everyone to use and enjoy.

It is not my place or desire to pass judgement, merely to educate, the spiritual karmic laws will be enough for that. However, I will not be persecuted for my hard earned talents without a fight and I will not bow to the pressure of misguided, ego driven authority. I am a free spirit and I work with the freely available spiritual energies which have been granted to mankind, as taught to any who would listen, by Jesus and others. I survive in the material world by my talents of being able to see and read subtle energy. I am sure I do not stand alone!

*David Ashworth*
Prestwich, December 2000

Love all, Serve all.
                Sai Baba

WHAT IS HEALING? WHAT IS A HEALER? WHEN I HAD MY
own healing awakening some years ago, I didn't have the answers to
these questions. It was only by talking to many ordinary people about
what was happening to me that eventually a lady took me to a Mind,
Body, Spirit exhibition and I met healers for the first time.

I was a serious emotional wreck, as I sat on the stand of the
National Federation of Spiritual Healers, while a lady healer stood in
different places around me with her hands held out, palms facing me.
I didn't know what she was doing, but as I had a lot of something
which looked and felt like lightning, when I thought I could see it,
or electricity shooting out from my hands uncontrollably, I assumed
her hands were doing a similar thing to mine. I didn't know at that
time that it was called channelling energy. I didn't even know what
energy was in respect to healing. With hindsight, I am not sure
whether or not I felt anything at all from this healing session. I was
too busy at the time praying to God to help me and asking was I in
the right place. As usual, God didn't answer me in the expected
blinding vision I was familiar with from Sunday School. Not even a

# WHAT IS HEALING?

whisper in my shell like ear. However, looking back I know that I was in the right place and indeed this guidance was his doing.

After the healing, I asked the lady for some details of where the group met, so that I might come along and see if they could help me with the concerns I was having about the things which were happening in my body. The feelings and emotions I was experiencing were upsetting me to a great degree and turning my whole life upside down and inside out.

The lady took my name and address and that was the last I ever heard. Perhaps God had intercepted the mail as well as refusing to give me an answer whilst I was on the stand in the midst of his healing workers. Looking back upon my unfoldment, I am sure that everything that happened or didn't happen, and everyone I came into contact with, was for a reason. If I was not meant to work with these particular healers at this time, then I suppose that was part of the divine plan. Who am I to question these things? Of course, when you are in the middle of a total life crisis, this does not appear to make much sense to you. So I had to continue for a little longer to find the people I was supposed to be with, who would provide training and guidance, to help me to understand what was happening to me and enable me to progress successfully through my first healing work.

Today, it is a little easier for people entering into healing, or light work as it is sometimes known, than it was just a few short years ago. There has been a veritable explosion in spirituality, healing and energy work of all descriptions. We have regular columns in some of the daily papers on alternative therapies which occasionally cover healing, first class healing exhibitions and very broad spectrum Mind, Body, Spirit events, which appear in the smaller towns these days as well as our larger cities, and even programmes on T.V. and radio. A wonderful array of informative books is available, even from high street book shops. At one time you would only find this specialised type of reading matter through esoteric book shops or specialist book clubs. If you were lucky a mainstream book shop might just order one for you.

However, all this available information doesn't make it any easier for someone going through an awakening, as I did, or opening up on a spiritual level. With no previous knowledge of energy or healing work, a person can still be as much in the dark as I was back then. The fact that the information is more readily available these days does not preclude the person from experiencing their awakening. As I write this piece a young man has come to me for help because over the last few months he has been undergoing an awakening and the energies are flowing powerfully from his hands. However, an awakening often brings with it what appears to be a very negative downside for some people, and without the benefit of hindsight or an understanding of how universal forces awaken those who are ready, this is understandable.

In this young man's case his wife is totally unable to accept his new gift and the marriage has come under great strain. He has told me that he will do anything for his wife and family but he feels this amazing power has been given to him for a reason and he needs help to understand what is happening to him. His first experience of the energy was when he was massaging a pain in his wife's back, when he became aware of a great magnetic force which attached itself to his hands. As he continued the massage, he pulled this energy blockage out of her body. Since that first incident he has accumulated a few more experiences, accompanied by grateful thanks from the people concerned. He has also found the helpful and understanding ear of a lady healer who runs a highly reputable healing clinic, but all this sudden change within his life has left his wife very uncomfortable and unable to cope with the changes taking place in her husband. In fact, her present opinion is that he has lost his mind and for the marriage to continue he must agree to see a psychiatrist.

Clearly the situation is very difficult, as is often the case in a relationship where one partner cannot accept changes that the other partner needs to make in their own life. A healing awakening can bring with it a great upheaval on the domestic front and I have seen very many cases where one partner is going through healing or spiritual evolution which results in the break-up of the relationship.

The young man in question cannot understand at present why such a wonderful and positive gift should be accompanied by such a negative reaction from his wife. It seems to have thrown his whole life into jeopardy. At this point there is still some hope, although his wife does seem to be immovable and will not go with him to see the healers he has met, so that things can be explained to reassure her.

Of course, what happens in a healing awakening is that universal or spiritual forces will conspire to throw off anything in the physical world which encumbers your progress in spiritual advancement. My own situation was very similar to this young man's position. As I tried to discuss what was happening to me with my wife, I was met with "all you want to do is go to one of those places where they all have sex with each other". I think she meant an Ashram! Needless to say, my wife was not able to accommodate the changes I was going through and so the union, under great stress, dissolved, which was very painful to both parties. Also in my case universal forces conspired against me on all fronts. My businesses collapsed against all the effort I could put into them. My physical body was going in and out of some kind of torment, building up so much real, physical pressure that I was convinced that at any moment I might explode. Spontaneous human combustion seemed a real possibility. I faced this situation many times and had to accept the distinct possibility that by the end of the day I might be a pile of ashes on the floor. The energy flow from my hands was increasing daily and I suffered mental and emotional breakdown. And of course … I became homeless.

Out of this dissolution of my previous existence, which took the best part of three years to pass through, were born new experiences, teachings and knowledge. I recovered my mental and emotional equilibrium and attained a new life direction of sorts. I met a new partner, Denise, who understands everything about who and what I am and she is my perfect guide and support through the continuing unfolding of my evolutionary healing process. Just as an aside, when I was looking through some of the astrological aspects of her Cancerian chart recently I came across a description which said of her … "might attract a powerful healer as a partner"! Wonderful stuff, astrology!

In order for the phoenix to rise from the ashes, … first of all there must be a conflagration of the old immovable objects which encumber the life direction being shown to you by our spiritual brothers and sisters. The universe has an uncanny way of setting fire to the whole situation around oneself to facilitate this rebirth, infusing and pervading one's whole being with a new and radiant light. It is a force which is almost irresistible! I say almost, because they only show us the way, or as it says in the Bible, the way, the truth and the life. We have free will, we have a choice whether to walk this path or not. However, they do not choose those who are not ready to receive. Therefore, surely it is folly to resist this gifted opportunity of guidance into a higher evolutionary state … therefore, it must be an irresistible force.

## The Electro-magnetic Universe

This is a huge subject which has never adequately been covered from a health and healing perspective and although I have long wanted to write a book on the subject of how energies in the environment can cause serious harm to the human electro-magnetic system, I have just not had the time. For our purposes here, a brief introduction will have to suffice.

We live in an electro-magnetic universe. Everything within the physical universe is composed of matter … sub-atomic particles which make up atoms, which in turn make up molecules. Each and every atom is in a state of vibration and movement and consists of electrical charges and magnetic forces, therefore every atom is electro-magnetic. As everything in the universe is made up of atoms, therefore everything in the universe is electro-magnetic.

We are composed of those same atoms. A water molecule in a lake is the same as a water molecule in our body. It has magnetic force and electrical charge. Every life force function within the living body is electro-magnetic. Electricity is created chemically in the brain. All thought processes are electrical. The nerve pathways are like little electrical wires which conduct signals from the brain to animate our body into movement. The acupuncture meridians facilitate electrical life force energy around the body and deliver it to all our organs. Every cell has electrical charge and magnetic potential. Substances are transported through cell walls electro-chemically.

From this very brief introduction we see that not only is our universe electro-magnetic, but we are also electro-magnetic beings. When the electricity is no longer within our being, our physical body ceases to function at the level we describe as living.

The Earth also has many electro-magnetic functions, earth energies, ley lines, power points, electric storms etc., which in the terms of my own experience define this planet as a living being. So, here we are, on the electro-magnetic earth, dancing within a massive spectrum of different electro-magnetic energies within a universe possibly consisting of an infinite number of different vibrations.

Each atom vibrates at a certain frequency. The frequency is determined by how many waves of the vibration pass a given point within a second of time, travelling at the speed of light. We call this speed of vibration Hertz. Mains electricity in the UK travels at a speed of 50Hz or 50 vibrations a second. If you've ever had an electric shock you will probably recall the vibration gripping you. Sunlight emits solar radiation, some of the frequencies making up daylight or the visible spectrum. Sunlight vibrates through seven different frequencies which give us the seven colours of the rainbow. All these colours being received by our eyes at the same time give us white light or daylight. There is also cosmic radiation travelling to us from deep space, so we see that we live within a complex soup of different frequencies of vibration.

## The Healer

A healer is somebody who has the ability to gain access to and process some of these very powerful vibrations or frequencies of energy which are available to us from the universe. They can pass these through their own being and into the body of another person. This is called channelling energy. So, channelling energy is the ability to open yourself at a certain level and receive these universal energies into your body and consciously direct them for healing purposes, either for yourself or to help others.

We all have the ability to do this. Some people are born with it, some, like me, have a powerful awakening, where the whole being goes into a sort of revolution, against itself, against your wishes and usually against any plans you have made for your life. You then begin to channel and transmit energy, of and through your being, at first uncontrollably and later you develop the ability to switch it on and off.

Then there are those who have an attunement to open up their system, whereby an experienced practitioner or Master with esoteric knowledge opens up their energy system in a specific way, so that they can begin to draw into their being additional energies which have previously not been available to them. Reiki is perhaps the most well known of the attunement processes in the west at this present time, although attunement of this type from a Master is probably as old as time itself. In this sense, Jesus and Moses were Masters who could pass attunements to their students or disciples. In fact, the correct term to describe Jesus is not as a Master, but an Avatar. An Avatar is a divine incarnation of one of the aspects of God, or God consciousness.

In India today we have Sai Baba who some say is a Yogi and some an Avatar. Those who claim him to be an Avatar, see him as a divine incarnation of love. Jesus was a divine incarnation of healing.

## Universal Consciousness

Healing energy appears to have, or is guided by it's own consciousness. If we look at the universe as a whole, it doesn't bear thinking about that this vast, somewhat incomprehensible mass of living, vibrating energies is all here by accident. Even if you wanted to say that it was, then how do we explain the form and function of so many repeated patterns in physical, material existence? The repeated patterns of stars, with planets held in orbit around them, moons in orbit around planets. Thousands of stars in each Galaxy and countless galaxies in their swirling, spiral patterns across a universe we know so little about. All these enormous bodies held in states of motion, circling each other in the vacuum of space, held together by unseen forces.

Just looking at the repeated patterns on this tiny rock we call Earth, we see physical living forms as diverse as fish, dinosaurs, birds, snakes, mammals, insects. They all have, broadly speaking, similar form and function to ourselves. Just take the heads for instance: most physical life forms have eyes on either side of the head, which are picking up and translating certain vibrational frequencies so that they can successfully navigate here and there. They have a mouth to take in fuel, which we call food, to nourish the needs of their individual life force system. They have ears, to perceive low or high frequency vibrations, taking the form of pressure waves which in turn create sound to assist in orientating themselves. And they have a nose to detect the many and varied aromas which pervade the atmosphere around them. Above all, they have a brain which guides most of their life force functions and instructs the autonomic nervous system to carry out these functions automatically and the central nervous system in the best way to achieve survival in their environment. The brain, of course, and the central nervous system function in an electro-magnetic fashion.

So why is it that so many creatures have similar features to our own? Tell me there is not some guiding principle created by an intelligence that has not modelled these individual forms, extremely diverse as they are, yet with similar form and function? Why is it that some prehistoric, sub aquatic animal, such as an Ichthyosaur (prehistoric dolphin type form) possessed a head with features much the same as ours? Coincidence?

As you begin to work with healing energies you become more and more aware that there is a consciousness at work which we don't really understand. A consciousness from a higher source. We can only speculate what that higher source may be, but there is no doubting that communication at a different level to that which the majority of people experience on a day to day basis, is most certainly taking place. As you work with energy, so the energy will work with you. It will work to unfold your dormant abilities and bring you more fully into a state of expanded awareness. The energy will ultimately connect your own consciousness with the consciousness of The Universal Mind or God Consciousness.

I have said that a healer can gain access to healing energies and pass these through their own being and into the body of another being. This statement needs some clarification. When channelling healing energy it is important to do just that, channel the energy. Channelling means presenting yourself as a channel or conduit for the healing energy to flow through, just as water will flow through a pipe. This means keeping your own consciousness, energy and ego out of the equation. This is easier said than done for many people. When learning to channel energy, it is natural for the aspiring healer to want to put their inquisitive mind into the job and to push the energy a little if they think nothing or not enough is happening. After all, it is natural that you want your client or the healee to be impressed by your powers or gifts, rather than say at the end of the session that they did not feel anything. If you are not careful, a little push turns into a shove and quite easily you can soon be pushing your own energy into the client. This can have disastrous consequences for both healer and client. So, just visualise the pipe with the water flowing through it for a moment. The water merely flows, it doesn't have any other force pushing it or interfering with it in any way at all. This is how energy should be channelled, with nothing interfering with the flow.

## Energy Follows Thought

The human body has it's own innate consciousness. Every atom within your being has consciousness and can be influenced by the mind. In simple terms, this is how many people have been cured of serious illness using visualisation. There is an important maxim that everyone should be aware of ... 'energy follows thought'!

In energy work, imagination plays a big part. If you imagine you can influence a situation, then you are putting the energy of thought into that situation. What starts with a little imagination builds a flow of energy via thought. Thought has form — thought forms. These thought forms are very powerful. Using visualisation, you can create visual thought forms. In the case of cancer, bringing energy to damaged cells by the use of imagery can create a healing flow energy. To do this, one would visualise the cancer cell being cleansed and healed or destroyed and eliminated from the body by an army of good guys such as white blood cells. If done with serious intent and practised regularly, this method can indeed bring about dramatic results or what is seen to be a miracle of healing.

Visualisation is the practice of changing your level of consciousness. Like all things, some people find this relatively easy to do and others take some considerable time before they think they can influence a situation. Indeed, there have been dramatic healing results for some people, while others feel that they have not, or cannot achieve anything substantial with these methods.

It is my own belief that everyone can influence a situation through visualisation. Whether this brings about the desired result or not is a different matter. With any such technique, practice and dedication are the key elements to success. You may need to spend many hours a day in meditation to bring about results. The other points to consider are that firstly, there might be outside forces undoing the good work the healing energy flow is trying to create. These could include earth radiation or other forms of Geopathic stress in the home. Secondly, not everyone is ready to face the life changes necessary to be healed; and thirdly, it might be the person's time to leave this incarnation.

On the subject of thought forms, there was a well known and very gifted clairvoyant named Wellesley Tudor Pole, who was famous for many things but especially for establishing the Chalice Well Gardens in Glastonbury as a trust in 1959. Previously owned by a Roman Catholic order, the gardens were purchased by W.T.P. and a group of friends so that persons of any race or religion could enjoy the atmosphere, inspiration and healing energy of this special place. I would recommend my readers to any of W.T.P.'s many written works on matters spiritual and humanitarian.

However, my point here is that as a child Wellesley first became aware of his psychic abilities as he watched the different colours of prayers rising upwards from the congregation as he sat in church each Sunday. It was his first awareness of thought forms.

In my own practice of what I call Guided Vibrational Healing, I can get the energy of a crystal to interact with a person's energy system from several feet away. The energy builds such power that a client can often feel it enter their body before I have told them what the energy is about to do for them.

Primarily I started this technique with the thought of an energy stream travelling from the crystal to the specific place within the client that I desired it should go. Secondly, after some practice, energy began to travel along this path, which was now a thought form, across space from the crystal to the target. Eventually this process became so attuned that I no longer had to create the thought form of the pathway. The consciousness of energy knows what I want it to do and it is now produced automatically. Thus we have 'energy following thought'.

When a healer presents their self within a client's energy field as a channel for healing energy, or places their hands on or near the body, the client's own energy system knows exactly what is happening. The consciousness of every atom in their body will recognise the healing energy which is being made available to them through the healer and will draw, automatically, without the healer's intervention, exactly what it needs from that energy source. If the client's energy system only draws a little, then that is all it needs or can process at that time. If this does not make sense to the healer, perhaps because the client is quite poorly and by all reasoning, you think they should need lots of energy, beware, it may be that the client's physical system is too weak to process a large amount of energy and this is the reason that only a little has been drawn on this, or perhaps subsequent occasions.

Some healers feel the energy flow in their hands turn on and off as the client's body draws energy and then stops as it processes what it has taken in. By sensing this 'on-off' energy flow, the healer can take full advantage by distributing the energy around the body. As the healer senses the energy turn down or off, they can then move their hands to a different part of the body where the client's energy system will again draw a full flow until that place has drawn as much as it can take for the moment. By moving around the body in this way, the healer optimises the distribution of healing energy during the treatment.

As a healer progresses in their art, they will learn to feel energy at different levels and become adept at detecting disturbances in the magnetic patterning or auric field of the body, sensing where there is disease, injury or energy blockage of some kind. They will be able to supply electro-magnetic healing energy to these areas to help rebalance the energy flow to the needy areas.

The human being is an amazingly sensitive piece of equipment. We can train our sensitivities to detect finer and finer vibrations. Science has great difficulty believing much of what we discuss in this book because scientific instruments capable of measuring such fine vibrations are exceedingly rare or none existent. However, at Stanford University in America, sensitive measuring equipment has been used to show the flow of energy entering the healer's body through the top of their head, or crown chakra, and flowing out through the hands as a healing treatment takes place. Kirlian photography, which is now becoming more common, also shows invisible energy patterns around the body. There is also the amazing Harry Oldfield and his electro-crystal therapy system, which can scan the body's subtle energies and display them on a computer in real time. Harry's equipment is far more advanced than anything in mainstream medicine or science to date. However, there is interest from the medical fraternity and he has trained a number of medical professionals in the use of this system.

## 02

"Don't believe what your eyes are telling you. All they show is limitation. Look with your understanding, find out what you already know, and you'll see the way to fly."

Jonathan Livingstone Seagull

## The Body Heals Itself!

IN ORDER TO BRING ABOUT HEALING WE NEED ACCESS TO energy, remembering of course that the healer does not heal, but that the body heals itself. The healer is merely facilitating an energy to the needy person which their body may be able to use in its own healing. The energy carries a consciousness, a knowing or blueprint and a cleansing pattern which the whole being can use to detoxify, cleanse, balance and realign itself at a subtle energy level, to the way it should be. When all life force energy is once again flowing as and where it should, then healing takes place. Therefore, 'the body heals itself'!

I assume within the grand universal plan that there is no limit to the ways in which we can ask for, or access, healing energy. However, there are two main ways with which we will concern ourselves here. Channelled energy is where the energy usually enters the healer via the crown of the head and passes downwards through the chakra energy centres to the heart centre. From here it usually

# THE CHAKRAS AND SUBTLE BODIES

continues down the arms and out through the palms of the hands. The second method is accessed energy. This is where the energy is brought in, or down from a spiritual source in a kind of vortex or whirlpool, to surround and inter-penetrate the healer. The energy then radiates outwards to encompass the client in a swirling mass.

 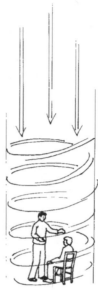 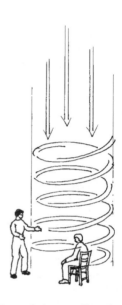

| Channelled energy entering the crown chakra, passing through the heart and out through the palm chakras. | Energy being brought down by the healer from a spiritual source to encompass himself and the client. | Energy being manifested around the client whilst the healer stands remotely orchestrating the event. |

## Healing Energy

In this book much of our focus is directed towards Reiki, pronounced 'Ray Key', channelled energy, as this has been the fastest growing aspect of energy work over recent years and many people can relate to it in one form or another. However, the references used to describe the use of energy hold true for any kind of healing using channelled or accessed energy, whether we choose to call it Hands-on Healing, Spiritual Healing, Faith Healing, Pranic Healing, Shamanic Healing, Usui Reiki, Tibetan Reiki, Karuna Reiki, Seichem or any one of many others.

The energy all comes from the same source; it is merely the modality of its application which differs, due to development by different peoples from diverse cultures at different times and places throughout history. The source and nature of the energy is the same, we are simply using different forms of knowledge and training and different methods to supply the healee with an energy which may help them. The important thing to note is that across all these cultural and time differences, there have occasionally been extremely gifted people who have had the intuition and insight to connect with this energy and the ability to access it and bring it forth for use on earth. From these beginnings, they have developed a knowledge of the energy and found ways not only to provide healing to others, but also to bring it into the being of others so that they might also use it for healing and again, pass it on through the generations.

Dr. Usui, the founder of Reiki, is one such person, whose tenacity, devotion and dedication brought him into contact with the universal healing energy. In the Christian Bible it is said 'ask and you shall receive' and 'seek and you shall find', and so it was that Dr. Usui asked, probably repeatedly, as I do myself on a daily basis, and eventually he did receive. These words 'ask and you shall receive', 'seek and you shall find', are a spiritual maxim, a reference to inner truth, to the inner light of what Christians call the Holy Spirit. These sayings purport to open doors to the divine, to the one true source of higher knowledge and ultimate spiritual attainment. The words do not allude to one true religion or belief system, as the energy has no rules or boundaries as to who can call it up and be one with it. The words address the one and only omnipotent consciousness or presence which pervades all of material existence and beyond. Although it is possible that many secret sects and mystical schools knew of this healing light prior to the arrival on earth of Jesus, it was he who came to spread the word to the masses. Jesus came primarily to give us this tool for our own salvation. He preached the message of light and spoke of his father of light, he said that God is Love and Light is Love. He did not preach that we should follow any one particular religion, but that we all have the ability to access his light. All we need to do is ask, in truth and from the heart, for help with our own spiritual advancement and we would receive the gift of love and truth in return, the gift which is of course ... Light.

'Ask and you shall receive' brings one into contact with the energy in an ever unfolding way. The more one is dedicated and the more one devotes time to prayer and the application of healing, the more one will be given the abilities to help humanity, the earth, the universe or indeed anything within creation which may benefit from healing energy.

Ultimately, no matter which techniques or modality we use with our clients when working with energy, the important thing to understand is that our subject matter is nothing more or less than energy. All energy is just energy, whether channelled or accessed, merely different frequencies of energy. Apart from the importance of a good grounding in the form and function of the subtle energies of the body and a sound knowledge of psychic forces and psychic protection, there is no right or wrong way to work with energy; plain, ordinary common sense is an excellent guide. When linked with a developing intuition, this can be a powerful combination.

Accessing and using healing energy changes you at a subtle energy level. You cannot work with healing energies or any other subtle energies, such as earth energies, and remain unchanged. As the energy pervades your being and courses through the subtle energy channels, it cleanses and purifies and with the purification of these channels your being becomes more sensitive to receiving information from a higher level. In some forms of healing the trainee merely works with other healers and eventually messages pass from the subtle energies of the healers into the subtle body of the trainee and at a higher conscious level the being of the trainee then begins to unfold and channel energies. In other forms of healing a specific attunement is passed from a Master to the student which opens up channels immediately for the energy to flow through. Reiki is a form of healing which is activated in the student in this way, by attunement.

Reiki initially acts upon your Light Body. By the Light Body I am describing your chakra system, aura, your core electro-magnetic being. This is the very essence of subtle energy which is both outside the physical body and at the same time, interweaving and pervading it at all levels. Every cell of your physical being exists within a field of subtle energy and to understand a little of what is happening with healing energies we need to look at the structures of the subtle energies which are part of our being.

The human being, or just the being, exists in several aspects. Most people are only aware of the physical aspect. In what can be described as the material planes of existence, we have the lower self and the higher self and beyond these are the higher planes of existence such as the intuitive and spiritual planes. However, we are going to limit ourselves to the lower and higher self in this book.

## The Lower Self

This aspect of our being consists of the physical body, the etheric body, the emotional body and the lower mental body. In terms of vibrations the physical body is very dense matter and vibrates at a comparatively low frequency to the other bodies. Our eyes are receptive only to the low frequencies of physical matter, hence we see material things by daylight. We cannot see the components of that light unless we split the white light, by using a prism, into its seven rays, which we call the rainbow or visible spectrum. Any frequencies of light outside the visible spectrum — beyond the red going into the slower infra-red at one end of the spectrum and beyond the violet going into the faster ultra-violet at the other — we cannot perceive with our eyes. We know from science that these frequencies exist but our sensors, our eyes, cannot perceive these different rates of vibration. This gives rise to many people believing that light does not exist beyond these points, but it does and it is this light which is seen by those with natural clairvoyant (clear seeing) vision or those trained in intuitive work who have worked to develop this type of vision.

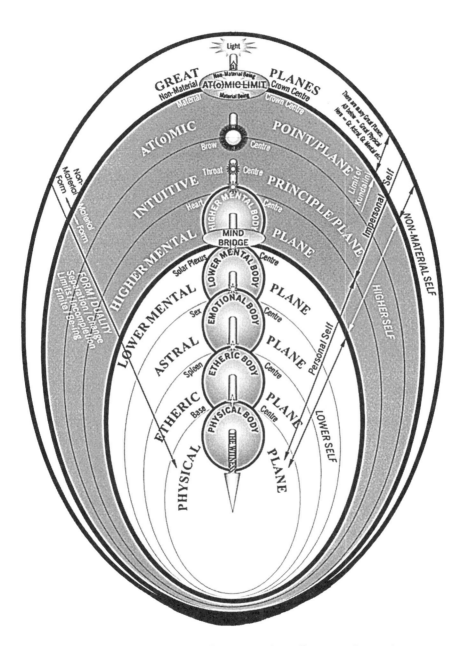

Representation of the Lower Self and the Higher Self. For complete version
see colour pages. (© Dr. Tim Duerden – for notes see www.duerden.com)

When we move upward beyond the physical body into the higher vibrations of light which comprise the etheric, emotional and lower mental bodies we cannot see them, for they are vibrating much faster than the atoms in physical matter.

**The physical body** exists on the physical plane and consists of all our physical structure such as skin, blood, bone, nervous system, tissues, vessels, cells, etc.

**The etheric body** exists on the etheric plane and acts as an interface or transducer, linking and transducing the energies of the higher frequency bodies down into the slower vibrations of the physical body. The etheric body is generated outwards from the physical body, usually up to about twenty inches (51cm).

**The emotional body** exists on the astral plane and processes our emotions. When the energy of emotions is activated, the energy imprints onto the physical body and manifests in feelings, usually in the solar plexus and sacral area. The emotional body usually extends between six to eight feet (183cm to 244cm) from the physical body.

**The lower mental body** exists on the lower mental plane and processes our day-to-day mental activity. This level of mental activity is composed of the regular thoughts which are needed for day to day functioning: thoughts of going to work, doing the ironing, planning the weekend; nothing out of the ordinary. The lower mental body is a narrower band of energy, usually in the region of 12 feet (366cm), extending from the outer limit of the emotional body.

Therefore we have a physical body and a number of other levels of existence which we call the light body or aura. It is called the light body because it vibrates at very high frequencies of light. This is not light as we see and understand it in the visible spectrum, but higher frequencies of light, visible in what we call the psychic realm. It is also called the lower self because it is exactly that. It is the lower frequencies of vibration of our physical and subtle bodies and we can interact with all of these levels of existence within the confines of the physical world. Using dowsing techniques, with a pendulum or rods, we can clearly interact and identify the limits of these bodies within the aura. In fact, the vibrations within the aura are so powerful that almost anyone can learn to sense or feel them with a few moments of training from someone who has the ability to tune them in and show them what to look for.

## The Realms of Light

The realms of light are all around us. Imagine the air which surrounds us, yet we do not see, feel, touch or smell it, this gas which pervades our whole environment and fills our lungs. The realms of light are other worlds, with other beings dwelling therein, which interpenetrate our own physical world, but unless we are attuned to these frequencies then we cannot see, feel, touch or smell them. If and when one gains clairvoyant vision through self-development or working with energy, one begins to see into these realms at what is called a psychic level. We can all do this to some extent, particularly when we are relaxed. The physical eyes have the ability to perceive higher frequencies of light in the area of their peripheral vision. If we are aware of this at an ordinary level we might be tuned to receive or perceive these higher frequencies of existence. For instance when we see a ghost or spirit or perhaps catch some movement out of the corner of the eye.

The reason so many people deny the existence of such things is that they are so rooted in the physical realm, with perhaps no flexibility or lateral movement of their higher or more delicate senses within their light body, that even in the most perfect conditions to perceive such phenomena, they would not have a hope of witnessing the event. However, all is not lost for these people, for if they are open-minded and wish to learn, I believe there is nobody who cannot achieve a certain level of attainment through self-development exercises, which will bring these invisible and marvellous other realms of existence within their reach.

Whereas air is all around us, the realms of light are both all around us and penetrate right through us, just as the very high frequency of vibration known as an X-ray will penetrate right through us, revealing on a photographic film the more dense parts of our body, depending on the length of exposure to these rays.

When trained in energy work and developed as a healer or light worker, clairvoyant vision is often achieved in some measure. Clairvoyance, meaning 'clear seeing' is the ability to see these particular frequencies of light in the etheric, emotional and mental bodies, collectively known as the aura. A clairvoyant can usually also see the chakras.

## The Higher Self

These aspects of ourselves are our higher functions. They are the higher mental body, the intuitive body and the atomic or atmic point. These bodies again are formed of progressively higher vibrations. At the present level of our discussion we are not really concerned with the energies at these higher levels.

## The Chakras

The chakras are energy centres of the light body. Chakra is a Sanskrit word meaning 'wheel'. When seen with clairvoyant sight they appear as spinning wheels of light. Throughout history, in cultures where spiritual development has formed part of the everyday lives of the people, the chakras have been known about and used by way of attuning ones perceptions to these fine vibrations. When working with subtle energy and attuning our senses to the finer vibrations, everyone's perception is slightly different in what they receive. Therefore as history unfolds, we see many different views of what the chakras actually look like. However, the general picture is approximately the same. To those who have seen them and catalogued them in drawings and artwork, they contain what appear to be petal-like divisions.

In the west we mainly concern ourselves with seven major chakras, but in Pranic healing we work with twelve major chakras, but my intention here is to give a fundamental working knowledge for the beginner, without over-complicating matters.

Illustration of the petals of a Chakra.

The chakras form an energy structure in an ascending frequency of vibrations which contains all the levels and aspects of existence from the physical world through to the world of spirit and the divine. There is thus a chain-like link from the gross lower frequency vibration rooted in the earth/physical plane, stepping upwards through to the highest spiritual access doors. The only trick is learning how to use the different levels.

Each chakra functions at a different speed or rate of vibration and contains a different number of divisions or petals within its wheel-like structure. The base chakra situated at the base of the spine being the slowest and consisting of four petals, works in anchoring us to the earth in a grounding fashion and provides a subtle energy link to the physical body. At the other end of the scale we have the crown chakra at the top of the head, which is the fastest rate of vibration with nine hundred and sixty petals, plus another twelve in the central core. This chakra connects us at a cosmic consciousness level. In many of the illustrations and carvings we see of the Buddha, his head is a clear representation of the crown chakra, open and flowing all over his head, usually with the centre section raised and projecting the higher central core of twelve petals outwards from his physical body, reaching forth into the spiritual beyond. This is also sometimes shown as a flame reaching upwards. To the uninitiated, this dressing of the head of the Buddha is usually perceived as stylised hair, a head-dress or a hat.

The seven major chakras we are going to concern ourselves with are positioned along the spinal column, from the base of the spine to the crown of the head. The heart chakra can wander about a bit, sometimes fairly central and sometimes quite a bit off-centre to the left, in the traditional place where the heart is drawn in illustrations.

Statues of Buddha showing the different representations of the crown chakra.

The chakras contain vital life force energy and breathe in and out, much the same as our lungs. They breathe in life force energy and distribute it around the body and they breathe out stale or negative energy. They can become blocked and dirty and when this happens they are in a state of congestion and malfunction. This can bring serious problems to the physical body if this energy state continues for any length of time.

Although it is said in some books that chakras cannot become closed down, in fact, they can. In one case, I had a lady who was suffering from a terrible headache and was completely disorientated and unbalanced, as well as being in considerable pain. I detected the crown chakra was completely closed and began various techniques to bring the chakra back into balance and functioning correctly. I spent half an hour on this lady before I could coax the chakra back into any form of movement or action and during the time I was working on her I could perceive the enormous pressure build-up in her subtle energy system caused by this blockage. Although she was unaware of any physical movement, her upper torso, neck and head were rocking back and forth under the pressure of energy which had no place to flow. I managed to get the lady to open an energy vent in the back of her neck which relieved some of the intense pressure. Dowsing and using a number of different vibrations of crystal I eventually began to bring the chakra into a functional state. Once it began to open, the pressure in her head released immediately and within a few moments the chakra was spinning quite happily and the lady was fully recovered.

In this illustration, the incredible physical discomfort was created by a malfunction in the subtle energy system. It seems difficult to comprehend that a mere blockage in this system can have such dramatic and painful effects at a physical level, but it is true. In this instance, taking a painkiller will do nothing to remedy the cause of the problem and may well contribute to further blockages, resulting in more painful physical problems later.

Most of the chakra material in modern literature came originally from the east where spiritual life and attainment have been part of everyday life for centuries. From this source the chakras are imbued with symbols and names foreign to our native western tongue. For simplicity I will adopt the western numerical system of identification.

## Attributes of the Chakras

Each chakra has a number of specific attributes associated with it.

**1st or Base Chakra:** Located at the base of the spine in the area of the perineum.
**Function:** Providing energy to all the visible physical parts and functions of the body. It is the lowest vibration, feeding the dense physical matter we see as reality: the skeletal structure, the muscles, blood, tissues and organs.
**Colour:** Red.
**Mantra:** I live.
The feet are rooted to the earth and the base chakra points downward, linking us with the physical earth. The base chakra says 'I live'. This is the very basest form of physical existence, the pure unthinking animal force of life, drawing energy from the mother earth which supports physical existence with her bounty.

**2nd or Sacral Chakra:** Located midway between the pubic bone and the navel.
**Function:** Providing energy to the bladder and sexual and reproductive organs.
**Colour:** Orange.
**Mantra:** I create.
The sacral chakra says 'I create'. This is the basic animal instinct to procreate, to reproduce ourselves through association with our opposite aspect of Yin or Yang.

**3rd or Solar Plexus Chakra:** Located just below where the ribs part at the solar plexus. Sometimes called the big motor, as this chakra can supply energy to all the other chakras.
**Function:** Providing energy to stomach, large intestine and liver.
**Colour:** Yellow.
**Mantra:** I know.
The solar plexus chakra says 'I know'. It is the centre of knowledge. This is not the knowledge we acquire by study, but when this chakra is activated it brings knowledge of who and what we are, it begins to bring awareness at a higher level of consciousness. We can see through it like we see through an eye, bringing us into focus with subtle energy around us.

**4th or Heart Chakra:** Located in the centre of the chest.
**Function:** Providing energy to the heart, thymus gland (which is the master gland of the endocrine system), and circulatory system.
**Colour:** Green.
**Mantra:** I love.
The heart chakra says 'I love'. This is the central chakra in our seven fold chakra system, the centre of our being which vibrates to both green and pink. It is the centre of compassion and love for our fellow man, our planet and ourselves. It is the knowledge that the whole of creation functions on and is love.

**5th or Throat Chakra:** Located at the throat.
**Function:** Providing energy to the throat, thyroid and para-thyroid glands
**Colour:** Sky blue.
**Mantra:** I speak.
The throat chakra says 'I speak'. This is the centre of communication: communication at all levels, with all peoples and with all animals, plants and spiritual beings. When this chakra is activated it brings clairvoyant vision, so that one begins to see that we are not alone but are surrounded by many other beings interweaving their high vibrational world of light throughout our own.

**6th or Brow Chakra:** Located between the eyebrow centre.
**Function:** Providing energy to the nervous system, pineal and pituitary glands and also linked to all the other chakras
**Colour:** Indigo Blue.
**Mantra:** I perceive.
The brow chakra says 'I perceive'. This is the centre of perception and intuition: perception and penetration into yet higher vibrational areas. Perceiving into the higher self and into the higher self of others this chakra brings the gift of intuitive messages and communication with Spirit Guides to take you higher in your own transformation. It brings perception that there is no death, only energy in different forms.

**7th or Crown Chakra:** Located on the crown of the head.
**Function:** Providing energy to the brain and linked through to all other aspects of the body.
**Colour:** Violet/white.
**Mantra:** I am.
The crown chakra says 'I am'. This is the centre of completeness, of oneness with the divine. This is the doorway to cosmic consciousness, the exit from the physical into the ethereal, which is the route by which the Yogis leave their physical body to travel amidst the ether and thence return with full consciousness of their journey.

## Mantras

A mantra is a sound, word or phrase which is usually chanted or pronounced in a repetitive, rhythmical manner in order to create a vibration. This vibration can then unlock aspects of consciousness and bring the person into a higher state of communion with their spiritual self, or bring about a connection with God-consciousness. But mantras associated with the chakras are not used in this way. This set of Mantras is an illustration of the potential creative journey of consciousness, from earth-bound gross physical reality at the base chakra end of the spectrum of human consciousness, through to the higher vibrations of the spiritual self as perceived outside of the physical body, within and above the crown chakra. As we move upwards from the base chakra, each chakra is vibrating faster through its increased number of divisions or petals, bringing a higher form of consciousness to bear at each level of existence attained.

We can now see from the descriptions above that a complete picture begins to emerge as to what we are. This picture displays a path of consciousness in terms of vibrations, beginning at the base chakra and rising in ever increasing vibrations through the other chakras to eventually exit the physical body at the spiritual centre or crown chakra. The Gurus and Yogis, the High Masters and Avatars can take their consciousness even higher, way beyond the crown chakra, up into the realms of pure spiritual essence. As we begin to work with our chakras to bring energy gently into them and expand our capabilities, we can see the various aspects which make up the whole ... "I live, I create, I know, I love, I communicate, I perceive ... therefore I am"!

## Chakra Perception

As we are dense physical matter and usually untrained in the perception of subtle energies, the concept of being able to work with our chakras is difficult to grasp for many of us. Patience and perseverance are the key to chakra perception, as with all manner of subtle energy exploration. Remembering we are dense physical beings in a dense physical world, we often need to make great effort to attain perception of the finer energy structures and bodies. Even those of us who have attained these abilities must on occasion work very hard to tune ourselves in. Don't forget, it takes hard work for most of us to gain these perceptions, but the work is worth it and one should not become despondent, even if it takes quite some time, months and even more months usually, before we get a little glimpse of things to come.

## Working with the Chakras

There are a number of ways you can begin to work with the chakras. One of the best is to work with a tape. A number of people have produced chakra meditation tapes over the years. The first one I had was given to me as a gift. It was very interesting, although it threw me in at the deep end, as it used a lot of the old traditional eastern terminology, which as an absolute beginner I found difficult to get my head and tongue around. However, it guided the listener's mind to the right places and that was the important thing. I used to take that tape everywhere with me and play it whenever I got the opportunity. I would play it every lunch time and evening. Once on a train from London to Manchester, I worked through the meditation, some forty minutes worth, on my portable tape player with headphones, to discover at the end that the speaker was switched on and that everyone within a radius of about twelve feet had heard it also. I bet they thought I was one strange person; very embarrassing.

A leader in meditation classes will often guide you through a chakra meditation, which can be quite instructional and supportive to the beginner. A teacher will ask for feedback, which will turn your tentative enquiries as to what might have happened during the meditation, into a positive affirmation that you did indeed experience aspects of awakening at a subtle level. Working alone with a tape is very good because you can find space during your day which is totally quiet and peaceful to practice in without the interference of noise often encountered in a group session.

Work through the tape over and over again, allowing the mind to meld with the instructor's tones. Let the consciousness move from its usual seat in the mind and the head and experience travel to new areas of the body. The power of the mind is incredible when you learn to use it and working with guided meditation of a Master or a tape is a very powerful starting point to any kind of energy work. Allow the mind to open up those spaces which have never had feeling, which you have never actually felt before in a subtle way and you will begin to experience new dimensions of your own being.

## A Simple Exercise

Try for a moment sitting in silence and allow your mind to move down to the toes. Open the energy of the toes by allowing the mind to move into this space, opening up feeling. Move the mind around a single toe, allowing it to come to life with feeling; sense the layers of skin, sense the structure of bone within the toe, tune your senses to smaller and smaller matter until you can feel the blood coursing through the tissue and feel every little cell at work. Spend fifteen minutes concentrating on just one toe and discover how much you can actually sense in that small part of you which has probably never had any detailed attention paid to it during its entire physical existence. Feel how powerful the mind can be at opening doorways into perception of things previously unrecognised.

Some of you will begin to perceive chakra energy quite quickly and others will take longer. For example, when trying to calm or still the mind and train it to do things it has not done before, it can take some time before any real measure of success is achieved. Some people will receive impressions of the energy within the chakras quite early in their practice while others will take longer to feel anything at all. Some will experience chakra colours almost straight away as their mind unlocks doorways to the energy. The important thing is to continue to work and practice regardless of what you receive and you will be rewarded for your efforts as and when the time is right.

You would do well to remember that bringing these new levels of light into your being often means that energy blockages and other structures which might otherwise restrict the flow of this light energy need to melt away. A healing session often facilitates and speeds up this necessary cleansing process.

## Chakra Stones

Crystal chakra sets are also available and those of you who are already sensitive to crystal energy will find these to be quite powerful aids to activating the chakra centres. To those who are not yet this sensitive, a set of chakra stones can certainly help bring your subtle energy to life and tune you in. A set of Chakra stones is usually seven specific stones, each of whose vibrational frequencies is attuned to each of the individual chakras. Quite often the stones occur in similar colours to the chakras. To use these stones, lie down on the floor, place the appropriate stone on the appropriate chakra and begin the meditation. It can help your relaxation if you use a bit of masking tape to hold the stones in place, so that you won't be disturbed if one falls off during the practice. Please take note that often the crystal placed at the brow or crown chakra can be quite uncomfortable in terms of the energy it activates. If you find this to be so, with the brow chakra in particular, remove this stone and place it above the head. Also, it is better to place the base chakra and crown chakra stone a few inches away from the body, but in line with the spinal column.

## An additional Experience, Bathing Luxury

For many years I have used crystals to energise the water as I run a bath. Using crystals in the bath is great fun. As well as clear quartz crystal points, we have in our bathroom a collection of quite large tumble-polished stones. I place them in the bath as I run the water. When the water is ready, add in a few drops of an appropriate aromatherapy oil. Choose the oil either by intuition or by dowsing and then distribute it through the water.

Arrange the quartz points into geometric patterns, which in themselves become powerful energy generators. I activate them with my mind. Arrange the tumble stones into groups or in a line from one end of the bath to the other. Leave the stones and oil for five minutes or so to begin their work of integrating and energising the water.

Before getting into the bath, move the stones into a pile so that you don't sit on them and, once you are immersed in the water, scoop up a handful of the stones to play with. Pass them from hand to hand and trickle their warm forms over your body or place them down the mid-line from throat to pelvic bone. You can also use the specific chakra stones on the chakra points. They feel wonderful to the touch and increase in fascination as their colours brighten with the wetness.

Included in your collection of tumbled stones can be a selection of appropriate chakra stones also, such as:

| | |
|---|---|
| Base | Carnelian or Red Tiger's Eye |
| Sacral | Orange Calcite |
| Solar Plexus | Citrine |
| Heart | Rose Quartz or Serpentine |
| Throat | Blue Topaz or Turquoise |
| Third Eye | Azurite or Sodalite |
| Crown | Amethyst |

Place these in their appropriate positions on the chakras and drift into a state of deep relaxation or even a meditative state. To add the final touch to this blissful state, if you have a battery operated tape player or Walkman, (do not use a mains powered machine in the bathroom) you can do your chakra meditation in the bath too. It's brilliant, the natural resonance of a typical bathroom gives wonderful vibrations from the sound, helping to take you deeper within your meditation and give you a unique experience of great depth and pleasure.

As I have increasingly worked and taught with crystals over recent years, I have noticed that those who have never previously been interested in crystals are often drawn to amethyst as their first introduction to the mineral kingdom. Of course it is obvious why this is so, but as with all things which stare you in the face, the obvious often goes right over your head.

The vibration of amethyst helps to activate the crown chakra, which is our spiritual connection. Our crown chakra becoming more open or starting to function at a higher level is always the first indication of spiritual evolution. So what we see when someone is first drawn to amethyst is a subconscious or unconscious reaching out for the tools which will help them to evolve, firstly on a more spiritual level and subsequently at other energy levels. I bought my first large chunk of amethyst when I was about 12 or 13 years old. It seems a shame it took me another 30 years to realise why this was. I've always been a slow learner!

## 03

If all the heavens were to open up,
And shower us with truth,
A thought alone would be enough,
To give the heart a roof.

Malcolm Cawley

MALCOLM CAWLEY'S LITTLE POEM ABOVE SPEAKS VOLUMES about the power of energy. In essence it speaks of truth. Truth is the only path we can take to evolve spiritually and break the cycle of reincarnation, if that is what one chooses to do as a soul. The poet also speaks of the power of thought. *"A thought alone would be enough"*. He speaks of a 'single thought' being enough to protect the heart. The heart chakra, of course, is the centre of the individual universe within each person. The energy of the heart is love. Love is what drives the whole of creation, be they the physical or metaphysical universes. God is love. The power of thought is tremendous when projected for good or evil. When used for good in healing, a single focused thought can create energy pathways to repair energy systems within a person. When used for evil, it can bond to a person and continually affect their energy and health in a negative way, until it is removed. We will look at this in more detail later under Psychic Attack. If we humans can do these things with a single human thought, then what could we do with a single thought from God or heaven, should we be granted one? Not only could a single

# UNDERSTANDING ENERGY

thought from heaven give the heart a roof, as alluded to in the poem, but I am sure it's truth could release all of human kind from it's present suffering in a second of time. After all, is not the whole of creation merely a thought? I wonder, did Mr. Cawley consider all this when he wrote the poem?!

The world is going mad for and with Reiki. It's a wonderful thing. The human race is crying out for this next phase in consciousness shift and it's not before time. People who are energy workers or on the spiritual path, working with other like-minded souls, or by themselves, look out at the world, at its leaders, it's politicians or representatives of the people, at it's leaders in industry, science, medicine and education and cannot believe they are from the same planet. Whose agenda are they serving? Certainly not that of the people they purport to represent!

In planetary terms, there is so much going on with control issues, bribery and corruption at every turn, people in their droves are turning away from old patterns and seeking a new way of living. New values are perhaps old values which have been forgotten and are now being restored to their rightful place, in the consciousness of the people. The way the world operates today has run out of time. Its little clockwork motor has run down and it is time to put this old world away in the toy box, to look back on nostalgically, as we look back on the Victorian age. The people are changing and therefore the structure of society and the process and priorities of governments must follow.

It is always refreshing to meet people new to the spiritual path, or people who are meeting dowsing, crystals, healing, homeopathy or energy work of any kind for the first time. When we had our Crystal Studio, people would regularly be drawn in to look at the goodies on display. After chatting with us for a while they would often find themselves leaving with a whole new vision and perspective on aspects of life they never knew existed. Recently, a retired gentleman came to see me because a lady friend of his had bought a crystal from our stall at a local Health and Healing Fair and he found that when he rubbed it on his painful legs it seemed to help. He and his son stayed for around an hour and a half while I demonstrated so many ways to feel energy and showed them dowsing techniques and aura work. They were very open to learn and fascinated by what they could feel as I tuned them in. The gentleman said to me as he left, "I've lived all these years and knew nothing of these things, this is all very interesting, I will definitely be back to see you again". It was wonderful to experience his surprise at his own abilities and see the enthusiasm in his eyes. This is just one example from many which illustrate how people are being drawn unconsciously to try the things which have been denied them for hundreds of years.

You meet the most unlikely people who are new on the spiritual path, people from most diverse sets of circumstances and backgrounds and many of them find Reiki as the first port of call on their new path. It is no coincidence either. I often say to people, you don't discover Reiki, rather, Reiki finds you when you are ready to receive it. This may be a strange concept to some of you reading this book, but when you understand a little of how Universal Wisdom is trying to guide us, if only we would stop for a moment and listen, then you would understand. Indeed if you are reading this book, then for certain you are on the path to having this truth revealed to you in due course. I hope this book gives you a few more clues, but the truth can only come from within yourself when you have accumulated the necessary experiences.

However, all is not well in the world of energy work and Reiki in particular and is likely to get worse unless people are taught correctly about the dangers of dabbling without a proper understanding of what they are actually doing. Proper training in how to bring energy into their system is essential to avoid unnecessary pitfalls. Nobody in their right mind would encourage a child, or another adult for that matter, to dabble with a ouija board if they understood the dangers. It is just the same with working with energy. Using a ouija board is all about using an intent. The intent is to contact other sources of consciousness outside our plane of existence. A ouija board opens doors into other dimensions and things can come through from these dimensions. When they do, it is not always easy to escape the consequences.

When you work with energy, even at the lowest of levels, you are beginning to tap the powers of your consciousness and as your consciousness awakens and your abilities begin to expand, you will begin to open doors into other dimensions, whether you care to or not. Energy work of any kind frequently crosses the boundaries between different worlds of existence. Be aware of what you are doing, so that when you encounter something unknown, you will know where it has come from and how to accept it, deal with it or send it back. Better still, know what is there before you enter, and carry the correct amount of psychic protection in order to avoid a disaster.

## What is Reiki?

You cannot adequately describe Reiki to anyone who has never experienced healing energy or working with energy. Reiki is an experience, and as all things experiential, it is a personal experience. One person's experience cannot be felt by or experienced by another person. Certainly one can describe the things one experienced, but unless the receiver of this information has had an experience to compare this description with, then they cannot know what you mean. And so it is with Reiki, unless you have had an experience of having your light body opened up, then you cannot know what it is like. With this in mind, let me now completely contradict myself and try to give you some clues about the subject.

## What will I Feel?

As we have said previously, Reiki is an attunement process and when they undergo their attunement, some students feel nothing at all. No visions, no sensations, no colours, no 'touched by the hand of God,' etc. Others will have the most amazing experiences, such as a kaleidoscope of colour in their mind's eye, visions of Spirit Guides welcoming them on their path of enlightenment, intuitive messages, astral travel to the pyramids or planets where they may receive a message or meet Spirit Guides, visions of past lives as a healer, a priest or priestess of Atlantis and more.

What needs to be understood is that each individual is at a different stage of spiritual evolution at the time of attunement and they will receive from the attunement exactly what they are capable of processing at that moment in time.

For instance, if the person entering into attunement is new to energy work and has lived a fairly sedentary life and does not eat a good diet in terms of life force energy food, i.e. live food, this does not mean eating live animals, but eating good fresh vegetables, organic if possible, the chances are that they will feel relatively little at the time of attunement and will have to work quite hard with the energy after attunement to bring the energy strongly into their system.

After the attunement there should be a series of meditational exercises to do for approximately an hour a day for a period of twenty one days. This is a detoxification process and is designed to bring the energy smoothly and firmly into the system and rebalance the chakras from this new, powerful and vibrant energy which is now flooding into and opening up your system.

During the twenty-one day cleansing process, a sedentary type of person may experience quite a big detox on the physical level. Strong smelling urine and occasional bouts of diahorea may occur within a day or two of attunement. This may continue from time to time during the following few weeks, depending on how much energy you bring into your system. Women often experience their menstrual cycle beginning the following day whether it is due or not. There may be spots or rashes on the skin that persist for months, even more than a year.

What the aspirant needs to understand is that the attunement has raised the vibrational level of the light body. This means the light body is now vibrating at a higher frequency, or faster than it previously was and the physical body is now trying to catch up. The physical body is much more dense than the light body and so when attunement takes place, the light body moves into its new, higher level of vibration immediately and becomes robust at this level of vibration during the coming weeks, usually, but not always, during the 21 day cleansing period.

# Resonance

Let's look at physical vibrations, for instance when a bus or lorry goes past your house and your windows rattle. What happens here is that the vibrational waves of the sound of the engine or exhaust hit your windows, some of which will vibrate in sympathy with that same frequency.

If you play middle 'C' on the piano with the damper pedal removed from the strings, all the other notes of 'C' up and down the piano will vibrate and sound in resonance with the original key which was struck. The original note is sending out a vibration and the other notes of the same type are 'in resonance' or 'in sympathy' with it and so they join in too.

It is the same with the physical body and the light body. The light body is vibrating at a certain frequency and all the atoms and molecules within the physical body are in resonance with this vibration. The frequencies of light are interpenetrating and interweaving throughout the whole sub-atomic, atomic and molecular structure of your physical body. Every molecule is in resonance with the vibration of its partner, the light body. When we change the vibration of the light body by attunement, by allowing in a broader array of frequencies, which by the same token speeds things up a bit, then the physical body must also adjust its vibration to the same frequency.

Because of the density of matter in the physical body, it cannot adjust its speed of vibration as quickly as the light body can, but nevertheless is forced to catch up. Frequencies of light are not constrained by physical matter and indeed can pass right through physical matter — as when we see a ghost pass through a wall, or X-rays reveal dense matter, such as bone, by passing through the less dense matter of the soft tissues of the physical body. Similarly, frequencies of light can accelerate in an instant, unhindered by physical constraints. The physical body cannot just change up a gear as the light body can and so it has to bring itself up to speed as quickly as it can and you can help it to do this. In order to catch up it must shed much dross which can no longer vibrate at the new, higher or faster vibrations of light which are now interpenetrating the physical body. Hence the physical body is thrown into a process of detoxification, usually called a healing process or healing crisis.

Preparation for a Reiki attunement will pay dividends in the form of the energy entering the system with less resistance. If you are thinking of taking an attunement, spend a few weeks prior to the appointed day in addressing your lifestyle. Firstly begin to prepare yourself spiritually by asking for guidance in meditation or prayer. Speak with your life guide or guardian angel and tell them what you are proposing to do. They will know anyway, but they will be pleased to be acknowledged and consulted. It makes a difference. Next, address your diet. In particular

After attunement the light body vibration is now much faster. The physical body must detox and shed some dross in order to catch up and once again be in resonance.

cut out all meat if you can, or just red meat if you can't. Bring fresh fruit and vegetables more into focus as your staple foods. Cut out all junk food. Cut out tea and coffee and bring in herbal or fruit teas, or best of all, just pure water and fruit juices. Take some time to be outside with nature, walking in woodland is very cleansing to the aura and subtle bodies. Sit beneath trees and ask the nature spirits for help in cleansing and healing. Be relaxed. Don't drink alcohol or smoke.

Any major changes in lifestyle should be approached over a period of time. Don't change your whole pattern of life in one day. This will shock your system and may bring about a major detox or flu-like symptoms. Take your time and plan the introduction of new patterns in a positive and healing way. Address your physical body and tell it you are going to make changes for the better. The cleaner your system the easier will be the transition during attunement and the more efficient and effective will be the power of the energy you now have access to.

## The Energy Source

Energy is governed by a higher source of consciousness. You can call this consciousness whatever you like. Some people call it God or God Consciousness, the Universal Mind or Universal Consciousness. If you have a belief system or religion you can call it after whatever Deity is at the head of your belief system, such as Buddha, Krishna, Jesus, Great Spirit, etc. It doesn't matter what you call it, it is just there and those who work with this force of creation know that it pervades everything and responds to all people equally, no matter what race, creed or colour, without discrimination. It is the one true mind of all creation, functioning on all levels.

This higher source of consciousness knows exactly what you need to attune the light body and oversees exactly how much you can process at the moment of attunement. It controls and monitors the energy during the coming days and weeks as you adjust to the new levels of light entering your being.

If you are a delicate flower, higher consciousness will allow your system to open more gently. If you are a robust person and capable of handling a rush of energy then that will be given to you in the moment. There are many considerations, some of which we may not be aware of in the physical world. After all, we know only a fraction of what there must be to know about energy. We are playing with an infinitesimal grain of energy in a universe which is too vast and complex to comprehend, created and governed as it must be, by an almighty consciousness, visible to most of us only in its physical form. How much more is there in other levels of consciousness?

There is yet another consideration. There are some people who, unbeknown to themselves, may be long overdue to walk this higher vibrational path, and perhaps have great latent healing talent which awaits them. In these cases, they are often given a great awakening, which can be very disturbing to their whole being. This is for a reason. Higher consciousness is saying that in order for you to understand your talent as it now rapidly unfolds, and hence you will develop the wisdom of working with energy, you need to have these exceptional, but frequently uncomfortable experiences.

This situation should not be confused with a student who is having a difficult time due to energy being unbalanced by an attunement which, for whatever reason, has not opened the light body perfectly, or who is in the grip of some kind of psychic attack. There is a huge difference, but unfortunately, the symptoms can be very similar. It takes a great deal of experience to determine this difference.

## A Look at the Traditional Master

A true Master of any school of learning will be available to guide you and for you to ask as many questions as you wish prior to making your decision to enter their teaching. One should be careful not to confuse the title Reiki Master with that of a true Yogic or Tantric Master of the Eastern traditions.

A Master is a very wise, very learned, very disciplined practitioner, teacher and guide who will oversee the advancement of his students through his own connection with higher knowledge. The Master has often been born more advanced than his contemporaries, having already attained a certain level of enlightenment in previous incarnations. He will teach the art and science of personal transformation using various disciplines such as yoga and meditation to learn to work safely with the energies which will connect you to higher consciousness and knowledge. As a Master it is often his life's mission to be detached from the material world to a sufficient extent to attain perfect union with the higher consciousness of his God, the universal consciousness.

Esoteric knowledge has always been passed down through dedicated Masters to students. As the numbers of students come through the Master's school of teaching, there will always be one or two exceptional people, who are destined to carry the torch onward after the Master has passed on, forming their own school.

Esoteric knowledge of energy is often passed down in a very personal and specific way. When the student is ready the Master will pass on the key to the knowledge. In many monastic type disciplines the student may study for many years without ever being asked to come forward for advancement. The student knows that they cannot ask for attunement or advancement; rather, it is offered at the appropriate time.

The Essene people, of whom Jesus was one, considered the development of the receptive energy centres, or chakras, was an essential part of the individual's evolution and that daily practice of correct methods were necessary. This was to bring the organs of the physical body into harmony with all beneficial currents of the earth and the cosmos, so that they can be utilised for the evolution of the individual and the planet. The techniques were handed down by word of mouth over thousands of years, but only passed on to the initiates after seven years of probationary training. (See The Teachings of the Essenes from Enoch to the Dead Sea Scrolls, translated by Edmond Bordeaux Szekely).

A true Master can see with his higher abilities when the student is ready. He will only bring the student forth by right of attainment. This is most importantly brought about by practice of the necessary skills and by dint of balanced personality qualities and balanced ego-structure and ability to hold the energy or light.

We are not talking about intellectual attainment. You may have the most brilliant mind intellectually, one which can memorise and recite hundreds of the sutras or teachings, but intellect is not all that matters in energy work. Intellect is the product of the left hemisphere of the brain and intellect can often get in the way of spiritual advancement and intuitive processes. We are talking about attainment of diversification of consciousness. This is the domain of the right hemisphere of the brain. The Master can see the consciousness of the student and see the places the student can reach with their consciousness. At the right moment the Master will summon the student for advancement.

Advancement through the levels of the esoteric arts is usually through attunement. Most often, the attunement is carried out by breath work. Unlocking the light body of the student requires a key and the key is contained in the Master's own light body as passed to him in turn by his Master, or attained in meditation or through an attuned intuition which is capable of receiving messages and the gifts of the universal mind.

In Reiki, the attunement is passed in this time honoured way, firstly by drawing a symbol in energy and then blowing it into the light body system through the crown and other chakras. This process is accessing spiritual assistance and the power for life-changing purposes in the physical realm.

## Understanding the Unbelievable Power of Energy

In the Eastern traditions, the Master, by use of the breath, opens the kundalini channels of the student, one level at a time over a long period, sometimes many years. This allows the serpent energy known as kundalini, which resides at the base of the spine, to stir and move from its three and half coiled sleeping position, into the three-fold channels of the Ida, Pingala and Shushumna. These channels pass through all the chakras and out through the crown chakra, linking us into communion with a much higher level of consciousness than is attainable through any other method.

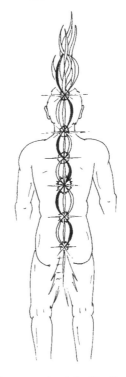

To release the energy of the kundalini inappropriately or too quickly can be very dangerous. This is why the student must study and practise for many years to attain the necessary discipline and control to be able to handle the tremendous power of this energy with safety. The release of this energy into the light body other than under the supervision of a Master is complete folly. Accidental awakening of the kundalini can bring instant psychological trauma, physical damage and pain, no sleep for months on end, or worse.

The three aspects of the Ida, Pingala and Shushumna channels rising up and piercing the chakras.

The kundalini energy is released from the base of the spine and moves upwards, lighting the chakras one by one and bringing in energy of untold force to these centres. The energy can only be brought in a little at a time, such is its power, and over a protracted period of time the light body, in combination with the consciousness, learns how to control this energy safely.

C.W. Leadbeater, the great clairvoyant and scholar of the mystery schools, describes kundalini in his seminal work entitled *The Chakras*. Gained from his knowledge of the Hindu Yogic teachings, he says that she is a "Devi or Goddess, luminous as lightning, who lies asleep in the root chakra coiled like a serpent three and half times round the Isvayambhu linga which is there, and closing the entrance to the shushumna with her head". It is well to remember, three and a half is a very powerful number in sacred geometry and esoteric energy work, appearing in nature as indeed it is present naturally in our light body.

Leadbeater also tells us what can happen when an inappropriate release of kundalini energy takes place.

"For the ordinary person it lies at the base of the spine unawakened, and its very presence unsuspected, during the whole of his life; and it is indeed far better to allow it thus to remain dormant until the man has made definite moral development, until his will is strong enough to control it and his thoughts pure enough to enable him to face its awakening without injury. No one should experiment with it without definite instruction from a teacher who thoroughly understands the subject, for the dangers connected with it are very real and terribly serious. Some of them are purely physical. Its uncontrolled movement often produces intense physical pain, and it may readily tear tissues and even destroy physical life ..." (which is) "the least of the evils of which it is capable, for it may do permanent injury to vehicles higher than the physical".

By 'higher than the physical' Leadbeater means injury or damage to the light body in the auric bodies of the lower self and higher self and possibly even as far out as soul level. This damage may cause serious problems through a number of incarnations until the person has sought and found help to correct it.

Leadbeater continues;

"One very common effect of arousing it prematurely is that it rushes downwards in the body instead of upwards, and thus excites the most undesirable passions — excites them and intensifies their effects to such a degree that it becomes impossible for the man to resist them, because a force has been brought into play in whose presence he is as helpless as a swimmer before the jaws of a shark. Such men become satyrs, monsters of depravity, because they are in the grasp of a force which is out of all proportion to the ordinary human power of resistance. They may probably gain certain supernormal powers, but these will be such as will bring them into touch with a lower order of evolution with which humanity is intended to hold no commerce, and to escape from its awful thraldom may take them more than one incarnation …"

"… Even apart from this greatest of its dangers, the premature unfoldment of the higher aspects of kundalini has many other unpleasant possibilities. It intensifies everything in the man's nature, and it reaches the lower and evil qualities more readily than the good. In the mental body, for example, ambition is very quickly aroused, and soon swells to an incredibly inordinate degree. It would be likely to bring with it a great intensification of the power of intellect, but at the same time it would produce abnormal and satanic pride, such as is quite inconceivable to the ordinary man. It is not wise for a man to think that he is prepared to cope with any force that may arise within his body; this is no ordinary energy, but something resistless".

"The force is a tremendous reality, one of the great basic facts of nature and most emphatically it is not a thing with which to play … for to experiment with it without understanding it is far more dangerous than it would be for a child to play with nitro-glycerine … It brings liberation to Yogis and bondage to fools".

## Reiki and Kundalini

Reiki is a kundalini process in some ways, but in reverse. The Yogic student through breath, meditation and chakra work will spend many hours a day for years to prepare their system for kundalini awakening. During this practice they will already have surpassed a level equivalent to a Reiki awakening. They will have the knowledge to empower the chakras and bring energy into the body in a very grounded way, through the base chakra, through the crown chakra in a direct cosmic flow, and indeed through any chakra they choose to focus upon. They will also be able to transmit energy from their body for energy exchange or healing. However, primarily the student will have consciously awakened this energy at the base chakra and manifested its path in an upward direction.

The Reiki attunement opens the chakras from the crown down through the brow, throat and into the heart, bringing us into a state of raised energy in the light body, where we can now, at will, channel higher frequencies of light into our system. So, whereas the kundalini student is brought into a higher state of being by the raising of energy from the base upwards, the Reiki student is brought into a higher state of being from the crown downwards. Remember though, the Yogic student has already attained and surpassed the level of a Reiki student before they ever begin to reach a point where they can undergo serious kundalini training with a suitably awakened Master.

## The Invisible Power of Breath

Breathwork has always been important in practices of transcendence and spiritual attainment. In this way we can say that Jesus probably attuned his disciples to energies similar to that of Reiki. Just because Jesus was an Avatar and an extremely high Master does not necessarily mean that he would have passed on the highest level of attunement to his followers, for they could only receive that with which they could cope at that point in their own evolution.

Jesus was born into the Essene people. The Essenes were a most enlightened and holy people, practising higher conscious thought and prayer, very in tune with the consciousness of the landscape and of many angelic aspects of the elements. Also very in tune with the consciousness of their own bodies, they practised cleanliness, colonic irrigation and a vegetarian regime. Where better for a son of God to be born, but within a spiritually enlightened community where he would prosper from a very early age with many Masters as teachers? Indeed, rather than being a Master who sat in meditation within his Ashram for many hours a day as we see in some cultures, Jesus was an active and busy person, learning, travelling, teaching and healing abroad in the world.

In the gospel according to John, we hear of Jesus on the first day after his crucifixion and burial by Joseph of Aramathea, appearing to Mary Magdelene beside his tomb and bidding her tell his brothers (disciples) that he is returning to his father and their father. Later that evening Jesus came and stood amongst the disciples and said "Peace be with you" and showed them his hands, feet and his side which had been pierced by the spear. Again he said "Peace be with you", and continued. "As the Father has sent me, so I am sending you". And with that he breathed on them and said "Receive the Holy Spirit". He continued "If you forgive anyone his sins, they are forgiven. If you do not forgive them, they are not forgiven".

In this scene we see three very powerful energy lessons taking place. Firstly we see Jesus speak of returning to his father or returning to pure spirit or a level of conscious energy which is everywhere at once. Transcending time and space, it encompasses every soul in creation in a knowledgeable dance of everlasting life. He tells them this conscious energy source is what He has been born of; it is his father, but also they are born of this same conscious matter.

But before he goes he passes on to his disciples, whom he now calls his brothers, the key to realising their own higher potential, by breathing upon them in turn and saying "receive the Holy Spirit". "As the Father has sent me, so I am sending you," says Jesus. In the second lesson, Jesus is saying, as I have the gift of communion and connection with God, the Father of all that is, so to you I pass on this gift. I am opening you, attuning you and sending this energy into you so that you also may have communion and connection with God. His parting gift to them then, is an attunement, the key to ever progressive unfoldment and attainment of healing power and spiritual evolution. Within this act of attunement of course, is the demonstration of the power of breath.

The third energy lesson is thought forms. After the attunement Jesus then speaks of the power of thought forms when He discusses forgiveness of sins. If someone sins against us, we harbour ill thoughts against that person. The harbouring of these thoughts constitutes negative energy which is held within our own being and at some level will work against us, holding us back on our own spiritual growth journey. Not only does it hold us back but it bonds us to the person whom we target with our thoughts, with silver chords of light. It burdens the other person and makes them the captive of our projected thought form. The thought form is also a type of psychic attack. These created and projected thought forms will survive as an energy imprint forever, unless dismantled, or withdrawn by forgiveness. So Jesus is saying to his brothers, forgive all sins against you for if you do not the thought form pattern will burden you and also those who have sinned against you, forever. The pattern will not dissolve. Therefore, He says "If you forgive anyone his sins, they are forgiven (the thought forms are dissolved). If you do not forgive them, they are not forgiven" (the thought forms remain binding indefinitely).

If we look further back in scripture to Moses, we see that Moses spent much time in communion with God and was chosen against his will to bring forth various messages to his people. In Deuteronomy 34,7 we read that "Moses was a hundred and twenty years old when he died, yet his eyes were not weak, nor his strength gone". This would be a good indicator of one who carried much kundalini energy in his being. Deuteronomy 34,9 continues... "Now Joshua, son of Nun was filled with the spirit of wisdom, because Moses had laid his hands on him". Again, here we see an attunement being passed from Moses to Joshua, the passing on of the torch of unfoldment from Master to Student. Quite probably there was breathwork involved in this attunement also, but for whatever reason it is not contained in the present scriptures.

I am not suggesting for one moment that there is any parallel between Moses, Jesus and a Reiki Master, but it is important to understand that the awakening of the light body has always been passed from Master to student by similar means. Although Jesus was a divine incarnation of the healing aspect of God, he will have no doubt undergone attunements during his studies with the Essene people. They were intuitives and scholars of the esoteric subjects and they will have known who Jesus was before he ever came amongst them and they will have helped him to develop.

## Releasing Kundalini – an Example

I was fascinated by Dr. Gabriel Cousin's description of his own kundalini awakening experience when I first read it several years ago in his book *Spiritual Nutrition and the Rainbow Diet*. It is a brilliant book by someone with a sure knowledge and grasp of energy principles and with permission I include his description here. I would ask the reader to note that he underwent much training and was under the guidance of his Master, Swami Muktananda Paramahansa at the time of his unfoldment.

> "At a special two day meditation retreat designed specifically to raise the kundalini energy, Muktananda employed a technique of spiritual transmission called Shaktipat, whereby one who has the energy of kundalini awakened within them sends this energy into the spiritual aspirant to awaken the serpent fire, kundalini which sleeps at the base of the spine in the first or base chakra."

Muktananda passed shaktipat to Gabriel by first hitting him with his peacock feather wand, I assume gently, and followed this by putting his hand over the mouth in a funnel shape and blowing directly into the mouth. He then squeezed the bridge of the nose and pushed the head backwards.

Gabriel continues...

> "After what seemed a few minutes I went into a deep meditation. In the midst of this, my mouth spontaneously opened and my tongue stuck out as far as it could go. These sorts of unusual physical movements are known as kryas, and they may occur on an emotional, mental, physical and spiritual level. They may be gentle pulsations or swirling feelings over the chakra area, very vigorous physical movements, sudden changes in emotional states, spontaneous crying, rapid thought production, or spiritual visions. They are evidence of the purifying movement of the kundalini as it travels through the nadis spontaneously working through blocked areas of energy. I later found out that my tongue sticking out is a yoga position known as the lion pose. While the lion pose was happening, I experienced a peaceful wavy bliss. At some point after this, I began to have a vision of Muktananda in which he guided me into a fusion and awareness of my Inner Divine Self. Following this, the experience of oneness between my inner world and the universe began to emerge into my awareness".

> "A little later in the meditation, I had the inner vision of my third, fourth, and fifth chakras in their anatomical locations all bathed in a full golden light. As the energy moved upward in my body, my eyes turned upward to the brow chakra to see Nityananda (Muktananda's guru) sitting in a lotus posture looking down at me. As my inner vision continued to turn upward, I experienced and saw the crown chakra blazing in what looked like thousands of lights. Sometime during this meditation, I began to experience intense pains in the sacral and lumbar areas. This back pain, in many people, is associated with the awakening of the kundalini".

The visions Gabriel experienced, while in meditation, of his Master Muktananda and his former Master Nityananda, are typical of how the Master can enter your consciousness to guide and protect you during your unfoldment. These are not just visions, they are the reality of the accompaniment by your Master on your journey of unfoldment.

Following this first part of the awakening Gabriel's meditations at home became more intense, with emotional issues coming up. The physical kriyas continued including spontaneous rapid and slow breathing known as pranayama, a technique often employed in awakening the kundalini. Some ten days after the awakening a red rash developed on his back, starting in the lower back and curling back and forth across the spine before it veered off to his left shoulder, lasting about a week. This gave the appearance of stigma similar to the Pingala or Ida channel, which was possibly opened during the awakening.

A few weeks later, Gabriel took a second meditation with Muktananda to enhance the awakened kundalini. Muktananda again directly channelled the energy into Gabriel resulting in an even more intense movement of the kundalini energy in the body and up the spine. Hot-cold shooting pains occurred in the upper back and neck and there were burning pains in the thyroid and throat region. The head and neck went through spontaneous movements.

At the final meditation of the retreat the energy moved up the spine with great heat and culminated in a great explosion of white light in the head and it felt as though he was exploding with energy. A great many visions of the chakras burning brightly and feelings of deep inner peace prevailed and pervaded his awareness. His body pulsed in total ecstasy and it was at this moment he realised that death did not exist ... for the self. The physical body might die, but the Truth, the I Am of his existence, was immortal.

During the following months Gabriel's desire for total communion with God was pursued relentlessly. His friends joked that he was like a bull in heat. He received his Master's permission to increase his daily meditations to four hours, the maximum his structure could tolerate. During this period of several sessions of meditations and chanting with his spiritual friends every day, he describes feeling,

"... like a plane reaching speeds and energies at which the wings were about ready to come off. My whole body, ego-mind, spirit integration was undergoing intense transformation".

In the following daily log Gabriel writes:

"In my afternoon meditation, it started again, with lots of energy. Nice visions of Baba (Muktananda) alternating with different energy forms. I was feeling joy and light. Then a brief sense of a negative energy feeling — vision came and quickly passed. Obviously the play of consciousness — it almost seemed psychedelic. Then the vas deferens spasm began; much pain, hot, painful erection. My whole pelvic area to lower solar area on the inside became flaming red hot.

My body began to undulate in orgasmic movements. Self-consciously I am relieved that I am the only one sitting in the meditation hall at that time of the day. But I had tinges of self-consciousness sitting in half lotus having spontaneous preorgasmic undulations. Then I realised that it was not going to stop. I was going to have an orgasm right in the middle of the meditation hall! I could not believe that this was happening. I was not even having any sexual thoughts or feelings. I then began vigorous dry ejaculation spasms with my whole lower pelvis involved. No semen was coming out. What a surprise! With each orgasmic spasm, I could feel and see (in meditation vision) the semen shooting directly up the shushumna, broadening it and extending the shushumna channel opening all the way to my brow chakra. It filled me with intense energy. It went on for what might have been 15 to 30 minutes. It took another 15 minutes for the erection to go down. It was another one and half hours before the perineal pain subsided".

"The next day, the nails of both my little toes spontaneously came off. It was as if the energy was so intense that my system could barely contain the energy. This whole process was very sobering. I felt a quiet joy in surrendering to a process that was more powerful than I and which was beyond my comprehension. But it is one thing to revel in the bliss of the divine communion and another to surrender to having my internal anatomy reorganised".

"Following this night and day long experience, whenever I even had the glimmerings of a sexual thought, that painful ten to twelve inch rod of energy would begin to activate. It seemed as if it were a shish kebab skewer piercing through the round discs of my first three innocent chakras".

Within the above text you may gather that energy work is a serious business. I work with energy on a daily basis at quite a high level, but I am not foolish enough to believe that I am anywhere near as enlightened as a student who works with an evolved Master for many years in the disciplines needed to attain this kind of awakening. But everyday I learn new things.

I would point out that during Gabriel's meditations you will notice that he often sees his Master. This is not merely a vision but this is the consciousness of his Master entering his own consciousness in order to guide and monitor his unfoldment. Evolved Masters have many abilities in the area of leaving their physical body in order to travel instantly, at the speed of thought, to be with whom they desire. Bilocation is also the ability to be in more than one place at a time.

For Gabriel to have reached this stage in his evolution, he will have attained a reasonable degree of enlightenment in former incarnations. A Master will not take a student to these heights until they have reached the appropriate level of spiritual evolution through energy work. As C.W. Leadbeater says, "the Masters always know when a student is ready for unfoldment. Their consciousness is everywhere, it pervades all that is in terms of the physical world and they see us and know when we are ready". So there is no point going out in search of a Master ... evolution begins within the self, at home, not on some high mountain in Tibet or Ashram in India. Yes it is good to be in the presence of the enlightened ones and to bathe in their light, but in reality you don't need to travel. The consciousness can reach out and ask for guidance and the enlightened ones will hear your call and assist you. Ask and you shall receive.

One day perhaps, I may be invited to follow the path of the kundalini fire, but for now I am very busy trying to understand the new things which unfold for me on a regular basis and as I look back on each previous twelve month period I am amazed at the new things I have seen and experienced.

Leaving the heady heights of kundalini behind us and coming back into the everyday world of healing at whatever level we mere mortals are working at, we should know that working with energy is not all sweetness and light. There is always a price to pay for any gift of power. In fact, gift is the wrong word. Exchange is more appropriate. We are given access to a level of energy with which to work, in exchange for our commitment to our own evolution. Evolve and you will be given a broader spectrum to work with. Evolution on a mental and emotional level is usually painful. The same lessons are constantly presented to us to deal with. To see the lesson is one thing, to evolve through it is quite another. Many times we kid ourselves that we have learned the lesson, but more often it is the case that we have seen it and tricked ourselves into placing it out of harm's way in the sub-conscious for now. Another great lesson we usually receive from a gift of power is enlargement of the ego. This is a good one to get stuck with for a few years ... or the rest of this incarnation. Tread carefully amongst all who wear the sign of Master.

When we work with energy it courses through our physical body and all our subtle bodies. This has the effect of moving energy and releasing energy and blockages whenever we work. This can have a very de-stabilising effect on the balance of the subtle bodies. For instance, the emotional and mental bodies are quite finely balanced in most people. Running energy through your system day after day can seriously upset the balance of these bodies and one can become quite unstable as the energies constantly purge your system. I don't mean unstable in a serious way, but emotionally you may become sensitive or your emotions may be very changeable. At a mental level you may become tired or stressed very easily. I have seen this to dramatic effect with students going through their Reiki second degree program of homework on many occasions. Their emotional body has not usually had this level of energy course through them previously.

When I am working in a healing session with Guides, those clients who are sensitive enough will often feel the whole room vibrating as the spiritual essence performs it's wondrous work. One cannot expect to work at this level, within such powerful vibrations without experiencing change. Change is evolution and evolution can be a painful process. In the Gnostic Gospels, Jesus says. "Let he who seeks, continue to seek. When he finds, he will become troubled". This is a reference to many aspects of realisation, particularly that we have many incarnations and that the soul is eternal. The deeper the insights mankind receives from and of the universe, the more he has to think about the way he passes every moment within an earth incarnation. The understanding of 'what we sow, so do we reap' in karmic terms becomes a reality. The realisations challenge everything you think and everything you do. Ultimately, the speed we evolve is up to us, the more work we do and the speed with which we can incorporate new realisations into our lives, the faster will be our progression.

Many healers who work at a high level, channelling many frequencies of energy, will tell you of these disturbances to their lives. Many will have periods where a kind of breakdown regularly takes place. The mental and emotional body can only take so much battering without it needing a serious rest. For some healers, this can be equated to the physical body suffering a whiplash injury in a car accident every day. The physical body would only be able to stand up for so long before needing a serious recovery period. Mental and emotional breakdown is often the beings way of saying, you need a rest, you can't take this anymore until you have re-balanced. The key point to remember is that the more we do, the more difficult our life may become. We can become overwhelmed by the changes of consciousness.

## 04

> All truth goes through three stages:-
> It is ridiculed …
> It is vehemently opposed …
> It is agreed to be self evident!
> Arthur Shopenhauer (1788–1860)

REIKI? … YOU ONLY KNOW THE HALF OF IT! THIS SUBJECT is really what prompted me to begin this book in the first place. Reiki is a wonderful thing and it has arrived for the people of this planet not a moment too soon. However I have had concerns for some time, that people taking up Reiki don't actually know or understand what it is they are getting into. Not only that, but many of the teachers opening the doors to this energy for their students also don't know much about what healing or energy work is, or the many pitfalls that can await them.

I don't say this as any criticism of any individual Reiki Master's teaching methods, as clearly, we can only teach what we know. That knowledge can only come from three sources, either what we have been taught by our teachers, from books, or from our own experiences. Experience is by far the best teacher, but this is only accumulated over time. Many of our Reiki Masters today are very new to the world of energy work, not having come from an energy or healing background originally. Therefore, they do not have the accumulated experiences under their belt which the benefits of time can bring about.

# REIKI? … YOU ONLY KNOW THE HALF OF IT!

I am certain that I will alienate some of my fellow Reiki Masters by what I have written in this book, but it needs saying and somebody has to have the courage to say it. I have also been pushed to write this book by Spirit Guides and not just my own Guides. By my hesitation to date, I have been told I am letting them down. I have been told that if I don't write it, I will be put in a position where I have no choice. Having been put in this position previously by Spirit, I know how effective and alarming it can be. I have also been told that this book should have been out before now. Time is running on and records need to be addressed and set straight.

To those of you who feel any negative emotion towards the author of this work, be it anger, frustration, hate or whatever, I ask you to stop and look inside and find the trigger for that emotion. With every emotion there is a message, with most negative emotions such as those mentioned above, the message is fear. Fear produces anger; fear of change, fear that we might have the information incorrect. If you can find the message you can learn a lesson. It takes courage to grasp the nettle of change, learning a new lesson can be a painful experience, but if we are to advance in our own evolution, then sooner or later we have to grasp that nettle. If you learn a lesson then these words will have value for you and I hope that is the case.

## Reiki – Old, yet New

Reiki is a new thing to most of us, myself included, new in terms of its availability to the masses. In days gone by, attunement to this type of energy was kept as a closely guarded secret. Initiates were usually selected by closed religious or spiritual orders and were trained over many years in various techniques before receiving an attunement. Receiving an attunement at Master level would be reserved for very few and by invitation only. This was usually not a path which could be chosen, one could only be invited to walk it.

The training through meditation, chakra work and energy work prepared people over a long period for the changes which were to take place within their being at a physical, mental, emotional or spiritual level. Today, we have a situation where people are fast tracking to Third Degree Reiki without any training or knowledge or, most importantly, experience of energy work at all.

I was recently at a meeting where I overheard a lady, flushed with the excitement of her recent attainment, say to a small group, "I am a Reiki Master now", to which I heard someone else reply, in a light hearted fashion "Who isn't!". This is where we are at in this moment in time in the healing and spiritual evolution world. Everyone is, or wants to be, a Reiki Master.

Somebody has to write down what is happening so that people may become more aware and knowledgeable and it looks as though it is my head which is above the spiritual parapet as this task is given out. There is bad practice all around us and there is back biting amongst us. I don't claim to have all the experiences or knowledge or to have all the answers, which I am sure no one else has either. However, I have decided to write this piece as an expression of my own knowledge and experience of energy work which is broad and extensive by many standards, particularly in the west, yet minuscule compared to that of other life long energy workers both here and in other cultures. Many cultures adopt a more open aspect to the spiritual dimension and other dimensions which surround their existence on the physical plane. Energy workers, Reiki students, Reiki Masters and teachers everywhere might glean from this book some of the dangers and pitfalls of energy work and gain a little more knowledge of how to assess their own readiness for advancement or their student's readiness to receive attunement to the Reiki or any other ray of energy. Also, as well as gleaning a little knowledge everyone should gain a healthy respect for the energy and learn what to do in a crisis, when things go wrong, both for the Reiki Masters and for their students. And yes, things do go wrong!

It is my opinion that everyone on the planet should have Reiki. If we did, then the crumbling fabric of our present so called 'civilised world' might well have a chance of progressing instead of remaining in its continual cycle of new technology and inventions which move society absolutely nowhere. As it is, society is in a state of total chaos. There are those of us who are trying to evolve and move forward and their are those of us who are stuck in a rut.

## Where Do We Start?

There are many questions the prospective student *should* have the answers to where Reiki or any other energy work is concerned. But as always, we never know in advance the questions we should ask before we have the problems to deal with after the event of a mishap.

When working in the area of energies, we are working in unknown dimensions of existence, with energy about which we know relatively little. We say the energy has it's own consciousness. This is a judgement made from experience: we know it goes where it is supposed to when we use it in a healing situation, but we don't really know the source. We say the source is from universal consciousness. This is only guesswork. Nobody knows for sure. For all we know it could be one of Satan's immaculate deceptions. The truth is, we don't know where it comes from.

We work with our Spirit Guides and the attunement is facilitated by Spirit Guides, but who are they really? We work from a centre of love and bring into our being light which we perceive is from a divine source. The work we do with this light, or energy, achieves results which benefit those whom we are trying to help, but the truth is, we cannot say for certain that we know what we are connecting with and what we are bringing through our system. The only real guidance we have is the knowledge obtained and disseminated by the great Gurus who have preceded us. Not many of us have attained the heady heights of transcending our physical bodies, therefore we cannot judge from our own experience.

At the end of the day it is only your own experience which will give you answers which you can call your own truth. Truth is individual to each person. Your truth is not my truth and the words of my truth which I have written in this book are not your truth. You must have the experience and then you have the truth as perceived by your own being ... these things will be true to you. When you have some truths you can share the experiences of these truths with like-minded souls. If you find the experiences have been similar you will be able to make judgements which may broaden your knowledge, but until then you must gather as many experiences as possible.

I will say that I subscribe to the belief that we are doing good work. Speaking for myself, my intentions are true and I can stand at the pearly gates at the end of this incarnation and say with honesty that I did what I thought was right and good. If I have got the whole picture wrong, then I will have some more learning to do the next time around. I subscribe to the belief that our Guides mean well and that the Reiki energy does have it's own consciousness, in as much as I think every atom in the universe has a consciousness. With the limited tools of investigation which we posses, namely our consciousness, we can only draw hypotheses from our own experiences. My main point is that as individuals, we should question everything, accept nothing and have the experience to provide us with our truth. Just because it seems to make sense is no reason to accept it. Beware ... Be aware ... Take care!

## Tuning the Light Body

My apologies for the masculine, left brained analogy here, but it serves very well to describe what happens when we alter the energy centres of the light body.

When you tune the engine of a motor car you get better or increased performance. When you tune the energy centres of your light body, namely your chakras, you get the same results: increased performance. The novice driver who gets behind the wheel of a high performance motor car without adequate training or knowledge sometimes gets into trouble, unable to control what is happening. Likewise, when you receive a tune-up to your light body with an attunement such as Reiki, again without the proper training or any previous knowledge or experience of working with energy, you sometimes have problems. Remember, Reiki is an attunement process, it is changing your core being at an energetic light level. Once you have the attunement you can't ask for it to be taken back or say you don't want it now. You must now move forward with the changes that will become a part of you and one must understand that if you work with the energy you need to know about protection.

## Protection

When an enlightened student asks the Reiki Master about protection, many bemused faces are often seen in the class. I say enlightened student, for many students of Reiki have never considered that there may be a danger in using this energy. The answer the Reiki Master often gives is that, Reiki is its own protection or Reiki will protect you, or even that Reiki will protect you from anything! They will continue by saying that Reiki brings protection with it and that there are no dangers working with Reiki.

I have seen the worried faces of students who are completely new to healing and energy work, when someone raises this question of protection. They are asking themselves: What do they mean by protection? Is this Reiki thing dangerous? Why do I need protection? What is it that can go wrong? What do I need protecting from? What *are* the dangers? In these situations I have seen uncertainty, I have seen confusion and I have seen fear.

Let us get this next most important point absolutely clear from the beginning. Reiki does not protect you! That's right, I'll repeat it ... Reiki does not protect you! When healers come to see me with energy problems — and more often than not they are Reiki healers and Reiki Masters — I take them back to basics. The basics are so simple and fundamental they have often never considered or comprehended what is happening. I ask them, "what does Reiki do?" After some time thinking and fumbling for an answer, I usually hand one to them ... Reiki opens you up! In their eyes I can see the incomprehension. What does he mean, opens me up?

Reiki opens you up, that is what it is designed to do. When you have your attunement, your chakras are opened up to a new level. They are bringing energy into your system at an increased rate and if you are not able to control what is happening at a chakra awareness level, you may end up with chakras which become locked open. Even if they do not become locked, the increased flow of energy can make a complete mess of the balance of your chakras and lead to patterns being released from your being which lodge firmly in the chakras, or energy structures being drawn into the chakras which can also get caught within them, as fish get caught in a net.

But there are dangers of this sort working with any form of energy, not only with Reiki. In Einsteinian theory, which is based upon physical laws, energy is matter and matter is energy. It is impossible to alter the energy state of one of these without it affecting the other. In the case of healing energy, we are dealing with completely different laws, universal laws, of which science knows little or nothing, because science cannot measure things in the spiritual world or in the realm of subtle energies. Reiki is a subtle and spiritual energy. Under universal laws, the energy we channel does not become matter, but it does affect the state of matter. So when we channel energy or work with manipulating energy in any form, we are entering into and progressing a potential situation where matter can and in all probability will be affected. For if anyone thinks that engaging in the manipulation of energy does not place you in a position of potential danger, they do not understand the very basic principles of what we are dealing with. When we work with energy we are working in dimensions that most of us do not understand, that most cannot see and that most have no control over. We are opening doors and we can access things accidentally that can cause us a great deal of anxiety, pain and discomfort. When I was studying one particular form of energy work some years ago, my tutor didn't exclude death from this list of possible side effects.

Without wishing to be alarmist I will say that the majority of Reiki students do not have problems, but when you begin working with energy you should be aware that sooner or later, and it may be that later is many years down the line, the odds are that you will meet a problem from absorbing an amount of negative energy which you cannot move out of your system. Students who work at Reiki One level for a considerable time seem to fare better than most. Reiki Masters, who have come up through the degrees at a fast rate, are more likely to suffer the consequences of a seriously unbalanced or damaged energy system. The side effects can be tiredness, constant lack of energy, spacy feelings in the head, (often mistaken for spiritual unfoldment) ungrounded feelings, extreme and persistent discomfort or pain in any part of the physical body, but usually associated with a chakra or chakras, emotional problems, relationship breakdown and a total lack of direction. More seriously still, you may encounter the first aspects of psychic attack from entities or spirit attachments. The stage of psychic attack, where beings become attached, is the thin end of the wedge and life can subsequently become very painful and difficult in a very short period of time.

As someone who specialises in psychic attack rescue, I have treated many extremely talented and experienced healers and energy workers, who because of their long experience of energy work have been very aware of the dangers they are exposed to and take precautions to make sure they have adequate protection at all times when working. Yet occasionally I find them knocking on my door for help. It is an unavoidable *side effect* of healing and energy work. At some time in their career, the majority of people will pick something up and need help to deal with it.

None of us is immune from psychic attack!, although I am perhaps more aware than most, because I help restore the energy systems of those psychic attack victims almost every day of the week. I am very privileged to have been chosen and trained by my Guides to do this kind of work; it has brought me much experience.

However, I am nevertheless humbled to know that my Guides continue to provide me with the most amazing psychic protection to do this work. In addition to the help they provide, they also continue to alter the structure of my being during healing sessions, which enables me to deal with ever more powerful and dangerous forms of psychic energy and malevolent beings.

Yet, I have still been caught out myself. Never when I have been working with energy, because I am at that time totally tuned into what I am doing and fully protected, but usually when I am completely switched off, minding my own business and doing something as mundane as shopping. All of sudden, whack, something has taken a bite out of my crown chakra — and the headache and pain starts immediately. The last time was around Christmas 1997, when I was nonchalantly drifting around one of the more select stores in Manchester, looking at the things I couldn't afford. This just goes to show that our little friends from other dimensions are clearly not choosy whom they feast on, rich and famous, or just you and me.

Mind, Body, Spirit fairs are particularly alive with entity activity by their very nature. As well as all the energy being raised by different folk in their various energy practices, many people needing help and healing come to these fairs carrying negative energies and entities. Extra protection should be sought if you know yourself to be vulnerable or susceptible to psychic attack. If you work with energy at the level I do and you become complacent, then a lesson is soon delivered, courtesy of the Universe, to remind you exactly what you are dealing with.

## In the Beginning

Let us take a journey back to the beginning of life in the Physical Plane of existence, here on Planet Earth. When we are born into the world, we all have a Guardian Angel or Spirit Guide. This is a Guide from the spiritual realms who accompanies us on this journey of incarnation in the physical body and physical world to help and assist us where possible. Sometimes this Guide is very powerful in the area of psychic energies and can provide protection for the person in certain areas of their lives.

You may have heard stories of people having inexplicably avoided accidents, from an inner message telling them not to go here or there today, or perhaps in a driving situation where it seems as if a hand has taken the wheel for a moment, avoiding certain collision. In some instances where the predestined path of the person is to work in healing or with energies, they may have a Guide who can provide psychic protection. In my experience though, it is not often that someone has a primary Guide who is with them specifically to provide psychic protection.

Some people may be born with more than one Guide in attendance. Usually this happens where the person has incarnated with a specific mission which involves working in psychic areas, healing or with subtle energies. Even in this type of scenario, a Guide will not be present to help with protection. Usually Guides are only in attendance for assisting with the chosen work of the present incarnation.

Let us have a look at what happens when things go wrong as we work with energy. The theory is very simple.

## The Inner Light

Out there in the big wide world, most of us only perceive what we sense through our five senses — sight, sound, smell, taste and touch. The majority of the time, this is the only *modus operandi* we are switched into, and we are not usually very acutely attuned at that. Clearly, we can't walk down the street in a meditational state with our perceptions heightened or totally tuned in, as we might be in a healing session with our intuition running high. Even if we were tuned in, the chances are we wouldn't be able to sense all of the baddies who are walking amongst us anyway.

Psychic energies are all around us. Psychic Vampires or Entities are everywhere and you would be amazed and most probably horrified to learn how many. People in the street are carrying them around with them and these energies are interested in only one thing: food. The food they crave is our energy; our electromagnetic life force energy; the energy within our chakras and our aura, which is the very essence of our light body or spirit body.

Entity: see colour section.
© Dinah Arnette

At an energetic level, we humans have tremendous power at the core of our being, an absolute powerhouse of subtle energy. Imagine for a moment that you are a light bulb. Most of us are born as a 60 watt light bulb and we give off a nice calm 60 watts of energy from our inner core, spreading out nicely into our aura, keeping us vibrant and protected. While the aura is whole and maintains its integrity we go through life without much of a problem, but should the aura get damaged in any way, we begin to leak our energy out into our surroundings, not only into our world, but into other dimensions of light. Our defences become breached so to speak and we become progressively drained and function on a constantly decreasing level of energy.

Now imagine you are wearing a raincoat with holes in it and this raincoat represents your aura. Imagine your inner core 60 watt light bulb, glowing away like a spotlight inside the coat. The rays of light are going to escape through the holes, making you look like a wartime night sky with spotlight beams shooting out into the blackness of the heavens above. In the subtle energy realms where other beings dwell, this is exactly how they see you. They are beings of light of one frequency or another and they dwell in the lower levels of the realms of light. These are the realms where your subtle energy, your core being, your chakras are seen. Your subtle energy functions in the realms of light and is completely visible to all and sundry out there.

Once the aura is damaged then your energy spills out all over the place. All we now need to complete the picture is an entity or psychic vampire, one which is attached to another person, who then sees your wonderful energy as it leaks from your system. As this entity has most likely drained a certain amount of energy from its current host, your energy will be shining much brighter than they are. Before you know it, the entity has jumped from that person's energy system right into your energy system. Depending how big and powerful the entity is, you will either feel it straight-away in the form of headache or pain in the back of the neck, or one of the chakras, or it will begin to feed more slowly and the discomfort creeps up over an hour or so. If you are really unlucky, it will paralyse you instantly in crippling pain as it bites huge chunks out of your aura or crown chakra as it lands on you. It can feel like being hit over the head with a baseball bat. I've seen it happen.

Light leaking from a damaged aura can be seen across other dimensions, like search lights in a night sky.

## Raising the Power

When you have a Reiki attunement you are 'raising the power', or increasing the amount of energy which flows into your system. In effect, you are no longer shining like the 60 watt light bulb we mentioned earlier. You are now shining like a 250 watt light bulb, putting out many times the light that was your previous self.

The Reiki attunement initially opens up the top four chakras, the Crown, Third Eye, Throat and Heart Chakra, and during the following 21 day cleansing period the other chakras come up to the same level, as the attunement filters through the system. The energy coming into these centres is vastly increased after attunement. In some instances the attunement can completely shock the system by the influx of the newly increased flow of energy, which may flood in with great force. However, as mentioned earlier, it is important to clarify that the Reiki energy does function with its own or a higher form of consciousness and will only open the student to the degree for which they are ready to unfold on an energetic level. This does not mean it will leave them in a state of balance!

When the energy enters your system many changes take place that we do not understand completely. We can only perceive what is happening by the changes which are taking place within our own being. As we are all different and all in a different energy state and spiritual state, then there is no way that a Reiki Master can predict exactly what will happen to the student after attunement. Indeed, we cannot predict what will happen to ourselves as students until it happens.

Many good books have been written on Reiki over the years, but no amount of reading can prepare you. Reiki is an experiential phenomenon. You have to experience it to understand what message others are trying to give you about it. In fact you could say that Reiki is the nearest thing to magic that you could imagine. When you have experienced the changes which take place with Reiki and understand something of how these are brought about between Reiki Master, Spirit Guides and Student, then from a lay perspective, it can only be seen as a magical right of passage.

## Back to Basics Again

We need to consider another point. Again, imagine going back to birth, coming into the world as a new physical being, but this time imagine you are a radio set. The crown chakra is the aerial linking us to the ethers of the cosmic consciousness, that infinity of channels of information broadcasting throughout the universe. However, in universal terms, here we are, an infinitesimal being, helpless, on a rock, in a solar system, in a spiral galaxy, somewhere in a universe and we are plugged in, we are receiving signals. When we begin our journey of life, the majority of us can only receive one station on our radio set, one frequency of vibration, the basic vibration of human life force function, the signal that says eat, sleep, procreate and survive. When we have a Reiki attunement, we can now receive an additional frequency. The frequency of the Reiki Energy, brings other vibrations into our being, providing unfoldment on a different level which previously we were unaware of. We can now move beyond the basic life force functions of existence in the physical plane.

So now we have access to two channels and each time we have an attunement we can begin to receive additional frequencies. The spectrum of receivable electro-magnetic frequencies becomes broader the more we work with energy; not just healing energy, but earth energies, psychic energies, meditation, prayer or any other form of subtle energy work will bring additional connections to channels of energy.

When we are born, most people receive only one channel.

In Pranic healing we talk of the spiritual channel, one single channel which is your connection to higher consciousness, and one can measure the width of this across the crown of the head. The more a person works with spiritual energies the broader this beam of energy grows. Many people who have been working with Reiki for a while will have a beam of spiritual energy some several inches in diameter going right through their body from head to foot and beyond in both directions, down into the earth and up into the heavens. My own spiritual channel when at it's minimum, is some 3ft. 3ins. in diameter. It is like a cylinder of light which surrounds one, which you stand in the middle of, like standing in a clear glass tube. When working and channelling energies this channel can increase in diameter. In my present state of spiritual evolution, my spiritual channel can expand to a maximum diameter of 17ft. 3ins. This is a quite enormous field of energy when I am plugged in and doing healing work. Frequently, I don't need to stand and practise hands on healing positions because the spiritual energy channel is so wide it encompasses the healee easily within its diameter. The energy in this space is swirling and dancing and you can imagine that this is a sort of spiritual aura provided for the duration and very necessary effect of the healing. The client is within this aura, they are in my aura and that is all that is needed. Just being there in that space brings all the healing energy that is needed.

Each attunement or leap in spiritual evolution brings more channels into your being.

I don't need to do anything in particular except be present and allow them to bathe in this amazing energy.

Of course it is not the same every time. When working with spiritual energy you are given what is required and by the same token, I am shown by my Guides only what I need to see. It may be that the work required is of a specific nature, in which crystals, vibrational essences or expanded and penetrating mind work is required. Sometimes it may be a channelled message or mantra for the healee to use on themselves. In these cases, they often do not need to be in that vortex of healing energy called the spiritual channel and therefore it is not opened up to it's maximum extent.

The growing Spiritual Channel which surrounds a person as they evolve.

There are those amongst us who are born already connected to many frequencies of energy or light: born healers, born channellers, mediums, clairvoyants. As children, if we were brought up in the right environment, an environment which fostered and encouraged the use of intuition and imagination, we would automatically develop access to some of these other light frequencies as part of our natural growth pattern. In the process we would attract more Spirit Guides and we would develop spiritually through our experiences.

The Aborigine and Native American Indian cultures demonstrate how a well developed intuition and communication on a higher level are inherent in people who foster these principles.

As an aside I shall tell you a little story to illustrate this point. A few years ago, my friend Jim met a Native American, a Jicarilla Apache, who was travelling with two other important elders of the tribe to catalogue their artefacts which were being held in various museums across America. The two men met on a fire escape and struck up an immediate rapport. During the following couple of evenings this gentleman and his companions shared dinner with Jim and also shared things that they had never told any white man before. This man was the cultural custodian for his people and in conversation he revealed that he was now trying to open to some of the old ways.

Although I cannot give you the full details here of the things which passed between them, I was very excited by what Jim had told me of this strange union and spiritual connection which resulted from that chance meeting on the fire escape. Later that year Jim and his wife Rita were to visit the gentleman and help him along his spiritual path. It was planned to bring him into the Reiki light by giving him a Reiki attunement plus some other spiritual instruction.

As the time approached for them to leave for the States, I was guided to send a gift of Medicine Cards to this man and also a poem to accompany them. When I am tuned in, I can channel very appropriate poetry from a soul level quite easily. In this instance I struggled and struggled for weeks and could only manage to raise two lines of verse just before my friends left. I couldn't believe it. Many, many times we are given the answer to a question intuitively but cannot see it for our intellect and consciousness getting in the way. Eventually, it dawned on me, with Jim and Rita's help, that these two insignificant lines were all that was required to accompany the gift. This is how it happened and this is what I wrote:

*Dear Friend,*

*This is a voice you do not know, but that of a spirit
bearing a gift, from afar, yet near to home.*

*It was my intention to write a poem to accompany
this gift, yet for weeks no words came to me.*

*Then, two days before the gift was to leave me,
To make it's long journey to you,
Two lines of verse came into my head.*

*Excitedly, I ran a bath and got in with pen and pad,
To take down the words in a relaxed atmosphere.
Alas, nothing else came, and I struggled with other
words which were ill fitting and clumsy.*

*The next day, I abandoned the poem, disappointed.
Sometimes we are blind to the truth.
Sometimes we cannot see the message.
And we doubt everything of a transcendent nature.*

*I should have learned by now to trust Great Spirit.*

*It was at the very last moment, as the gift and I parted
company for the next stage of its journey that my good
friends Jim and Rita guided me ... and then I could see.*

*I realised, with their help, that the two lines of verse
were the only message to be sent to you. It may be that
you understand more of them than do I.*

*The two lines bear all the beauty and knowledge you*
*will need to begin your journey into the light.*
*Take them to your heart and they will serve you well.*

*And so now, I bid you farewell and leave*
*you to contemplate these words:-*

        *'When the wind speaks,*
           *The man must listen.'*

I received a gift in return and a short letter. In the letter my new found friend wrote:

> "... *It's quite amazing that you talk of listening to the wind, as my grandfather could talk to the wind!! The wind carried the safe news of his Son's return from World War Two!*"

> "*I have learned of this news from my last remaining Aunt and have since taken keen interest in communicating with Mother Earth in whatever form becomes evident to me ...*"

Here is an illustration of how the native cultures foster communication with and through the natural elements, brought about initially by parent to child communion and during the passage of time by higher conscious connection and tuning your subtle energies to the environment. The second point in the illustration is that of intuition. This man was entering his own spiritual awakening and, aware of this, I tried to send him a poem of great depth and profound meaning to help him on his journey. But even though I can channel some excellent words from time to time, I was firmly being told from above that this was not needed, yet I could not see the message.

In fact, the two simple lines, which I was forced to accept, due to the complete absence of anything else coming through which made any sense, couldn't have been more accurately phrased as guidance for one of his paths of spiritual unfoldment. Clearly communication with the wind was in his blood and to reinforce what his aunt was giving to him as guidance, the same message came to him from an unknown source from the other side of the world.

Therefore, if we adopt the energy of our surroundings as our teacher, many things will be revealed to us and we will grow connected to many energies which can bring us help, guidance and personal power. Reiki is just one of these energies, but also a key to many others.

## Fast Tracking to Emptiness and Burnout

Now we have a picture of some of the fundamentals of energy and how we access it, let's have a further look at our Reiki world in particular. In the Reiki world at present, many Reiki Masters seem to have developed a complete lack of responsibility. Is this a criticism? No, I don't think so. It is an observation. I think this lack of responsibility is brought about because of lack of knowledge.

Many Reiki Masters will accept students who come to them asking for attunements with little knowledge about them and without enquiring why they wish to receive an attunement. They will attune them through the different Degrees of Reiki much too quickly for the students' own well-being. Some careful Reiki Masters who may have advised a student that they should work with the energy for longer before taking the next level, find that the student has then gone to another Reiki Master to get what they want sooner, ignoring the advice. The student would only do this if they did not fully understand what it is they were entering into with Reiki, or alternatively they were seeking the perceived power of advancement over the considerations of safety and knowledge. This would indicate an energy imbalance at an ego level, which of course is provided very conveniently and powerfully as one of our lessons by the Reiki energy itself, as it enters our system. There are many, many Reiki Masters out there these days, practising and teaching, but there are relatively few who have had the necessary experiences of energy work to advise a student when they should take their next step with Reiki, or any other form of healing energy for that matter.

When you fast track through Reiki, you learn absolutely nothing about energy, about what it is, what it is doing for you, what it is doing to you and how it interacts between you and the person you are working on with it. When a teacher allows a student to progress too quickly through the Degrees of Reiki, they are denying the student their apprenticeship with subtle energy. For that is what all the stages of progression with Reiki are. It should be a gentle unfoldment, steady progression and confident attainment of abilities and skills brought about by the different, but subtle experiences that Reiki will bring to you as you work with each different level.

Many students know when they are ready to advance and it is wonderful to have a student who says "I am not ready yet". This shows a great degree of maturity in their inner attunement to their own energy and ego state. Unless a Reiki Master can read a student's energy system, they have no idea whether or not the student is ready to take either their first, or subsequent steps into light work.

If it is the case that a Reiki Master cannot see clairvoyantly or read clairsentiently, dowse or muscle test the energy state of a student, or consult with Spirit Guides, there should be a considerable length of time between First and Second Degree. It is up to each individual Reiki Master to determine what this period should be for each of his or her students, as the well-being of these students depends upon the Reiki Master correctly identifying their readiness, either for starting the Reiki process or preparing for advancement to the next level. Speaking for myself and based on my extensive experience, working full time on a daily basis with energy over a number of years, I councel twelve to eighteen months between first and second degree. Unless the student has considerable prior experience of healing or other energy work such as Health Kinesiology, Intuitive Acupuncture, Dowsing, Yoga, Tantric practice or similar, then their energy system is rarely ready to have a high frequency energy, such as Reiki, pushed through it at different levels of intensity without giving it adequate time to adjust, balance and strengthen. In addition to reading the student's system in the methods outlined above, I also consult their Spirit Guides and my own Guides on the matter. Spirit Guides are keen to get people attuned, to move us all up in our evolution, they do not want to slow us down. However, they will not encourage us to move forward if there is some impediment to the health or ability of the student to move forward in safety.

## Why Long Periods Between Attunements?

During the second part of this chapter, we will continue to return to the point of why we should spend long periods between attunements as the energy picture unfolds. The problem with working with energy is that it fuels desire as you bring it into the system, and we will look at this problem, or lesson, later in the book.

Many Reiki Masters think that three months between first and second degree attunements is adequate. First of all, this assumes we are all equal. Where energy work is concerned and in the way it affects us, we are not all equal. Some people are robust and solid, with a powerful aura and strong and powerful chakras, with relatively little in the way of energy patterns to be released in order to evolve. Other people can be extremely sensitive, with a weak etheric aura and delicate chakras, in terms of their energy make-up. Just as we have people who are physically strong, there are those who are less strong, it is the same with the subtle energy system of a person. One additional thing is for certain, we all unfold from our experiences in working with energy in our own individual ways.

After a first attunement, some students will have cleansed and unfolded on an initial level very quickly, within a few months. However, others may still be unfolding many months later. If we take these two scenarios and study the energy systems of the people, we may find that both energy systems are fine and functioning one hundred percent. If we then consult the Guides, we may find that even though the one person is still unfolding, the Guides will say that their system is robust enough to continue to the next level. This does not mean that they advise it, frequently they don't. There is a big difference between being 'robust enough', 'balanced enough' or 'developed enough' to progress, and being in a position where the Guides consider that the student has gained sufficiently valuable experiences of that level of the energy.

If they are robust enough, but the Guides advise against the attunement for whatever reason, then I will not attune the person. If the person decides to go elsewhere and ignore the advice, then that is their choice and I respect that. We all have free will and the Guides and I can only advise on the situation. If the period is less than twelve months between first and second degree and the person is balanced and ready in terms of their energy structure, and the Guides give their approval and permission, then I will consider it. However, this consideration is based upon the student understanding very clearly that by progressing too quickly, they may miss out on important experiences and the subsequent knowledge gained.

Another point to consider: if the student is intent on becoming a Reiki teacher, then it is imperative they must have many answers for their own students. True answers are gathered from one's own experience. Another source of answers can be from one's Spirit Guides, if you are suitably connected to receive this information. If the person has rushed through their Reiki path, then they will not have had the necessary experiences to draw from and cannot therefore advise with any authority. It is paramount in a teacher of energy work, that they have experience.

Where is the responsibility of Reiki Masters today? A Reiki Master *must* take responsibility for their students' well-being. In traditional energy apprenticeships such as Yoga, Meditation and Healing, Feng Shui and many other disciplines, the student is assigned a Master, or the Master selects a student, and it is the Master's responsibility to appraise the student's progress continuously, usually for a great length of time, if not for the lifetime of the Master or student, whoever passes over first. In all of these disciplines the Master is exactly that, a Master: a Master of Feng Shui, a Master of Krya Yoga, a Buddhist Master, a Tantric Master, etc., and it has taken this Master many years of hard work, practice and experience to reach the point where they may be referred to as Master. They have reached a point where they can answer any question, based on their own experiences, which the student poses. More often than not, they have been born into this position through attaining a high degree of advancement and working through and healing their karmic lessons in previous lifetimes.

There is little or no responsibility being taken in Reiki circles by many Reiki Masters, and again I point out that this is not necessarily a criticism of these individuals. People are coming into Reiki from diverse backgrounds with no knowledge of any form of energy work and little or nothing in the way of developed intuition.

## Intuition

The majority of souls in the west have been brought up in typical western society with its extremely limited view of things esoteric, spiritual and intuitive. It is a society for the most part, which does not acknowledge a spiritual dimension to our lives. We learn through, and live in a society which thinks we should not have intuition because this is unscientific and cannot be measured or proved. Further, we are mocked for suggesting that there may be other dimensions. Astrology and numerology are examples of very powerful tools which can help show you your skills and talents, or your life's path, and unravel the complexities of your personality, so that you may better understand yourself. Palmistry and tarot are examples of very accurate divination tools, which can provide valuable guidance in the hands of an experienced, intuitive practitioner.

If someone has a spiritual or mystical experience in their life, virtually everyone around them tries to explain it away via one of the five senses. In Dr. Elizabeth Kubler-Ross's book, *On Life after Death*, she says that in the hundreds of cases of people who have had out-of-body experiences during medical operations in hospital, the Doctors always put the experience down to too much oxygen or something similar.

Western society has great difficulty in acknowledging or accepting anything or anyone who is different. We are educated in a system which does not acknowledge any of the right brained intuitive functions, except perhaps for art and music. Most of our teaching mechanisms in the educational curriculum in Britain are geared towards left brained activity such as the three Rs, which of course will bring about an imbalance in our development. The exclusion of right brain training in turn brings about repression of a very necessary facet of our being.

My school report from Bury Church School, which my Mum produced for me recently, and which I am now very proud of, although I bet she wasn't when I first brought it home, contains the headmasters summary note at the end of the first year, which states:- *"There is no reason why he should not be producing better work; one can only conclude that he is quite indifferent to the value of education."* I prefer to think that their education system was quite indifferent to and unable to comprehend this boy's talents and gifts!

Many children with learning difficulties such as dyslexia have very dominant and well-developed right brain faculties and capabilities. An example of this is my own son Nick, who suffered terribly at the hands of the education system in England. The bullying and torture, (emotive words I know), which were perpetrated on him by those who are supposed to have had his interests at heart, in a so called professional capacity, had to be witnessed to be believed. The local education authority was no better! Unfortunately, at that time, due to the knowledge I did not possess and the misguided trust I placed in those in authority, I was unable to support him in his struggle, discovering far too late how the system undermined us and twisted the truth in order to subjugate those who did not fit the educational model, which of course is geared to everyone being the same.

When I arrived home from work one evening and went into Nick's room, I found that on the wallpaper, this seven year old had drawn in crayon a Ninja Turtle, (remember those heroes of the 1980s). It was bigger than he was, it covered the whole of a wall, some five feet tall and in the most amazing visual proportion, almost three dimensional it was so perfect. Most parents would have gone mad to find the wallpaper covered in crayon, but to me, his skill was astonishing. I'd never seen him do anything like this before. On another occasion, when he was perhaps twelve or thirteen we were out walking and I asked him could he feel auras. He said "I don't know", I proffered that we try it on the next tree we came to. He duly felt the energy of the tree and showed me where the aura extended to. He was right of course.

These illustrations show that many people with so called learning difficulties possess wonderful talents which our western society doesn't acknowledge, let alone value. There is no place for these people in our education system for it doesn't cater for their natural skills; rather, it tries to force down their throats an education which is unnatural and difficult for them. The very sad part is that for a great many children in our schools, the result of struggle to adhere to the unbending rules is that they become psychologically damaged by their experience. In the worst cases they become social misfits, because that is what the system has told them they are.

Scepticism of psychic or intuitive abilities is born of fear; fear of acknowledging that some people may have talents that others do not, or fear of not understanding. To those with psychic or intuitive talents, this leads to fear of speaking their truth in front of colleagues, fear of being ridiculed and labelled a crackpot. This attitude is all bound up with fear!

We need to learn to accept. We do not need to understand everything in a clear-cut scientific way, labelled, packaged and put into a compartment, that we can take off the shelf now and then and say this is it and these are its limits, we know because we have measured them. It is true that the universe and our consciousness have no definable limits, but most people are afraid to push back the barriers, push out their consciousness into new areas. Others are unaware that one can be taught to do this, therefore in both instances the people become limited; limited by their fear of being different, limited by their unquestioning acceptance of the conformity which is all around us which, of course, is comfortable and safe. They cannot be blamed for this, for conformity is what our society forces down our throats constantly. It makes it very easy to govern a people if they are all the same and all function to the same set of rules in society. We have looked at the education system already, which is geared to turning all the pupils out the same, one set of ideals for all to attain. Business and commerce also has to conform to a set of rules and regulations.

At present all the governments of Europe are doing everything they can to bring into existence Europe-wide conformity. Currency, tax structures, Rapid Reaction Force, measurement. Each member state is in fear of being left outside of the structure, so everyone goes along with it, whether it suits them or not, Hence the individual identity of nations, cultures and people become lost. What is the basis of their fear? Fear is brought about by having no faith in yourself and your abilities, no courage to stand alone and ultimately no self respect for who you are. Also, this fear is manifest particularly where individuals or a society have no sense of spiritual connection. To live day by day, in the here and now, negates the need for fear. So we see that fear breeds limitation.

Scientists are the most limited of all. They are limited by the five senses, the governing principles which their science must conform to. We are told that their bold experimentations are labouring on the frontiers of scientific discovery. Often, it is more true that they are labouring on the frontiers of ignorance, for that which they do not know or understand, they are ignorant of. Until they accept that there are aspects of the whole of the material universe and ourselves as beings within it which they cannot measure with their instruments or understand with their approach, they will remain limited. Spare a thought for the fact that science cannot define the nature of consciousness, yet this is the tool which they use to evaluate their science.

Returning to the original point then, intuition is a powerful, trustworthy and valuable tool. It is also a very necessary tool for the successful healer and energy worker. In fact it is the key to success as a healer and teacher. If a Reiki Master is not a natural intuitive or does not possesses a natural psychic aspect to their nature, then they have much work to do to accomplish this faculty. They have to work with energy and learn how to tune in, how to perceive. Only the passage of time and much practice will unfold the intuition and possibly develop clairvoyant abilities. Remembering we are brought up in a left brain orientated society, most of us have much work to do to develop the faculties of the right hemisphere of our brain. Working with energy will unfold a person to a certain degree, but they must also work on themselves in other ways to help unfold, integrate and balance the right brain energies with those of the left. When all is in balance, then they will move forward into clairsentience, clairvoyance or clairaudience. Until they develop these skills, they can have no knowledge of what they are actually doing during the attunement of a student into the Reiki energy.

When a Reiki Master attunes a student, they are primarily accessing and interfering with the student's energy system on many levels: physical, mental, emotional and spiritual. You are opening a gate for energy to surge into the chakra system. Is the student's system capable of handling the energy? Is the system balanced and fully functioning in the first place? Is this person ready for Reiki? Although I have stated that Reiki carries its own consciousness, as do many other Reiki Masters, things can still go wrong. Reiki is an energy stream which rushes into your system. If your system is damaged or malfunctioning at a chakra or auric level, then the Reiki energy will not, I repeat, will not sort out and repair the problem. The Reiki energy will just blast on through the system. This is it's nature, certainly clearing some things out of the way in its rush, but incapable of repairing damage in the light body. The essence of it's consciousness is to guide it to areas where the individual blueprint of a substance or essence is incorrect, at whatever level of the being.

You can liken the energy to that of a raging river of water travelling down a pipe. You are the pipe. If the pipe has a small hole in it to begin with, you cannot expect the water to avoid going into the hole as it rushes through the pipe. As the water passes through the hole, the wear and tear creates more damage. Now imagine the hole is a chakra or your aura: the effect is the same. As the energy blasts through the system, it cannot repair any damage that is already there, it merely passes through and exacerbates the problem, until eventually you have a situation where there is even more serious energy system damage.

If a person has a damaged or malfunctioning energy system when you attune them to Reiki, or any other energy for that matter, their problems and symptoms will become much worse. I have seen many situations where the student is having a difficult time coping with the energy after attunement because of this type of problem. Sometimes they have suffered for months whilst the problem gets worse. Their Reiki Master is often unable to help them because they don't understand what is happening and they can't see that there was a problem with the student's energy system prior to attunement.

Frequently the Reiki Master will try to help by giving a healing session or advising working more with the energy. If there is damage to the aura or chakras then a healing session will do very little to remedy the situation and in fact, it can make it much worse, as we have seen with the analogy of water and the pipe. The very best the healing session can hope to do is perhaps bring a little more balance to the person. However, because of the damage to the system, this balance will be short lived.

When approached for help, I have seen many Reiki Masters say to their student that "this is all part of your clearing or healing process and everything will be fine"; or, "the Reiki will take care of it". Well, I'm afraid it won't take care of it at all. The student will usually suffer a progressively worsening energy system and be in an unbalanced and sometimes desperate state until they have the good fortune to find somebody who can help them.

Another problem area is the person who is suffering on many levels, emotional, mental or psychological, who thinks that Reiki will help them sort their problems out. A bigger problem is the Reiki Master who also thinks the same. Reiki Masters are often keen to attune such people, thinking this will help solve their problems. Often, psychological problems are present simply because there is damage to the aura or the person is under psychic attack and any energies which penetrate the person's aura can then create panic attacks, delusions and many other situations of imbalance. A Reiki attunement will exacerbate the problem because this type of person is already leaking light out into other realms. The increased energy from Reiki will double the amount they leak, not forgetting of course that there whole being is now shining brighter and is a bigger target for unwelcome visitors.

## An Example

I recall being at a Reiki exchange many years ago, before I had developed my present abilities or knowledge, and I was sitting next to a young lady in her early thirties and her mother, both of whom had attained Reiki second degree. The younger woman was in tears through the whole of the evening. We were expressing our experiences to the Reiki Master one at a time moving around the circle, in which some thirty or so students were present. When it came to the turn of the young woman, she poured out her heart in a desperate attempt to receive some help or comfort from her Reiki Master. When she had finished, the Reiki Master said "Thank you for sharing that with us. The Reiki will take care of it". At that time I didn't have many answers to things that were happening to people, but for certain I knew this woman had a serious problem either in the aura or chakras.

When it was my turn to speak, after the young woman's mother had spoken, I suggested to the Reiki Master what I thought the problem might be, that I considered that she probably had serious spin problems or blockages in some of the chakras, which was why her emotions were totally uncontrollable. I suggested that perhaps she could get some help with other forms of therapy. I was specific in the field of help I mentioned. My suggestions were very forcefully put down by the Reiki Master's assistant and I was told in no uncertain terms that she would be OK and that ... yes, you've guessed it ... "the Reiki will sort it out".

Later, when we had time to ourselves, I spoke with the ladies and gave them some telephone numbers of people who I thought might be able to help. I was astonished to find that this lady had been in this emotional state for four months without help from her Reiki Master and without any knowledge of where she could go for help.

It is time for all Reiki Masters to learn what is going on and have the courage and decency to act responsibly. There is no shame in honestly saying 'I don't know how to help you'. There is much shame in covering up for lack of knowledge. Eventually, the Ego will catch everyone out who is not being truthful. There is no room for deception when working with higher power. There is room only for truth.

## Another Example

Recently, a young girl who was training in holistic therapy came to my attention. She was having a terrible time, picking up negative energy from her clients in class. This was happening every time the class had to perform practical therapy work with other students or the general public. A well meaning Reiki Master suggested that she should take her Reiki First Degree and that this would help her deal with the problem. In reality this is the last thing the young girl should have done. Clearly her system is wide open, and has no inherent protection from the energies of other people, let alone the energies of powerful predators, such as entities. The Reiki Master was probably labouring under the illusion that the Reiki energy would protect the girl, and went ahead with the attunement.

After she had undergone her Reiki attunement, the poor girl's system was still just as wide open as it previously was, but because of the attunement, her chakras were now processing energy at a much higher rate, with nothing to filter what might come in to her system along with the Reiki energy. Not only that, but because of the attunement, she was now also carrying and leaking a lot more light from her system. She was shining like a veritable beacon and her light body was just waiting to be the feeding ground for some powerful inter-dimensional beings.

In this situation, this girl should have been taken under the wing of someone who could control what was happening in her chakras and aura. Firstly, the chakras should have been balanced and cleansed and then the aura checked for damage and repaired if and where necessary. She should then have been closed right down so that no light energy was leaking from her system. The next stage would be to monitor every job she did and check her regularly until satisfied that her energy system was robust and sealed for protection. Other aspects of her life also needed to be looked into. It is important to understand why this girl had the problem in the first place. Diet is very important to the energy state of the aura. Medication is another prime factor in evaluating energy and strength in the aura. Finally, when she had worked for a period of about four months without picking up anything untoward and her aura was vibrant and her chakras have remained in balance without assistance, then she would be ready to receive an attunement, providing all other aspects of her life were in a state of harmony also. How can one be a therapist without the necessary balance?

The Reiki Master needs to consider the overall state of harmony, because when you bring the Reiki energy into someone's system it will highlight any matters of disharmony. This can be positive in as much as the energy brings the problems to the fore so that they can be addressed, but the question which must be asked is whether the person is well balanced enough to deal with the situation at that time or would they be better to wait?

The example of a complementary therapist being drained by her clients is, unfortunately, not uncommon. I have not experienced a college yet which understands the issues presented by one-to-one energy work, whether this be massage, reflexology, aromatherapy or even hairdressing. Nobody is teaching their students psychic protection. I firmly believe that this is because the majority of tutors do not understand that beings do exist which can jump from one person to another. Further to this, they do not understand what happens between any two people in a 'one-to-one' energy exchange situation or that negative energies can be absorbed and overwhelm a person.

We can see that intuition, clairvoyance or any of the other methods of 'knowing' which we have discussed, are of vital importance to a Reiki Master and teacher. Having access to a method which will give you answers for your students and which you can trust is paramount to your success and their safety in your hands.

## Back to Fast Tracking

Fast tracking does not always bring problems immediately. A light body which has been opened too quickly can store up problems for years later, when all of a sudden, the energy system begins to fail and there is a total energy drain upon the person. They lose all integrity in the aura and become wide open, without the protection against outside forces which they had previously enjoyed. They will then pick something up in the aura and this causes immediate devastation to the structure of the aura, frequently tearing the chakras, allowing what little energy or light they still have to leak away.

Using a Gas Discharge Visualisation (GDV) kirliograph technique, which is one of the photographic/computer scanning auric energy display systems available today, shows very clearly the aura's energy structure around the body. Recently a number of Reiki healers and Masters I know underwent this scan, which revealed that their energy systems were seriously under-performing and were shot full of holes. Their scans were compared with two others: one a man who was on sick leave from work with a cracked elbow, and another man who has had his share of fairly major health problems over the last few years, including open heart surgery. Well, I expect you've guessed by now, the two people who should have been write-offs had brilliant energy structures compared to the healers, who by the state of their scans should have been checking into a convalescent home for six months!

The poor healers were quite alarmed, but the lesson here is simple. With reference once again to our motor car, once you tune something up, it performs more efficiently. In the case of the car and most other things that you tune up, the tolerances become finer and therefore the state of tuning *must* be maintained, otherwise the performance drops off very quickly. In the instance of the motor car, the performance would reduce to a level below that of its previous level in its standard state of tune. So it is with your light body after a Reiki attunement. Once you have been tuned up, you perform more efficiently, but you can now go out of tune or lose energy much more easily than before you had the attunement.

It is true that while we are giving a healing treatment using straightforward Reiki techniques, we are channelling the energy through our system and so we benefit from the energy. Some people believe that we actually get a full Reiki treatment during the process, which of course is untrue. Whilst a healing session is in progress, we are particularly open. As well as the Reiki energy which is flowing through us, we create around ourselves and our client a complete energy system functioning on many levels, often including unknown assistance by Spirit Guides. This energy system interpenetrates the auras of the healer and the client and can deplete your energy quite dramatically if you are not aware of what is happening.

This expanded healing situation arises as your healing talents begin to expand and your ability to channel energy increases. Additional healing Guides will come to assist and it is they who tap into the flow of energy and manipulate it for the benefit of the client. They also make sure that you are protected whilst the healing is taking place, but after that it is incumbent upon the healer to make sure they are closed down sufficiently to avoid any further energy depletion.

The vibrational frequency of each of the Degrees of Reiki is very different and therefore receiving an attunement for Reiki II very soon after Reiki I is not advisable. The vibration of Reiki I is very fine and subtle, and designed to unfold you gently, over a period of time. The energy of Reiki II is very coarse in comparison. Therefore, if you have your attunements within a short period of time, within a few months of each other, your system does not have the necessary time to unfold properly. In addition, you lose the very necessary experiences of the first degree vibration before moving into the different vibration of the second degree.

We also need to consider what is happening at the different levels of our being. When considering the First Degree of Reiki, many Reiki Masters and students assume that this is working only on the physical level. This is not true. The energy carries out adjustments at **all** levels of our being. By all levels, I am referring to all the levels in the lower self: the physical, etheric, emotional and lower mental; and also all the levels in the higher self: the higher mental, intuitive and atmic, making seven levels in all. Remembering that we cannot alter one state of energy without it having consequences on all other states of energy within it's sphere of existence, we can see that a Reiki I attunement must filter through to all other levels of our being. As we have observed, we are all different, and some of us will unfold more quickly than others. Some of us are more sensitive, some of us are more robust, some will struggle as the energy begins to release patterns from many lifetimes as well as the present one, some will sail through it without a second look.

I have observed Reiki One students who have followed all the rules of cleansing, yet whose systems are still adjusting many months, even more than a year later. It is not until the energy has done it's work at all levels of our being that true unfoldment with the energy begins. Once the initial attunement has done its work and all levels of our being have come to a position of fruition, and therefore balance, then we can begin to work with the energy in a balanced and coherent state, to experience what unfoldment actually means.

An even worse situation than receiving an attunement too soon after the previous one, is when a student receives the first and second degree attunement at the same time, or within the same weekend. They will never have the opportunity to learn what that first level vibration is all about. They will never learn to feel the difference between the two levels. They will never experience the unfolding at that first vibrational level, which is designed by the Universe to be very subtle and gentle for specific reasons. Nor will they ever have the knowledge to pass on to their own students. By opening too quickly to energy you lose an awful lot of essential experience and subsequent knowledge. In effect you lose your apprenticeship with the energy. You cannot go back and do it again. It's like making your first parachute jump, you can't step out of the plane and then ask yourself am I ready for this and did I bring my parachute? There is no going back.

I reiterate that it is up to the individual Reiki Master to determine with the student the best period for their first initiation or their continued progression through the Degrees of Reiki. As more and more students are falling foul of bad practice and experiencing problems with energy, it is only a matter of time before somebody gets very upset with the bad advice and or attunement and takes the matter to a legal representative. Where will we all be then? Responsibility is the key note for Reiki Masters. They are taking the energy systems of students into their hands and altering them by the use of a spiritual vehicle and a force, which I repeat, we do not fully understand. If anything goes wrong for the student, then somebody has to be held accountable. After all, the students do not attune themselves.

## 05

When a man does a piece of work which is admired by all, we say that it is wonderful; but when we see the changes of day and night, the sun, the moon, and the stars in the sky, and the changing seasons upon the earth, with their ripening fruits, anyone must realise that it is the work of someone more powerful than man.

Chased-by-Bears (1843–1915)
Santee-Yanktonai Sioux

YOUR UNFOLDMENT WITH REIKI IS APPROACHED THROUGH three different levels, called degrees. We sometimes refer to these levels as Reiki One, Reiki Two and Reiki Three.

## The First Degree

The First Degree of Reiki, for many people, opens the chakras to energy for the first time in their lives. The subsequent influx of energy at this first level is focused within the physical being. The First Degree attunement is designed specifically to begin to cleanse the physical body of toxins and energy blockages. Thus, the cleansing process will allow the physical body to vibrate at a higher frequency. When looking back over a period of months after their attunement, the student often finds that subtle changes in their life have begun. Preferences for food and drink for instance are often highlighted by a movement towards a more balanced, nutritious and wholesome diet. Beginning to dislike some foods and even becoming vegetarian is not uncommon. This is the physical body communicating at a subconscious level and saying that things need to change in order to

# THE DEGREES OF REIKI

support the new, higher level of vibration of the physical being. Smokers often cut down or give up altogether during this first phase of cleansing and evolution. I have seen colour become more important to many people at this early stage of change: re-decorating favourite rooms or buying new clothes with more vibrant colours for example. Again the subconscious is getting the message through that the vibrational energy of colour is a powerful transformative ally in the process of spiritual attainment.

As you work at bringing the energy into your system at this first level, the physical cleansing continues incessantly. This first degree of Reiki is by far the most important to you and vastly underestimated by many Reiki Masters, teachers and students. This is the level at which energy is filtered into your system for the very first time and in a very gentle way. If you go no further through the Reiki Degrees, as you work with this level of energy over the coming months and years, it will constantly but delicately unfold you to finer and finer energy perceptions. These will be new perceptions which you have never experienced before. As I have already said, this is the most important level to spend time at. You should be unhurried in your approach to energy work and allow yourself to unfold gently, but with the clarity of what is happening to you.

Your Reiki Master will give a specific exercise known as the Twelve Positions to practice upon yourself everyday for an hour. This brings the energy strongly into your system and progresses the detox through you during the twenty-one day cleansing process. The first degree provides very useful energies to work with, particularly by yourself and on yourself. You should not consider using this energy on others until you have worked on yourself through the twenty-one day cleansing period, as negative energy patterns releasing from yourself can be passed across to others. It is even better if you extend this period of self-healing to, say, two or three months. There are no guidelines for this period, but do not underestimate the importance of self-cleansing and self-preparation to enable you to move forward. When you feel ready, then practise with other Reiki students or on family members or very close friends. Allow your progress to be gentle and positive and try to understand what is happening in every healing session you participate in.

Try to get plenty of experience at this first level of energy work. When practised regularly, Reiki One is very powerful in its own right. I know students who can give a straightforward healing treatment as powerful as any Reiki Master with this level alone. Don't underestimate your capability, you can achieve much and your power will accumulate, the more you work with the energy.

## The Second Degree

At the Second Degree, the energy becomes much more powerful: most teachers say it multiplies at least four fold, which I would not disagree with. The energy at this level can flood very powerfully into the system as it pushes open and further enhances the levels of energy held in the chakras. Second Degree is primarily concerned with cleansing of the emotional and mental bodies. Whereas at level one you will experience the detox primarily at a physical level which can be relatively easy to deal with, detox on an emotional level can be quite tough sometimes. Bear in mind that the energy is now coming into the system at an amplified rate. You need to be ready to deal with any unresolved mental and emotional issues, for they will without doubt be presented to you.

The emotional issues are by far the more painful of the two and these are presented at a conscious level. Thoughts and patterns repeat themselves until you resolve them; until you do they will constantly return to hamper your evolutionary process. They will not prevent you evolving spiritually or as a healer or energy worker, but they will continually sabotage you by returning to upset your mental or emotional balance. Remember of course, that your being, now existing at a higher vibration, is also in a more delicate state of tune, more refined. These issues will de-stabilise you more easily than if you had not begun your evolutionary process. However, if you had not begun the process, they probably wouldn't have come up as an issue to be dealt with. Be positive and welcome any issue as an opportunity to heal or understand yourself further. Remember ... you chose the path, it wasn't forced upon you ... or was it?

The Second Degree provides energy which brings advancement for you and is very powerful in its application when working with others, particularly at the mental and emotional level. The introduction of symbols helps your clients to deal with mental and emotional issues too. When working at this higher level with the use of symbols it is important to have gained a good deal of healing experience. Your clients may well begin to release emotional blockages while you are working on them, which can deliver them into an instant emotional crisis. You need to have the ability to help counsel them through the crisis, and at an energy level understand what is happening within their emotional body. You need to know how to calm and rebalance these energies in order to facilitate the passing of the trauma. The healing session needs to be brought to a successful conclusion. You cannot send your client out into the world in a severe state of distress, to deal with the issues which have been released by the energy you have channelled into them.

## The Third Degree

At the Third Degree level, the energy is an extremely fine vibration, moving into the spiritual aspect of your being. Many people think that because the second degree of Reiki is a hefty increase in power, the third degree will likewise give them a great power boost. This is not necessarily the case. We start with Reiki on the physical level and we evolve through the emotional and mental level and now, at Third Degree, we are arriving at the door of the spiritual level. In essence, we have moved through the gross, coarse vibration of the physical body, through the finer mental and emotional vibrations within the aura to arrive at the very fine vibration of the spiritual level, which is expanding our awareness into completely new areas of our being. Because of the subtlety of the spiritual, many people will feel no perceptible difference. The spiritual aspects of being will unfold extremely slowly, over many, many years, and this only if one continues to work upon ones self with the specific goal of personal evolution. That is, evolution at the physical, emotional, mental and spiritual level.

## The Nature of Evolution

To evolve generally, we need to do a great deal of work on ourselves. In order to unfold at a spiritual level, this work needs to be done at the lower levels. One cannot move upwards at a spiritual level if there are blockages and restraining patterns at the lower levels of our being. For instance, at the physical level, the detox through the 21 day cleansing period is very powerful and does release many things. If we continue to practice these techniques beyond the 21 days, then the cleansing will continue to a certain degree whenever we use the energy. At the physical level, there is always a relatively straightforward level of blockages which will be dissolved more or less automatically. However, blockages at all levels can be very complex phenomena to identify and deal with.

In my work of guided vibrational healing, I use high energy vibrational tools with the help of Spirit Guides. Our primary task is to remove blockages at a subtle energy level, that is removing the energy pattern, not an actual physical thing. For example, in homoeopathy, an energy pattern is given to the client, to take as a remedy. This might be the energy pattern of a flower, a crystal, a toxin or a virus. It makes no difference what the substance is, it is the way it is processed that is important. The homoeopath imprints the electro-magnetic life force (or atomic) energy pattern of the substance, either into a liquid or a tablet. The actual substance does not exist in the remedy, only the energy pattern. In the case of the homoeopath, he or she is identifying a problem with the client and prescribing an energy pattern which will release the energy blockage which is causing the client's problem.

In my guided vibrational healing, I am doing a similar thing. The difference is that firstly, I am placing the energy pattern required for change either on the body or within the aura, rather than it being administered within the body as a remedy, and secondly, my Spirit Guides are determining the priority with which the energy blockages should be dealt, according to their higher knowledge of the state of all levels of a person's being. They are guiding me to use the energy patterns needed to release these obstructions thereby allowing evolution or healing, which of course are the same thing. If we are healed, then we evolve, because there is less in the way of restrictive patterning holding back our progress. Whether we realise it or not, we all need healing at some level. In some instances, the blockages have been created in this lifetime, in others, they have been created in past lives.

## Past Life Energy Blockages

Where past life traumas or blockages are concerned, the energy patterns can carry over mental, emotional or physical problems into the present life. Damage which has been present at a physical level in a previous incarnation can create an energy pattern which is capable of carrying over via our eternal spiritual essence, into a later incarnation, and again causing physical problems if not identified and dealt with. This imprint or recording is frequently in the mental or emotional body or energy field, and is created as a result of shock or trauma to the whole personality structure. Catherine provides a case history of this type.

While working with Catherine, she commented that someone had asked her to ask me whether she had got a tear in her aura. As we had worked together previously, I knew that she hadn't, but checked anyway. I asked my Guides to show me why this person should think Catherine had aura damage. They showed me a great red slash rising from her back, vertically, slightly to the right of the centre of her head as I viewed her from the front. I could see straightaway why someone might think this was a tear, as clearly it did look like a great rent in the fabric of her light body. However, it was not. It was the energy pattern of a trauma, and you might wonder why I had not seen it previously. Priority is the answer. The Guides only show me what I need to see and in the order we should work on it.

Catherine asked me to look at the pain she was experiencing above her left breast, where she had previously had some operations. The pain had caused her problems in this area and upwards through her neck and into her head for a long time. My Guides told me there were things we could do to help this problem, but not at present. We must work in priority order. On this particular visit, we were trying to calm and balance certain energies, as Catherine was struggling a little with her healing crisis from previous energy blockage releases. However, during the session, as we were processing certain things, the Guides decided to show me pictures in more detail of how Catherine's physical problems had been caused.

I could see her clearly, dressed in a long dress of grey and burgundy, a white bonnet on her head. She was walking among the dead and wounded in a battlefield. She bent down towards a man dressed in uniform and armour. The Guides said "France, Joan of Arc period". As she bent down, I saw his helmet clearly. I was obviously seeing through Catherine's eyes at the time. He raised a huge sword and pushed it straight through her. It entered her in the upper left breast and exited just to the right of her left shoulder blade. He then cleaved the sword up and down so that the entry wound became a pivot point and the blade at the back cut a broader wound. She died immediately.

The shock of the incident was what did the greatest damage. She didn't see it coming and the sheer violence and impact, as well as the physical damage to some degree, literally traumatised her to death. Because this physical incarnation was now terminated, she had no opportunity to recover from her injuries or work off the trauma. Therefore, it impacted her personality at a soul level. At the next point in time when the soul made the choice to project a personality structure into human form, this energy pattern was at the forefront, waiting to be dealt with in the only place it could be, namely the physical realm or the world of mankind. As soon as the personality structure entered the new physical body, the energy impacted upon that body, resulting in Catherine's present day condition.

The scar in Catherine's aura from the energy of the sword thrust.

You will notice in the illustration that it would not be possible to create such a huge wound in physical terms with the sword thrust as is shown. In energy terms however, the violence of the act projected an enormous energy into Catherine's whole being, which rendered a wound larger than the physical path of the sword.

Catherine told me that the pain was a constant problem. She said that she had always felt that if she had her whole left shoulder and arm cut off, it would solve her problems and that the pain felt exactly as she imagined a sword thrust would feel. I drew a picture of the soldier's helmet, which was very distinctive — I could even see the rivets on it — and she said she had seen exactly the same helmet in her mind's eye as I was describing the scene. She also said she often had visions and dreams of walking on a battlefield which seemed odd for a girl. I touched the place next to her shoulder blade to show where the sword wound had been and drew a picture of the energy pattern of the wound.

She told me that all the details felt exactly right and fitted perfectly with what she experiences.

This is an example of how the energy pattern of a physical trauma can manifest in a physical way in a later incarnation. Of course there is damage at the subtle energy level as well in Catherine's case, as evidenced by the deep red blockage visible to anyone with clairvoyant or psychic vision. In the same way, energy blockages at a purely subtle level can also carry over into a later incarnation. These can be the energies of things with which people have perhaps been working or casually come into contact with during their lives, which have been absorbed into their subtle energy system. Examples would be patterns from toxins, viruses, illnesses or energy patterns of powerful substances like plant essences, alcohol, narcotics, etc.

## Present Life Energy Blockages

Blockages may be created by the absorption of any material we come into contact with. There may be blockages caused by vaccines when a child, or later in life. A vaccine is a very powerful energy pattern and can cause blockages as soon as it is introduced into the body. Surely, vaccination is the greatest disservice we can do to a new born child, along with depriving them of their mother's milk, enriched as it is with all the very special ingredients needed for the best start to life!

To illustrate a case in point by reference to myself, in my early days of dowsing I used dowsing rods and worked mainly in the area of earth energies. As I progressed, I found that I could not use a pendulum. No matter how I tried I could not get it to work. Eventually, I saw a healer about the problem. He worked at a high vibrational level, as I do now. I knew that I could feel the dowsing response vibrations in my body, but they would not work at the level of the pendulum. He diagnosed the problem in a few moments. I had energy blockages caused by the absorption of the energy patterns of nylon as a child. These blockages were in my upper arms and probably originated from nylon shirts. He used a vibrational remedy on my arms to remove the energy pattern causing the blockage. This took about an hour, and the pendulum has worked perfectly for me ever since. My body's subtle energy, or chi, now flows into places where previously it did not.

So you can see that we pick up blockages from all kinds of sources. Everything in the universe has an energy pattern. Anything we put into our bodies or which comes into contact with our bodies has a subtle energy pattern. These energy patterns can be absorbed and interact in a negative way in terms of our life force function, but because the patterns are on a subtle level we often get by without too much of a problem. In some cases they cause allergies or food intolerances, but we can usually cope and we don't look too deeply to solve the problem.

However, if we are trying to evolve via our interaction with energy work or healing, then we are working in the realms of subtle energy and energy patterns, and they can become something we need to understand and deal with.

We also need to consider another source of energy pattern blockages. As we have seen with Catherine, it was a serious life trauma which set up the pattern. A combination of powerful factors so imprinted this pattern into her being, that it carried over in such a way as to cause her life-long problems to date in this physical existence. There are probably shock, fear, anxiety, tremendous emotion and mental realisation taking place at the same time: the shock of the event, the sheer horror of the unexpected sword thrusting through her body; the paralysing fear of being unable to do anything about it, with the realisation that death within the moment is upon her; searing pain and trauma imprinted into those last living seconds of her physical life.

Unexpected and violent death can cause many problems to the spirit, often leaving it roaming the physical realm as a lost soul. Certainly the event will have created an instant and enormous mental and emotional pattern, which may well not have had time to balance out in the panic and terror of those last moments.

Emotional and mental patterns can be powerful creators of energy blockages. From the time we are in the womb, we are subject to our Mother's emotional patterns. Anything that upsets her emotions, we will feel and record. If this is a serious upset, then it can create within us a serious trauma, which may or may not play itself out in our present lifetime. From the moment we are born and in our formative years, we are subject to all kinds of mental and emotional experiences as we grow and learn. We will experience many situations which we do not like and at a subconscious level we will repress and retain this information. These experiences do leave an energy pattern, the energy of a negative experience, a mental or emotional pattern. Remember thought forms and the power of thought, and 'energy follows thought'. At some level, we often shut down certain systems unconsciously to protect ourselves. If systems are shut down, the life force energy will not flow to those places, as demonstrated by the problem with my dowsing arm through the absorption of the nylon energy pattern. Mental and emotional energy patterns are generated from within rather than absorbed, but can have an equally powerful effect.

M.E. and M.S. are late twentieth century illnesses. They are both body energy related. Consider for a moment how many chemicals have been introduced into our environment, and particularly the food processing chain, since the middle of the 1900s. It is literally thousands, and they contain new, scientifically developed energy patterns. In essence, new molecules which previously did not exist on earth. Science has invented them. We have only relatively recently, within the last two generations, come into contact with these substances. I know for certain that some sufferers of M.E. for instance can pin down a specific pattern to do with vaccines or other chemicals which they have used, immediately prior to developing the illness. Does this give you some food for thought?

Whatever happens at one energy level of existence will affect the performance at another, whether we are talking about ourselves as humans, or about other life force systems within the universe. If we come back now to the cleansing at the mental and emotional level, the issues will repeatedly present themselves to you, and as those who have experienced this will attest, it is easy to see the issues when they come up, but in reality it is very difficult to process and deal with them. Frequently they are pushed back down again because the fear of dealing with the issue is far too great to cope with. Often these issues involve changing life-long attitudes and learning to see or behave differently. On the surface we often think we have made progress with these, only to see them reappear from whence we have pushed them away.

Changes at the core level of your being can take a lifetime of continual self analysis and appraisal, and even then they may still be too painful to deal with or too illusive to comprehend. The main point here is that you can spend a lot of time working on yourself to remove blockages, and this is the most important thing you can do to aid your evolution. Every blockage you remove will mean your whole being begins to function at a higher level, and subsequently the removal of this dross will allow you to evolve. I have been very lucky in having a very good friend, Anne, who has worked on me over a number of years with Health Kinesiology to remove blockages.

However, you cannot rush this work. After each blockage is removed, the being, on all levels, must re-adjust its balance. This can sometimes take a considerable length of time. The only true way you can measure this is via spiritual information or information from some higher source. This can be arrived at in many ways. In kinesiology, the practitioner asks the higher intelligence of the body for the answers and receives these via muscle responses. For instance, when can we next work with this person? Is it one week, one month, three months, etc.? An experienced practitioner working at a high level, whether they know it or not, will actually be accessing answers from a spiritual level as well as the body's or being's own higher self. These answers can be from the client's life guide, their own healing Guides or other spiritual beings who may wish to help, for whatever reason. Dowsing is another form of accessing information from a higher source. Mediumship, clairvoyance, clairaudience, clairsentience are all methods of receiving messages from spiritual helpers and development classes exist for people wishing to train in these techniques. When we get information from such a high and knowledgeable source we can maximise our potential for change.

Spirit Guides have our best interests at heart and know in what order we should carry out the necessary work. They understand the laws of karma, often translated to mean righteous action, far better than we do, and it may be that they are working with us for their own reasons and to further their own ends in terms of their own karmic mission, they help us to help others whilst also helping themselves, working for humanity and also working for the soul. It does not matter what their reason is. When you begin to trust in the consciousness of the Universe to bring you what you need, then you will receive the help which is most appropriate for you to work with. In a healing session, sometimes my Guides tell me what is happening and why, and sometimes they tell me next to nothing. Sometimes they tell me that with the limited comprehension we have on earth, I wouldn't understand. My clients and I just have to trust the process. In essence, this is spiritual healing!

Finally, after some digression, of an illuminating nature I hope, we arrive back at the spiritual level and you can now see that to advance at this level it is essential to have advanced at the physical, mental and emotional levels first. Remember the words of C.W. Leadbeater, with reference to the awakening of the kundalini energy: "… it is far better to allow it thus to remain dormant until the man has made definite moral development, until his will is strong enough to control it and his thoughts pure enough to enable him to face its awakening without injury". Thus we are reminded that although we are not working to awaken the kundalini energy in particular, while working with Reiki, we are still working with energy which does affect the kundalini channels. Thus, parallels to moral development and pure thought are still relevant. Working with the energy will release issues for us to deal with. This is a certainty. Until we have dealt with these on the lower levels, particularly the emotional and mental, there will be impediments to our spiritual advancement.

The other aspect to consider when third degree has been attained, is attuning others. This is not automatic, as there is a special symbol to enable a person to carry out attunements, which we will look at separately.

## Reiki Training

All Reiki Masters are different and they practise their art slightly differently. Reiki has not been passed down to us in the west with a strict code of conduct or practice, such as exists with some other healing modalities, such as Bowen Technique, Kinesiology or Pranic Healing, where the teachers must work extremely hard to attain the necessary skills and the approval of the tutors or Master before they are allowed to teach or present courses to students.

There is much debate about Reiki training and many questions are asked about why some Reiki training is covered in a day and some courses are over a weekend. There are a number of reasons why this may be the case. Some Reiki Masters will pass the attunement in one go, where others split the attunement into four parts. They will pass two parts of the attunement in the first day and two parts in the second day. The reasons for this can be varied also. Some of these Reiki Masters have been taught this way and hence they continue to teach what they have been taught. Others know of different ways to pass the attunements, but if they have not had training in energy exercises, they may not be able to raise enough energy to pass the attunement in one go. Passing attunements requires a lot of energy from the Reiki Master if it is to be done efficiently.

There are many techniques to raise energy within the light body and physical system. One such is the Micro-cosmic Orbit where, using your chakra and visualisation skills, you can move energy around the body in an orbital manner, which raises your core energy to a very high level. Breathwork is also an important factor in raising the energy in your core being. Pranayama is the Indian term for this practice. Pranic Healing also uses breath techniques to raise energy. When a Reiki Master can perform these controlled tasks of energy raising, they can pass a tremendously powerful attunement in a few moments. This is one reason that a Reiki training might be completed in one day.

## My Way of Teaching

I usually teach a one day course, partly because I can raise the energy in the above manner and thus pass the attunement in a relatively short time, but mainly because I restrict the course material to the very basics. If you give a student too much to learn at an early stage, their concentration becomes scattered. Secondly, I think it is very important to concentrate efforts on the very fundamentals of energy work without dressing these up with mysterious or mystic overtones. Starting people off on the right foot is about keeping it simple. They have plenty time to learn all the add-ons. I want my students to be equipped with a very basic understanding of energy principles. This will give them the tools to begin channelling energy, powerfully, but with safety.

I also approach the subject of Reiki as a tool for self transformation rather than purely as a healing development course. I am primarily interested in introducing

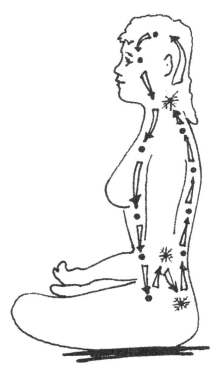

The Micro-cosmic Orbit moves energy around the body.

the tool of Reiki to my students as a powerful way to bring about changes in their lives. I want them to understand the concepts of light and the light body and the unlimited power we have at our disposal for change. I also want them to know who and what they are in terms of energy, and what they are capable of. A good foundation in energy principles shows that Reiki can be used as a powerful first step into self transformation. The fact we can also use this energy for healing is merely a by-product of it's nature. Work with energy, with knowledge and respect, and it will reward you with extremely powerful gifts of healing ability.

This is not to say I don't pay heed to the healing aspects of Reiki. I cover all the healing basics, probably including many aspects others leave out or are unaware of. There is meditation, focus, preparation to use energy, fundamental hand positions and practical experience at the couch, full healing sessions and aura cleansing. Everyone gets a turn on the couch to experience the energy of their colleagues and in turn give of their own new channelling abilities. This is a full eight hour day of hard work and by the end of it I guarantee that everyone will be able to feel auras, such is the level of transformation in energy-sensing ability.

Let me compare my methods with those of a good friend of mine who is an excellent and very talented healer, teacher and Reiki Master. She takes her Reiki First Degree course over two days. She is a very powerful energy worker with many different talents and can perform the energy raising exercises mentioned above. Like myself, she passes the attunement in one go. She gives her students a very good grounding in many different aspects of healing techniques, not just Reiki. Her students get much, much more than just basic Reiki training and this requires intensive individual instruction and practice at the couch. With this amount of content, it is better to take the course over two days, so that it can be done in a more unhurried way than if you tried to pack too much into a single day.

Although much of the fundamental Reiki teaching between our two methods is similar, the overall picture is quite different. Neither of these two methods is right or wrong; each of us has our own particular focus. This is why it is important that a student should make sure they know what they are getting from their teacher. One teacher's focus might be more appropriate than another's for the needs and desires of a particular student.

There can be many individual reasons why some Reiki Masters give two days training and others only one. The above illustration can be used as a guide to what you should expect. Some Reiki Masters will fill two days with little more than very basic Reiki techniques, repeating these over and over again. Practice is important, but once you know the basics, you can take this home and begin working on yourself. If you are unsure you can refer to the Reiki Manual which all good Reiki Masters will supply with the course.

Of course, there is also the ever present issue of that root of all evil, money! Many people have great difficulty in dealing with this one. Students want to know how the charge is justified and teachers have different ways of justifying it. At the end of the day money is only a form of energy which we can use almost universally to exchange for something we want. If you feel that the energy exchange being requested is not balanced, then don't proceed. Find another route to take. You would also do well to remember that old addage that you get what you pay for. Everyone has a different level of connection with energy. Reiki Masters are no different. Look beyond the veil and use your intuition.

## Reiki Manuals

The Reiki manual can be almost as mysterious and legendary as the unicorn. Some Reiki Masters supply only a scruffy photocopy of some basic hand positions or symbols, others produce masterpieces containing esoteric knowledge of the mystery schools, and wonders of a divine nature, spanning some 40 to 50 pages. My own Reiki First Degree manual is some 25 pages in length.

A manual is important for the student to take home with them. There is a lot of information to absorb on a well planned Reiki First Degree course, which for many is completely new and very unusual. Reiki initiation is a right of passage into a new dimension of light and needs to be supported with some basic knowledge, firstly about Reiki and secondly about other aspects of light work. A clear but concise introduction to what Reiki is and how to use it is needed, along with a little information on auras and chakras. The understanding of these energy centres is the very essence of what energy work and healing is all about.

Detoxification and the 21 day cleansing process are important too. Details on the twelve positions of Reiki are essential. Giving a Reiki treatment should be laid out as clear guidance to refer back to if you have forgotten any particular procedure. There should also be an introduction to psychic protection and psychic attack. Finish this off with a little bit of history and the student's Reiki lineage, *ét voila*, the students won't go far wrong. If there are any uncertainties or interpretation queries, then the student should be able to contact the Reiki Master by telephone. Essentially though, they should have as much as they need provided for them in the manual.

A manual is also important for the Second and Third Degrees. The Second Degree attunement involves symbols which some people will find more complex to deal with than others. When we were originally taught Reiki in the west, many Reiki Masters showed pictures of the symbols to the students and made them learn them on the day. The students were not allowed to take a copy, as they were considered sacred. Indeed they are sacred and powerful and should be respected. However, they have been published in a number of books to date and are not as secret as they once were. The important thing to understand is that the symbol is useless to a person unless it has been placed within that person's light body by a

Reiki Master and thus activated within their being. I do provide copies of the symbols to my students because I want them to 'get it right', and not worry about whether they have remembered them correctly. However, I do instil in them the importance of respect. In the final analysis, if people do not respect the sacred knowledge, they will have to answer with their karma.

The Third Degree Manual should contain the basic Reiki Master content, but this is also the place where you can expand, if you wish to, into other areas of healing and esoteric knowledge.

## History

I don't intend to go into the history of Reiki: I am not qualified to do so. Rather, I would refer the reader to the works of Frank Arjava Petter who has much first hand knowledge, due to his extensive research and immense efforts to find the truth.

## Homework

At Reiki First Degree level, the homework is primarily the 21 day cleansing process. The most important aspect of First Degree is to go away and just use it as much as you can, primarily on yourself. However, homework at Second Degree level is very important. Sadly, many Reiki Masters not only don't supply a manual at this level but do not give homework either.

My own Reiki Second Degree teachers were excellent and gave us very important homework to do. In energy terms, this homework is paramount to bringing the energy into the mental and emotional bodies and clearing or detoxing at a very deep level, not only back to birth, but beyond into the womb and back through your mother's pregnancy term. Unless you are well versed in energy work you will not understand the many traumas which can be set up while still in the mother's womb. When a mother suffers shock or trauma this is passed on to the unborn child. Just living a normal daily life has its ups and downs and if the mother goes through even slight emotional or mental upset, this will affect the baby in her womb at some subtle level. This usually results in subtle energy blockages, leaving us unable to process certain things. This type of energy blockage can result, for instance, in allergies or learning difficulties. In fact, almost anything you can imagine may have stemmed from trauma in the womb.

Reiki Second Degree equips you with the tools to create a pathway back to conception and beyond if you wish to go that far, where much needed healing must, and I repeat, **must** be done in order to progress in your upward evolution. A great problem with healing is that people limit themselves by thinking that they have only ever existed from birth. It is not until you experience light work and your perceptions begin to expand that the possibility arises that in fact we may have had many lifetimes. Healing past lives is often as important as healing this life-time; not only that, but healing past lifetimes can often heal things in the present lifetime. In the case studies we see a lady who incarnated into this life in a state of demonic possession. What sort of life did she have prior to this one, with the accompaniment of her guest? Certainly, this lifetime has given her a very rough ride health-wise. How much of it was to do with the thirty odd years of carrying around a parasitic demonic energy?

The nature of the homework is to travel backwards in time, using the Reiki symbols to transcend time and space. As you go, you clear mental and emotional patterns and blockages which at some level, conscious, sub-conscious or even higher conscious, are preventing your evolution. This should be done in a very controlled way over a period of months, taking yourself back a year at a time. This process can release enormous emotional trauma which has to be dealt with and worked through and should not be taken lightly. You usually won't recognise the emotional problem, as the release is in pure energy. When done properly under guidance with your Reiki Master the results will release you to move forward powerfully over the coming years. Many times I have seen people underestimating the seriousness with which this process should be attempted. Rushing through the process, they then become almost unable to function as the resultant energy releases have severely burdened them emotionally and mentally.

## Healing Crisis

The term healing crisis or healing process is often heard in light work circles. When we carry out healing work on ourselves, or others carry out work on us, we release energy. When this energy is released it must travel out of our being from whatever level it has been released, physical, emotional, mental or spiritual and the space it previously occupied must be replaced by something else. When people go to visit Sai Baba or Mother Meera or any of the other great Yogis or Gurus, they are making their journey specifically to ask for healing for themselves. They may not even have discourse with the Guru, but it matters not. Merely by being within their presence, within that person's aura, which in one so evolved may spread outwards over great distances, even continents, the Master knows that they are here with intent, silently asking for help in their evolution. The Master will also know at what level they require help.

After experiencing the presence of a Guru, blockages are removed, patterns dissolved and subsequently, people's lives often fall apart. They become emotional wrecks, nothing seems to go right for them and they find it difficult to function in the life they previously had. The removal of energy patterns leaves a void and something needs to fill the void. The substance which fills the void is light. Light comes into the void and raises the vibration of the being further. The process of the vibratory rate increasing may remove further blockages, bring further evolution and so we can get into a cycle lasting many months before things begin to settle down again and a more comfortable emotional and mental life re-emerges.

Healing is the path of the spiritual warrior. As the saying goes, there's no gain without pain!

## Attunements

I do not intend to go into the specific details of attunements in this book — there are other good Reiki books available which deal with this subject admirably and I don't wish to cover ground which can easily be accessed from other sources.

However, I am often asked about attunement at Third Degree or Reiki Master Level. The question that usually follows is, how much is it? I tell them my fee, which being in line with many other Reiki Masters' fees, I call an investment. I then say, "If you are interested, we should make an appointment to discuss it". I then often don't hear from the person again.

Because I am cautious and don't jump straight in and book them there and then to 'do' their Masters within the week, I am probably perceived as not really interested. This is not the case. I take my student's advancement very seriously. Perhaps too seriously — you be the judge. However, this suits me just fine, because if people are in a hurry, then they are not taking care and pitfalls await the unwary. However, we must all walk this path of discovery our own way.

But there are those who see that what I am actually doing, is saying ... "we need to be together in calm surroundings so that I can tune into you and you can tune into me, and we can see is there a balance between us. If there is balance then let us proceed. You can examine my credentials and ask as many questions as you like and judge me by my answers. Am I the Reiki Master who you would like to take this step with, or not?" Or indeed, do you think it is not important who you take your attunements with? I can understand why some students would think this. They are coming into an area which is new, exciting and baffling. They don't realise what actually happens at the moment of attunement and whose hands they are actually in!

In calm space and in mutuality, we can look at your history of energy work and how you have arrived at this point in time. I can look into your chakras and see your issues, see and feel how your energy is at present, whether you have any psychic attachments or negative energies which need attention, whether your light body is in balance or needs a tune up. Communicate with your Spirit Guides for their opinion and generally check that everything is in order to proceed. Ask my own Guides if you are ready, or if there is any work we need to do together in preparation, so that you can receive the attunement at the appropriate level.

## On-going Support

Support is important to some people, less so to others. Some people take on the Reiki mantle and fly with it, never to be seen again. Others, especially working through the homework of Reiki Two, sometimes need counselling, help and support. Occasionally students, even Reiki Masters, need confirmation or feedback on something they may have experienced, or advice on how to approach a problem. We are all constantly learning, even Masters. As the saying goes, the more you learn, the less you realise you know.

As a Reiki Master, making yourself available for your students is important. You don't have to call up all your students every couple of weeks to see how they are getting on, unless you want to of course, but let them know that they can call you if they need to. There is nothing worse than going on a weekend course in another part of the country to then find later that there are things you don't understand or which need clarification, or you are experiencing problems and there is nobody to turn to for the answers.

To solve the problem of contact, Reiki exchange evenings are a good way to bring everyone together now and again. An exchange evening is an event where Reiki students, practitioners and Reiki Masters can get together informally to exchange information and experiences and practice Reiki on one another. Some Reiki Masters provide these once a month, which is admirable. Others provide them less frequently, of which I am guilty. But it is a good way to stay in touch and a great opportunity for the students to share energy with their Reiki Master and their fellow healers.

The important point is that students know where their Reiki Master can be contacted, so that help is at hand for any problems or uncertainties they may have.

**06**

"Those gulls where you came from are standing on the ground squawking and fighting amongst themselves. They're a thousand miles from heaven — and you say you want to show them heaven from where they stand! Jon, they can't see their own wingtips! Stay here. Help the new gulls here, the ones who are high enough to see what you have to tell them".

Jonathan Livingstone Seagull

CHOOSING A REIKI MASTER CAN BE EASY OR DIFFICULT. AS with everything in nature, there is simplicity and complexity. Pick up a pebble from the beach and what have you got? You have a simple pebble! Now look at it in more detail. You will usually have a mixture of different materials. It can be one of three kinds of rock to begin with. It can be igneous rock, born of fire spewed out from the earth's molten core. It can be metamorphic rock, born of the changing temperatures and pressures within the earth's crust, as it moves over millennia, or it can be sedimentary rock, born of millions of years of sediment slowly drifting downwards, compressed by the ever increasing weight of material and bonded together by the calcium of decomposing sea creatures falling to the sea floor, to be raised above sea level at some future time by earthquake as the tectonic plates of our earth's surface move.

Look again: the pebble may be made up of a number of minerals of which each has its own specific pattern of atomic structure, unique to itself, showing it's imprint to the world in terms of the way its atoms vibrate. Each has its own fingerprint. Now pick

# CHOOSING A REIKI MASTER

up the pebble next to it and it could be completely different in every respect. So, we have the simplicity of the pebble in one view and the complexity of its personality in another.

Therefore, we see that choosing a Reiki Master can similarly be simple and complex. On the one hand we can intuitively choose someone who is right for us. On the other we can look deeply into many aspects of their personality to find out what makes them tick. What we need to do is strike a balance. We can appreciate the aesthetic beauty of the pebble, its look and feel in our hand, and likewise we can evaluate a Reiki Master from a few well chosen questions and how they feel to our inner knowing, our intuition. Just as we meet people in everyday life and either like or dislike them.

## Reiki, Victim or Victor?

Reiki is going through its own transformation as it unfolds across the planet, just as its students are going through theirs. Unfortunately, in some ways, Reiki is becoming the exact opposite of what it is supposed to be: a vehicle which brings about healing, health and transformation for the better. In reality it can bring about negative transformation into destructive ego power instead. The power of Reiki is seductive. It is a seducer of the ego, and therefore of the self. It is very easy for the student, new to Reiki, to become seduced by this power ... perhaps more alarmingly, it is even easier for the Reiki Master to succumb. We should remain vigilant and not become blind to the fact that the Reiki student, no matter at what level, can be the victim of their own success, as indeed the whole practice of Reiki is becoming the victim of its own success in many ways.

How can Reiki be the victim of its own success? Quite simply because of the power element of the energy and the way it accesses the ego. Reiki groups and organisations across the globe have been falling out over various issues to do with Reiki. Allegedly, individuals have tried to set themselves up as overall leaders, fostering titles such as Grandmaster. Some have tried to take from others by attempting to trade mark the Reiki name and practise. Some have proposed total control (there's an issue in itself!) to extract large amounts of money from people for the right to use the name Reiki Master. Others have developed new healing modalities and bolted them on to the Reiki name. Legal action has been perpetrated by so called healers, against other healers.

Some Reiki organisations have tried to apply specific 'form' to the practice of Reiki, passing judgement on who can and cannot swell the ranks of their membership. All this when anyone who knows anything about healing understands that we are all individuals, seeing our colours and receiving our messages in our own individual way. An enormous aspect of healing ability is perception and intuition. Many years ago, I allowed my membership of a large healing organisation to lapse, because the permitted form of practice was too restrictive and the structure too political. If one is not allowed to use one's natural talents to their maximum effect because of rules, where does that leave us?

It is all about power! It is all about money! Reiki, in some circles, has become dirty. More accurately though, it is about ego power, brought about by the energy fuelling a weak moral fibre within the individual. The Universe grants us power and we misuse it; it grants us power and we become jealous of others who also have it; it grants us power and we become possessive and controlling. This is how Reiki is becoming the victim of its own success!

## Ego, Your Inner Mistress or Master

You've all heard it, flushed with that special pride in the breast, with the thrill of attainment in the voice, "I'm a Reiki Master now"! Those amongst us who haven't reached these dizzy heights yet, stand with mouths agape, admiration tinged with a little envy crossing our minds. We promise ourselves that we are going to concentrate on nothing else but achieving the status of this same goal.

Little do we know that the one who has just spoken thus is probably completely lost, totally unsure of themselves in their new role and wondering what happens next? Often they feel obliged to rush into putting on workshops and attuning others. Or worse, they have attained Reiki Master status in a hurry, specifically to make money from attuning others; terrified in case the attunements don't work and not knowing how to judge whether indeed they have worked. Into the abyss, with great trepidation, leaps the new Reiki Master, trying to be spiritual, praying for help and guidance and never really knowing what will or will not happen.

Without really hearing it, we connect very powerfully and deeply with the energy of "I Am". It is the personal ego which speaks to you of "I Am". Beware of the seduction within … the "I Am important … the I Am a Reiki Master … the I Am of achieving a higher status than we really possess … the I Am calling out to be recognised and the ego's fear that it won't be. You may end up worshipping at the temple of I Am, which of course sets one apart from the multitudes. For "I Am" stands alone, in fear and competition with their fellow healers. But in reality, you will not be alone, because there is already a multitude of "I Ams" worshipping at the same shrine!

Energy is power and as we know from the adage, all power corrupts and absolute power corrupts absolutely. This is more pertinent in Reiki than in many other walks of life. Power and control issues are strongly bound up in the energy of some Reiki Masters. It is easy to fall into the trap of taking your Reiki attunements for the wrong reasons and possibly with the wrong Reiki Masters. As with all things which concern interaction between people, there is quite often a hidden personal agenda and this may even be on a subconscious level. In some cases it is on a conscious level and the practitioner may be aware of it, but the seduction is too strong to resist. When powerful energies are brought into the chakra system, they have powerful effects at all levels of our being.

Greater energy activity at base and sacral chakra level will increase the grounding and sexual functions; at solar plexus level it will increase certain aspects of perception and the amount of energy spinning out to all the other chakras; at heart level it can balance emotions and increase self love, at throat and brow it will increase sensitivity to inner sight or clairvoyance and at crown level it will create space for spiritual attainment. In reality, the lower centres, those which are rooted in the physical functions and provide the drive for our existence and survival in the physical world, are easier to identify with, without having to learn new skills. Emotional projection and sexual control issues can quickly become more difficult to control as energy comes into the system at base and sacral chakra level fuelling desire.

Reiki *is* power, self-transformational power, mental and emotional power, healing power, psychic power, mystical power, financial power and personal power. Reiki should be regarded as power by those who are already initiated, and treated with great respect! It should also be regarded as power, indeed even more so, by the uninitiated and it should be understood very clearly that the Reiki Master carries this power and can influence many things through it, not least through thought and projection. Unscrupulous Reiki Masters will also use this power in a manipulative and sexual way.

Reiki is life changing. It is instantly life changing at a subtle energy level. It can be almost instantly changing on a physical, emotional and mental level also. The surge in energy and the new abilities one inherits from using the Reiki energy are a powerful seducer of the ego.

To anyone who has attained Reiki First Degree, the title of Reiki Master can seem very distant and awe-inspiring. The student thinks, that if I have so much power at First Degree, then the Master must be incredibly powerful. Students put Masters on a pedestal, and who would not wish to be in this place if we were completely honest? It is a good feeling to be looked up to. It feeds one of our basic needs as a human being, ego. The unscrupulous amongst us would cultivate and feed off the energy of adoration of our students, instead of wearing the invisible robe of true Master/Teacher and feeding our students from our own energy, knowledge and experience. A true Master of any art gives of themselves and their energy. In Reiki, we often see the reverse taking place.

Reiki One brings an enormous buzz to a person. In the beginning there can be uncertainty, but as the energy begins to come through more powerfully, the student soon becomes confident. They cannot get their hands on people quickly enough to try out this powerful energy, and again they get caught up in the ego trap of thinking that they can heal anyone of anything: tummy ache and stiff joints to M.E. and cancer itself. With some people, the ego becomes so animated from the energy, that I am sure even death itself would not pose an insurmountable problem, such is the power of this new healing energy coursing through their being.

Many people go through this stage. It is understandable and almost undeniable, it shows that the energy is doing it's job and it is a great leveller for those who can see it for what it is. An excellent and talented natural healer who lives not far from me, cites in his own book his similar experiences, and although not a Reiki practitioner, he says that at one point he even began to think that he was the second coming of the Lord, he became so carried away. When you have power like this and you begin to get out of control as the energy fuels the ego, the powerful hand from above soon comes to teach you a lesson. And so it was in this case. One morning, his talents had all but disappeared. He didn't see it coming and indeed, it *was* a great leveller. You have to get down on your hands and knees and learn a few lessons fast as to who's in charge here. This is not our energy to use as we wish without paying for the consequences of its misuse. It is seeded to us as responsible guardians and facilitators, to use with humility for the benefit of mankind. Those in so-called positions of Reiki power will not get away with what they are doing. At some time, there will be a karmic debt to pay. They of all people should know this.

Power! It's a roller coaster with no brakes in some instances. People understandably want more of this power. Healing power is good; power is King; power is all. I can use this power to heal the world. Give me Reiki Two!

Another little thing to look out for from your Reiki Master, which is bound up with ego, fear and control issues, comes at Third Degree level. The attunement really consists of two parts. There is the initiation into Third Degree, which opens you at a spiritual level and then an additional symbol is placed into your energy system which enables you to attune others. Some Reiki Masters have a great fear of creating other Reiki Masters, they see them as a threat or competition. They like to take your money and put you through as many of the degrees as they can, but when it gets to placing that extra symbol within your light body, they cannot, or choose not, to do it. This is something that they would like to keep for themselves or rather, their ego is trying to keep it. Their ego is saying to them that if their student becomes a Reiki Master, then he or she will know all their secrets, so reducing the power and mystique which they try so hard to cultivate and retain. However, the only person to whom they do a disservice is themself. This is a fear and control issue. The Reiki energy is fuelling the ego to a point which has elevated them into a state of fear; fear to let go, fear to pass on to others the gift of light. So ultimately the fear sets up the control aspect which tries at all costs to avoid opening up and sharing. The universe, and the earth in particular, is in need of this energy right now. The more Reiki Masters that exist, the better.

What some Reiki Masters do is initiate the student into the third degree as a practitioner only and not pass the symbol which then enables the student to attune others. Some Reiki Masters will do this and then charge an additional fee to raise the student up to true Reiki Master/Teacher status. Others will not pass this symbol at all. Make sure you understand what is being offered to you.

Fortunately, all Reiki Masters are not so limited in their vision. Some are actively proud of the number of Reiki Masters they have created and continue to share and teach with those people for as long as they wish to maintain contact. However ... some things get worse!

## It Gets Worse

I hear it regularly. "So and so is doing Reiki One and Two this weekend and has booked to do their Masters in a couple of weeks time". He's organising his first Reiki workshop a fortnight later" or, even worse: "So and so is doing a four day intensive, all the degrees of Reiki in one go. She will begin teaching then".

Teaching what? I ask myself! What will this new Reiki Master/Teacher be able to offer their students? The intellectual knowledge acquired during four days of workshops? Workshops which may have been taught by someone who themselves have only done three or four days of workshops? This type of Reiki Master is not fit to teach someone to make tea, let alone attune people into the high frequency vibration of a life changing transformational energy like Reiki. Where is the experience? What support systems do they have for their students? For the record, the very best of these crash courses I have come across was a person who did all the Reiki degrees by distant attunement across the Atlantic Ocean over three weekends. Never even met the Reiki Master!

These are not isolated theoretical situations. It is happening all around us and students need to be aware of their chosen Reiki Master's abilities or records of achievement in other fields of energy work. I am not saying, don't go to a newly qualified Reiki Master, but you certainly need to know a good deal about who and what they are. Ask for references and names of other students if they have carried out attunements previously. Ask for an introductory session of Reiki and observe the procedure, making sure others are present. If you have a friend who is knowledgeable, take them along too and get some feedback from someone in the know.

## Non-Spiritual Healing!

Not all Reiki Masters are spiritual people, in fact some of them are positively materialistic and will cold-bloodedly drag as many students in for workshops as they can, purely for the monetary gain.

A sales representative I know called on us one day, and seeing our vast selection of crystals in the studio began to tell me about his wife who was selling crystals and who also had started doing 'a thing' called Reiki. I established that she had received her first attunement about two months previously. He was over the moon how much money they could make out of it, telling me that she had received a donation of £100 from one person already. In his own excited words ... "its a brilliant, brilliant way to make money". I know quite a bit more about the background of these people and I can assure the readers that you would not wish to be involved if they were dispensing the Reiki.

In another instance, a good friend who supplies us occasionally with beautiful hand-carved crystal healing wands telephoned me one day to warn me not to supply a certain shop with crystals because the two people who owned and ran the business had cheated a series of suppliers, some of which we knew, himself included. He had supplied them in good faith with some beautiful items and they would not pay him. They came out with all the excuses under the sun, you know, the ones that we have all heard before as to where the payment was, but he never received it. Daily he called them and was told it was in the post.

Although my friend is a powerful natural healer and intuitive, he does not move in wide healing circles and one day he asked me about Reiki. After I had finished giving him some fundamental information he told me that the couple who had cheated him out of his payment were both Reiki Masters. He had great difficulty reconciling the notion that Reiki was a good thing when these crooks and charlatans, who actively promoted their Reiki courses in the mainstream spiritual press, were totally untrustworthy, without either morals or ethics in their business dealings.

There are Reiki Masters who will give you an attunement in the back of a booth at a fair for a few quid. No instruction, no manual, no support and definitely no responsibility. There are others who will attune you over the telephone. I suppose, next, there will be mass attunements on the Internet, who knows where the madness and money grabbing ideas will end!

Some colleges are now offering Reiki to their students. In one case I know of in detail, the college paid for the Reiki Master's training and when this was complete the college wanted to push as many students through Reiki as possible. The idea is to maximise the revenue for its corporate purse, but without offering anything in the way of backup or support to the students. The attitude was to let them get on with it!

The Reiki Master was put in a very difficult situation and was horrified at the way the college wanted to approach Reiki. If the college is taking the fee, then the college needs to show some responsibility to the students. Reiki is not a commodity or a therapy which can be taught by just anybody, it is a subtle energy, self-transformational process which needs to be taught by a qualified and experienced Reiki Master. The Reiki Master must have total control of every aspect of the Reiki process, for the very necessary well-being of the students. Faced with this terrible predicament, and to her great credit in this difficult and pressured situation, the Reiki Master eventually refused to teach the students under this regime.

## Choosing a Reiki Master

Earlier, we discussed resonance. When one thing is in resonance with another, they are in harmony or in sympathy. Essentially they are attuned to each other. Like two people of the astrological water signs, such as Cancer and Scorpio, their energies will flow and blend with each other, causing little tension in a relationship, but if you mix a water and a fire sign there will be a vibrational imbalance at some level. It is unavoidable.

When deciding you are going to tread the Reiki path, it is important to choose the right Reiki Master for you; a Reiki Master who resonates with you and with whom you resonate. I am not suggesting that you choose a Reiki Master who is astrologically resonating with you, this is merely to illustrate the point about resonance and how we can feel naturally in tune with some people and not others. After all, you are probably not planning on having a long term personal relationship with your Reiki Master, although stranger things have happened.

As we have seen, a Reiki Master can be anyone, no matter what their level of knowledge, wisdom, enlightenment, power, or most importantly, experience. They may have attained the title Reiki Master within a week or so. They may have no prior training in any healing therapy or a discipline which fosters spiritual enlightenment or expansion of the senses through training or energy work. The title Reiki Master does not denote any knowledge, experience or wisdom of any kind. All you can deduce from the title of Reiki Master is that this person has the key to unlock a door within your light body to access higher energies.

The title Reiki Master does not denote any aspect of a spiritual nature. There are many Reiki Masters who don't have a spiritual bone in their bodies. They may be liars, cheats or charlatans. They may even sell you crystals which have been acquired dishonestly. In short, find out as much as you can about the person, if you don't know them already or they haven't come to you by recommendation of a trusted friend, which is always the best way, providing the person knows how to judge these matters. A good long chat with the Reiki Master, with your mind and your heart open, and a sprinkling of common sense will usually tell you if things feel right.

# Remember!

Although it is difficult in the west to work with a true Master of the traditional kind and in the traditional ways, because of the many restrictions placed on us by the demands of our modern lifestyle and also because there are not many places we can do this without a serious time commitment, be as certain as you can that your chosen Reiki Master is as near to a True Master as can be. Remember that we are brought up in a society and an education system which do not foster the spiritual aspects of our being or acknowledge the intuitive functioning of the right hemisphere of the brain.

It is therefore incumbent upon you, the student, to ascertain for yourself what qualities your prospective Reiki Master possesses. It may be beneficial to consider a Reiki Master who actively works in healing or has their own practise, someone who works with energy all the time. It is up to you to ask the questions, evaluate the answers and then decide for yourself whether you consider your chosen Reiki Master to be a safe pair of hands, capable of supporting you through any situation you may then find yourself in, once your light body has been opened.

> A true Master will be available and encourage you to discuss your motives and reasons for taking this form of healing and spiritual advancement now.
>
> A true Master will encourage you to speak with other Masters to gain a broader knowledge of the subject matter, which will help you to decide.
>
> A true Master will not try to possess you or cajole you into taking a course before you are ready.
>
> A true Master will encourage you to consider taking different Degrees of Reiki with different Reiki Masters. This will allow you to experience different energies and acquire different perspectives, knowledge and experiences.
>
> A true Master will encourage you to take your time in your unfoldment and be sure you are ready for the next level, when you think the time has come.
>
> A true Master will be there to help put you back together if things go wrong.

Let us return to that word resonance. No single Reiki Master has all the answers. Be cautious and take your time and move into the light at a steady pace with confidence and security and with a Reiki Master with whom you feel in resonance.

## A Thought for Your Fellow Light Workers

Healers should not be in competition with one another. They should be standing four-square beside each other, channelling the light together for the common good. If you think you are in competition then you are allowing your ego to come out and display itself. Envy, jealousy and fear *do* rear their ugly heads from time to time. These are natural human emotional tendencies and none of us is immune from them. The first important thing in one's growth is to recognise them when they are active. The second important thing is to accept them as part of you, and try to understand their message. The third is to allow the energy of the emotion to dissolve, thereby achieving evolution.

> It is by the pathway of diversity,
>     That our journey brings experience.
> It is by the pathway of experience,
>     That our journey brings knowledge.
> It is by the pathway of knowledge,
>     That our journey brings truth.
> It is by the pathway of truth,
>     That our journey brings wisdom.
> It is by the pathway of wisdom,
>     That our journey brings wholeness.
> It is by the pathway of wholeness,
>     That our journey brings light.

Since the first printing of this book, the feedback has been phenomenal. Many Reiki Masters have commented on how much they've learned about enegy work which they had been ignorant of for so long. Many have recommended it to their students and some have even bought copies as gifts for their students.

## 07

"Teacher, I beg you to look at my son, for he is my only child. A spirit seizes him and he suddenly screams; it throws him into convulsions so that he foams at the mouth. It scarcely ever leaves him and is destroying him ..." Even while the boy was coming, the demon threw him to the ground in a convulsion. But Jesus rebuked the evil spirit, healed the boy and gave him back to his father. And they were all amazed at the greatness of God.

Luke 9:37-43

IT IS A WONDERFUL THING THAT SO MANY PEOPLE ARE changing and moving up in their energy, evolution and spiritual attainment and connectedness. As the changing vibration of the planet is forcing change upon us, those who are ready find it difficult to resist. It is wonderful that young people are training in the intuitive and healing arts, dowsing, channelling, alternative and complementary therapies and Feng Shui. It is also wonderful that more and more people are creating new energy tools, such as vibrational essences, flower and tree remedies for use by intuitive therapists, kinesiologists, homoeopaths and healers such as myself, in my guided vibrational healing.

In addition to my healing work with people, the universe has always sent me Geopathic Stress cases and major Earth Healing and Geomancy projects. I get a great buzz when a healer comes to me with an energy problem and I can see it in their chakras or aura and fix it for them. Sometimes I see my role like that of the old fashioned country garage mechanic, in days when motoring was more pleasant. You would call in with a problem, have a chat while he fixed up your

# PSYCHIC ATTACK

motor, and you were on your way again in no time. One of my jobs is fixing energy systems so that you can go on your way and channel more light with the increased confidence that comes from understanding what went wrong. When one fixes energy system problems properly, the effect is very often instant, followed by a dramatic change in the quality of life.

Healing of any kind is brilliant, it's fascinating, it's fun and it's rewarding … it can also be devastating when things go wrong. And things do go wrong, both for the novice and for the experienced healer alike. Often they arrive at the door of their teacher or Reiki Master for help, and frequently there is not the accumulated knowledge or experience to provide that help. If they are extremely lucky, someone will know where they can get some assistance or psychic first aid, for there are not many places where the type of help they really need is forthcoming. Although it is true that there are quite a few people who can deal with some aspects of psychic attack, there are not many who can deal with the greater spectrum of problems which might befall the unfortunate light worker.

My practice is busy all the time. My diary is usually full for several weeks in advance with different types of work. For instance, I have a number of clients who come to me for spiritual evolutionary work. Vibrational energy work can be fundamentally transformational if a person's being is ready for change. Guided Vibrational Healing is about moving people forward at an energetic level. Therefore, when someone has a session, it triggers a healing process by which energy blockages or barriers to evolutionary progress are removed. The person can then move forward during the ensuing months. As their energy system goes through these changes, it is inappropriate to do more work until the light body has transformed itself to a new level. Once the light body has moved forward and settled on a higher plane, the physical body has some catching up to do and it is not until this new plateau is reached that we can continue the work. Sometimes this can be several months between sessions. In another example, if someone with M.E. comes for treatment, because their energy systems are so delicate, only very gentle balancing is possible on some occasions. The Guides telling me what and how much we can do. I am then often told that we cannot see the person again for several weeks or even a couple of months, as their system processes the work. Many of my clients are one-off psychic rescue cases, people who know that there is something seriously wrong with them, but they can't put a finger on what it is. Many healers and energy teachers come for energy system balancing, realigning, chakra cleansing or spiritual evolutionary work. In addition to my healing work, my 'proper job' is really Geopathic Stress Investigation or house surveys. This work keeps me as busy as the healing work and often includes psychic energy problems of many kinds which either inhabit a building or are encompassed within the fabric of the building. Often the building is the cause of the whole problem where a person's health and well-being are concerned. I will be explaining more about Geopathic Stress and how it affects health in a subsequent book.

I sometimes receive several calls a week from experienced healers or the general public who are the victims of psychic attack. In some cases they may have suffered mildly for a short period of time, in others their lives may have been devastated for many months or even years before they discovered what the problem was. They arrive for help with many different energy system problems. Chakra damage ranging from mild misalignment through to leaking, blocked, torn, locked open, malfunctioning, distorted or with foreign energy inclusions, to a complex combination of all of these and more. The aura may be completely out of alignment with the physical body. The different levels of the etheric, emotional and lower mental bodies within the aura may be misaligned and out of balance in relationship to each other. Perhaps the outer essence or fabric of the aura is ripped or holed, leaking energy and light across other dimensions or realms of light, attracting all kinds of black and negative forces of one sort or another into one's being, to torture at a mental and emotional level the unsuspecting victim, often driving them into a terror filled existence. I frequently see things I've not previously encountered.

The effect this has on people's lives can range from mildly disturbed or lack of sleep at one end of the spectrum, through to constant nightmares, if and when they can get any rest at all. When things begin to deteriorate, the victim can move downward into dramatic mood swings, anxiety, panic attacks, fear attacks, hallucinations, depression, more serious psychological problems and even personality disorder. Without some help or an enormous but unlikely stroke of good fortune, the condition continues to deteriorate.

One cannot say that there is anything like a typical case of psychic attack, although there can be a general pattern in the majority of cases. There are many levels of psychic activity, and predicting what will happen is not an exact science. However, what I can say with a fair degree of certainty is that, once it begins, it very rarely sorts itself out without help from someone who is well

The subtle energy body, or aura, which is out of alignment with the physical body.

versed and skilled in the matter. The first signs of psychic activity either in the home or around the self are, quite literally, the thin end of the wedge and as the wedge begins to drive home, the psychic activity becomes greater. Let us take a very straightforward look at how psychic attack can occur even with the most grounded and protected of experienced healers or therapists, let alone inexperienced Reiki students or ordinary folk going about their daily business.

## Identifying Psychic Attack

As well as the general public, healers and therapists of all kinds can be prone to psychic attack. Hairdressers, beauty therapists, masseurs or those who are in close proximity to other people in their daily work, but specifically those in a hands-on situation, are more prone than others to the risks of psychic attack. Many of them suffer mild attacks without really knowing what has happened and after a little while these manifestations will usually dissipate to a certain degree and then fade away altogether over a couple of days.

A common scenario is this. After treating a client, or perhaps a number of clients, you may notice that you feel off-colour, not one hundred percent, or even quite drained. You may feel a little sick or have a headache. Most people will put this down to workload or being tired, or perhaps you had a late night the night before, etc. In many cases the reason that you feel this way is due to picking up negative energy from one or more of your clients. This negative energy 'pick up' is accumulating with each client you treat. When you actually know and understand how it feels to pick up negative energy or to have psychic attack, then you can recognise it immediately.

As healers and therapists, take a moment to look at who your clients are. They are usually people who are unwell in one form or another or they would not be coming for help. It may be that these clients are just a little under the weather or not feeling up to par. Alternatively, it might be that they are suffering quite severely. Sometimes they will have straightforward physical symptoms or exhaustion, but in other instances it is quite often the case that they are unwell because they are carrying a fair degree of negative energy of many different kinds.

Reflexology, aromatherapy or massage are great examples to take for this type of case because, firstly, these therapies are becoming more common and accepted in our western society and more widely and easily available. Forward-looking medical practitioners and doctors are even suggesting these therapies to their patients. Secondly, because they are becoming more common and acceptable, the problems of psychic attack are increasing amongst practitioners.

A typical day in a typical health or healing clinic may begin with the therapist having a bright and breezy outlook as the clients begin to arrive. After a treatment has been performed, the client often says how wonderful they feel. They say

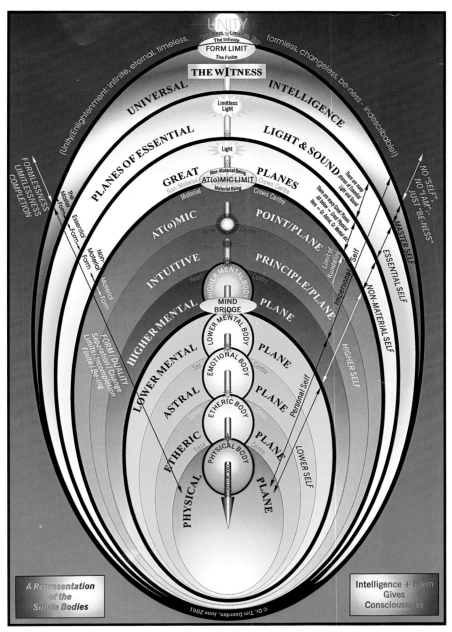

Plate I: Representation of The Subtle Bodies
(© Dr. Tim Duerden – for notes see www.duerden.com)

Plate II: Illustration of the Light Body and Chakras.
(Illustration by Nick Clarke.)

Plate III: An Entity hanging in space above the corner of a doorway.
An ideal place to attack the energy of the Crown Chakra.
(Photograph © Dinah Arnette.)

Plate IV: We were always a little unsure about the provenance of this image, but as I and many others had seen similar beings, usually about 16 inches high, we thought it worthy of inclusion as an example of the types of gremlin you or your clients may encounter. Don't see them as dangerous, just other forms of consciousness with a life-force of their own.

In February 2007, after six years of publication, we eventually discovered the origin of the image and it proved to be part of a display in the Cheddar Caves.

that they feel ten feet tall or that a great weight has been lifted from them. Indeed, the latter is often very true in a psychic energy sense.

This great weight may be a number of things. In its mildest form it may just be an accumulation of negative energies, literally dark clouds of energy which were clinging to the client's aura and blocking them up. Sometimes this is referred to as auric mucus or fog, which releases and lifts during the therapy. As it lifts from the client, it is absorbed by the therapist. Hence the client feels wonderful and the therapist, at the least feels weighed down and tired, or at the worst feels awful with a number of different symptoms.

This type of energy has a magnetic attraction, as does all psychic energy. Once you absorb a little, it can then accumulate from many sources and places. For instance, if a person works in the vicinity of negative people, then they stand a good chance of absorbing into their aura some of this dark energy. Negative people also pattern their environment with such energies, and so merely being in a negative place can have similar consequences. Places such as psychological institutions, prisons, police stations and hospitals are classic examples of places where there is a great deal of energy interaction on a human level. One-to-one energy exchanges as doctors or nurses treat patients, releases mental and emotional energy which can be absorbed by others. Some places, like psychological institutions, contain very sick people. It is often the case that certain aspects of their sickness are due to psychic forces being attached to them. In other situations such as policing, the officers have to deal with some very bad and very negative people. When these interactions take place, energy is released from the people involved. This energy has to go somewhere. It doesn't just disappear. At a deeper and more worrying level, drug addicts are often possessed by serious forces such as drug entities, which manipulate their personalities. These can be powerful beings, and counsellors, social workers and others who work with these people are at real risk of psychic attack from this source. You cannot work around negative people and not expect to pick up some of their energy.

When any therapist engages in therapy with a client, they are entering into an active energy exchange. You are working within that person's aura or subtle energy field and they within yours. Remember that the aura can extend many feet from the physical body and it is made up of a combination of powerful electromagnetic energies which interact on many levels with the same energies of other people. As well as the negative aspect, picking up the things we don't want from someone else's aura, we can also learn to use our auric energies to pick up things that we do want.

The aura acts like a sponge, soaking up energy. My own aura does exactly that when I am reading the energy of a person, a house, an office or open space environment. I soak up the energy through outer levels of my aura and transmute the vibrations through my etheric aura into the mind/brain, which then translates the energies into words, pictures and perceptions which I can relate to. The energy is then processed back out of my physical and subtle energy system via a yawning process, leaving my energy clean and vibrant. This is also how a clairvoyant reads the information within a person's aura.

This yawning process is an interesting phenomenon. Many therapists will notice that they want to yawn a lot when giving a treatment. This happens more so with healing and energy work such as kinesiology and cranio-sacral therapy, rather than straightforward massage, reflexology etc., as the person is working at a deeper level in subtle energy terms. I often see therapists trying to stifle a yawn. You should not do this. It is important that you allow this process to happen unhindered. Explain to your client that the yawning is an automatic response of your body's consciousness as it transmutes and releases energy from your system, which you are in the process of continually absorbing as a consequence of the subtle energy interaction, between the two of you, brought about by the practise you are performing in your healing work.

If you are subject to this yawning phenomenon, try to notice that it is not like a normal yawn as when you are tired, it is completely different. I call it an energy yawn. You will notice that it can be very deep and prolonged and sometimes feels as though it will break your jaw because the energy release opens the mouth so wide. This yawning is sometimes accompanied by very watery eyes. My friend Anne, yawns constantly as she works with her clients, her eyes water and her nose runs too, poor girl. She always works with a box of tissues at hand.

This yawning process may affect anyone who has particularly open chakras and is drawing in energy at a high level. One of my students reported that she has always had this type of energy yawn and she was always getting into trouble from the teachers at school for yawning. She says she was never tired, she just kept yawning and describes her yawns as being "almost too big for my mouth". In her case, she does have certain chakras which are particularly open. There is nothing wrong with them, this is just the way her energy system is formed. Now that she understands the process and why it happens to her, she can relate it to her subtle energy system and how it is functioning.

Sometimes this type of energy release comes from very deep within you. I occasionally have a situation where the energy rises up in a big lump from the diaphragm and gets stuck at the throat, beneath the Adam's apple. It needs quite a push of energy to release it and can feel as if it might choke you if you don't get it out. Anne also gets this very deep energy release and puts this down to when there is the energy of an issue within herself which is trying to be released at the same time that she is working on a client. The vibrations being used for the client just happen to be appropriate for the therapist too. I can agree with that although I tend to get this happening more often when working with earth radiation than healing clients. Of course, earth radiation is much more powerful than auric energy and perhaps this is why it moves such a lump of energy in one go. It's great to know that Mother Earth is helping release stuff from me, as I am helping vent toxic energy from her.

As soon as I tune-in to anything, within seconds I am yawning. This is always a good sign that I have connected with who or whatever situation I might be looking into. When appraising the energy of a house, the occupants who may be accompanying me from room to room will often start to yawn as my consciousness pervades the living space and releases things which then change their energy. It is also a sign of a highly tuned subtle energy system and a fine degree of sensitivity to subtle energy. Essential for a good therapist or healer. For instance, when making a call on an ordinary land line telephone, I constantly yawn.

So we can summarise that in a hands-on situation, where the therapist feels tired or drained after a session with the client, they have usually absorbed a certain amount of the negative energy carried by the person they are treating. Subsequently, the therapist may feel tired or drained. Given a little time, this will usually dissipate on its own if the therapist is strong and healthy with a powerful aura and chakras in balance. However, if you take on a small amount of energy from each client who comes through your door during the course of the day, then you will become very drained and may get symptoms such as headache, aching neck and shoulders or cold symptoms. Constantly absorbing and accumulating energy in this way compounds the situation and the energy becomes more difficult to dissipate. In fact it may take quite a bit of effort on the part of the therapist to remove it. This of course is providing they know some procedures to psychically cleanse themselves, procedures we will look at later.

Consider what might happen, if we have absorbed energy and our next client is someone who is frail or sick, or someone with an energy system disorder such as M.E. or chronic fatigue syndrome. This energy build up within the therapist may then discharge into the client's aura adding further trauma to their already difficult state of health. In cases of M.E. sufferers, I have seen cases where healers have put the client in bed for as much as three weeks after a treatment, such has been the devastation to their very delicate energy system, which of course has little chance of recharging itself.

One further scenario for your consideration. I am aware of situations in reflexology and massage classes at college, where regular clients coming for treatment with the students will almost fight to have a treatment with a certain therapist because they always feel brilliant afterwards. This is usually where the therapist is also channelling natural healing energies similar to Reiki. As well as practising the prime therapy which the client has come to class to receive, such as reflexology, they also get treated to a healing session too. The client doesn't understand why that particular student makes them feel so good, but at a subtle energy level they are absorbing a mass of positive energy, which releases blockages and lifts their energies dramatically. Often this type of client may be a psychic vampire, hungering for energy. They are very good at identifying, at a sub-conscious level, those who can feed their need for energy. If this type of person gets a therapist who is perhaps a little open, they will drain them totally within a few minutes. Recently a young trainee therapist came to my attention with exactly this kind of problem. In this case, the poor girl was drained by her client so quickly that she had to run to the window and was physically sick within a few minutes of starting the treatment. She didn't recover at all that day.

To avoid these situations we need to understand about psychic protection to provide ourselves with a shield against this type of energy transference when we are working. We also need to understand and practice some techniques of psychically cleansing down both ourselves and our treatment room between clients and also learn grounding techniques to make certain our energy is at least balanced in one direction.

## The Forms of Psychic Attack

There are two main forms of psychic attack, passive attack and active attack. The method of attack can be accidental or deliberate. Deliberate attack can be malicious or non-malicious.

## Passive Psychic Attack

Passive means undirected. In some ways passive attack is not really attack because it has not been focused deliberately at you from a third party source. However, we deal with it as attack because essentially that is what it is doing to you when it is absorbed into your energy system. Quite simply it's negative energy state is attacking the normal functioning of your own balanced energy state as contained within your aura and chakra system.

Passive attack is when you pick up negative energy from any source, whether a person, building or a place or site of some sort. For instance, there are many people practising dark arts at sacred sites and leaving very nasty energies behind them to contaminate the unwary. Most usually though, it comes from another person whom you have come into close contact with. This form of attack is called energy transference, where the energy literally rubs off them and clings onto you. Remember that the aura can extend some twelve feet or so quite easily. When we are going about our daily business, the aura is passing through many other peoples' auras and it is at this time that transference of negative energy takes place. Imagine walking through a crowded street or market and then think how vulnerable you are if you are open at a subtle energy level. Visualise yourself wearing a white suit and accidentally brushing up against people in dirty overalls. You will get a transference of dirt onto your clothes which can be seen. It is just the same with picking up negative energy from someone who is carrying it around with them. Get close enough without any psychic protection and some of it will brush off their energy system and enter your aura. Remember also that it has magnetic attraction, so once you pick up a little bit, the chances are vastly increased of you picking up more which will enhance the size and power of that which is already attached to you, and of course, exacerbate your problems.

## Active Psychic Attack

Active psychic attack is when the energy form attacking you usually has a life force. This means that it is some kind of being, as you and I are beings, but existing within dimensions other than the physical dimension which we inhabit. We know for instance that we exist in the physical realm, but that our aura also exists within other dimensions of light. The beings of which we speak can sometimes cross between dimensions and even co-exist in different dimensions at the same time. Imagine a bear that could be both on land and under the sea at the same time. This is co-existence in different realms, or dimensions.

There is also psychic attack of a malicious sort, targeted by one person upon another. This can be done with passive or active energy which is driven by thought forms activated by people who have energy knowledge, but have enlisted the help of the dark forces to aid their agenda. In the passive energy state this can be particularly debilitating if the thought forms enter your light body at a vulnerable moment, i.e. when you are particularly open. Voodoo with dolls can be classed as this type of attack. Some assaults can become more powerful if the attacker maintains the attack with some form of constant energy stream towards the intended target.

Another aspect of the above is when a person has the ability to manipulate beings within other dimensions and target people or places with them. An example is similar to the work I do with distant spirit clearances. With the assistance of my Spirit Guides we can transcend time and space and remove entities, spirits and certain other forms of being at a distance, within seconds, anywhere on the planet. When doing this type of work for people suffering from serious hauntings, the effect is immediate and they are usually on the phone the next morning to say how wonderful the changes are. It is through the feedback that one learns of the effectiveness of these techniques. However, there are those amongst us who have these abilities but work with the dark side, maliciously attacking people, rather than taking away their suffering.

## Attunements and Psychic Attack

When an attunement is in process, the individual is in a state of union with spiritual forces at a subtle energy level. In other words, spiritual beings are manipulating and adjusting the energy channels of the person. In those moments a form of operation, akin to a physical operation as carried out by a surgeon, takes place within the chakras and the subtle energy system in general. Any interference from outside energy sources during this process can upset the balance of the attunement. Even worse than this, it can result in damage to the subtle energy system of the person. This damage can remain permanent unless the individual first of all, begins to comprehend that things are not quite as they should be and secondly, is able to find somebody who is capable of performing psychic rescue and repair work.

During the attunement, great respect and reverence should be accorded to the ritual, and sincere acknowledgement paid by the Reiki Master to the spiritual beings present. Physical movements should be balanced and flowing, with nothing rushed. Time should be taken with each student before and after passing the symbols. During the process of attunement the auras are wide open as the Reiki Master blends his or her own aura with that of the students. The energies flow between both while the spiritual third party essence blends harmoniously in attendance. Be as aware as you can of what is taking place on a higher plane and allow it the due time and space to complete the process.

If an attunement is not completed satisfactorily or the connection is broken during attunement causing a subsequent imbalance, then channelling Reiki to yourself or receiving a Reiki healing from others will not fix the problem. Damage to chakras and aura is specialist work which is successfully carried out by only a very few. If you are treading the light worker's path, then be sure to have the telephone number of someone you can turn to if you feel that your energy does not feel right. This should be someone you can get to quickly or someone who has the ability to work with Guides at a distance to repair the damage.

During the process of attunement, the Reiki Master's physical energy is used by the Spirit Guides as a sort of battery, allowing them to interact more easily in the physical dimension. If the Reiki Master does not enter into the process properly, then our spiritual brothers and sisters cannot perform their part of the job properly either.

I can cite many instances in which for one reason or another, a person has not received an attunement correctly. Sometimes only a little bit of work needs to be done to connect them up properly; in other cases there is severe damage or blockage to chakras and aura. In some cases there has been no Reiki Guide attending the person, as indeed there should be after every successful attunement.

There can be an accidental oversight or a little uncertainty on the part of the

Reiki Master, especially with Reiki Masters in their infancy with the art and unsure of procedure. In other cases there is negligence and even gross incompetence, but at the end of the day it is the student who suffers. It is the student who leaves with a bad attunement, one which doesn't work properly or perhaps not even at all. At the other end of the spectrum the student may be severely damaged by the experience at a light body level and left in a vulnerable condition.

It is time students who are not happy with what has happened to them returned to their Reiki Master asking for a refund. I do know of some Reiki Masters who are recommending this when Reiki students come to them with this type of problem, asking for help or re-attunement. Perhaps they should also ask for a refund and the cost of treatment to have the damage repaired, plus the cost of attending the workshop of a competent Reiki Master who has the experience necessary to guarantee their safety.

There is nothing to stop anyone from being a Reiki Master, Teacher or Practitioner, therefore it is incumbent upon each of us to strive for high standards. No amount of academic study or qualifications can guarantee you the development of intuition or can prepare you for working with Spirit Guides or becoming an intimate, co-creator with spiritual forces. Only dedication, perseverance and experience will bring you close enough to know what is happening. I cannot say often enough, that the dissolution of ego is paramount to attaining communion on a higher level. Ask those who have experienced the loss of their spiritual connection, or power if you like, and how it is attributed to that moment where they became 'too big for their boots'. It's a great leveller to approach a healing situation and nothing happens. You soon realise where the power comes from and upon what terms it is granted.

## A Case in Point

A lady called me to make an enquiry about the cost of a Reiki First Degree attunement. I talked to her in depth and explained my methods, encouraged her to speak to other Reiki Masters and guided her in the questions she should ask, so that she could get a good feel for what she was getting into. It was at this point that she told me she had already received an attunement in the March of that year. It was now September and she had not felt right since the attunement.

I asked her about her attunement and she told me that during the process, she had been in a deep meditative state when the telephone, which was next to her on a table, rang out. It startled her to such an extent that she had felt extremely shocked. Since that time she had been unbalanced and felt that the attunement was not right. Her friends had encouraged her to have it done again and she had spoken to several Reiki Masters about a re-attunement. This primarily is why she had called me.

She had come to the conclusion that many of the Reiki Masters she had spoken to were on an ego path, controlling their students, a view that people who would interview a number of Reiki Masters would come to. She was very unsure who to take the re-attunement with.

I explained that before she even considered having a re-attunement she must be checked out for damage to the energy system and that with my clairsentient abilities I could do this for her now over the telephone.

I took a couple of minutes to tune-in, sent my Guides over to the lady and then dowsed her energy system. I tuned my senses into her body so that I could feel what she was feeling and told her that she had damage to the solar plexus, heart and throat chakras. Although my sensing told me that she could not feel the damage in the solar plexus chakra, I could feel sensations on the left side of the heart chakra and directly in the centre of the throat chakra. The damage here was so great that I was certain that she must be able to feel discomfort. She confirmed that this was the case and she could indeed feel that things were not right in these areas.

Although the crown, brow, throat and heart chakras are the main chakras which are attended to and manipulated during a Reiki attunement, the other chakras have to be adjusted also to accommodate the increased flow of energy. You can't tune half a musical instrument and expect it to sound sweet. The vibrations have to be in balance across the whole spectrum of the instrument and with a Reiki attunement, all of the chakras must be tuned to the correct pitch. So it is, that although the major change takes place initially in the top four chakras, the other chakras are also brought into alignment at the correct pitch, so that the whole of the light body vibrates to the right tune.

I dowsed that the shock when the 'phone rang had broken her connection with spiritual forces during the attunement and that it had not been re-established. The attunement was however, about 70% correct and she was channelling the Reiki energies. I dowsed that she could use her Reiki on herself and even on others if she wished, without worsening her situation, although I recommended that she didn't work with other people until she had undergone repair work for the damage which had been done to her subtle energy system.

This lady was lucky in some respects, in as much as she had not suffered any damage to the aura, which was still intact and very strong. She had a very strong aura to begin with and this is perhaps what saved her from a worse situation. She could have been left wide open after the attunement and then been vulnerable to all kinds of psychic attack.

She told me that I was the first person to tell her anything about the various processes which made any sense of her situation. I told her to take some time to think about what I had said and then if it seemed right to give me another call and we could take it further. It is important to give people time to think things through, to reflect on other things they have been told, and consider any experiences they may have had. If everything is as it should be, then they will know which way to turn without the pressure of somebody trying to manipulate them.

Be clear that when you are open or left in an open condition after an attunement, it is not some unfortunate occurrence if you are psychically attacked: you will definitely be attacked by some form of psychic matter. This may be a passive negative energy such as auric mucus, which can readily adhere to you, or an active energy in the case of entities or spirits. It is merely a matter of time until something of this nature befalls you.

This lady was fortunate that her chakras were not left open and she was particularly strong within the aura, probably due to the fact that she maintained a very good diet in terms of powerful energy food. However, wherever there is damage in the subtle energy system, even in somebody who is doing all the right things to support their system, at some level the system will not be performing at an optimum level. The aura is not being fed by all the subtle forces from the chakras and sooner or later its strength will be compromised.

In this particular case, the lady called back the following day and made an appointment to come over for a psychic repair session. During the process of repair to the chakras it was confirmed that the attunement was functioning quite well and the lady was channelling the Reiki energies successfully. It took about an hour and a half to repair the chakra damage and at the same time the Reiki Guides perfected the attunement, saving the lady having to go through the process again at additional time and cost.

## Another Example

To illustrate another case, a client came to me encumbered with six entities and a badly damaged aura. In itself, this is everyday work for me, nothing out of the ordinary. She was in her late thirties and had suffered various forms of psychic attack since puberty. Puberty can be a difficult time for psychic attack for young girls. The emotional changes which take place as the endocrine system metamorphoses into maturity send out powerful emotional signals through the aura. Anyone with a weak or damaged aura will pick up entities very easily. More often than not, though, this type of energy change attracts spirits around them. It is also interesting to note that this particular time in the development of young girls is also strongly linked with the onset of M.E. where the sleeping site is in the vicinity of earth radiation and electro-magnetic radiation.

This lady had graduated through Reiki First Degree and then three months later had done Reiki Two. A couple of years after that she had done the Third Degree.

She told me she had never felt things were right with her Reiki and after I had done the entity clearance and aura repair, taking around an hour and a half, I tuned-in to her chakras and dowsed the attunements. All three attunements had been performed correctly by the different Reiki Masters but I detected a serious problem which had occurred at the time of the Reiki Two attunement. This was nothing the Reiki Master had done wrong and was actually outside the time that the actual attunement took place, but while her aura was still open.

I told the lady that all attunements had been performed correctly but the problem began on the day the Reiki Two attunement was performed. She then told me that she had known that things were not right after that attunement and had subsequently been to another Reiki Master to be re-attuned to Reiki Two again, but this had not solved her problem.

Accidentally she let this Reiki Master's name slip. I know this particular person and have very great respect for their abilities and integrity and found it difficult to believe that anything would be wrong with an attunement from this source. Upon checking out the attunement, I found that everything had been in order. My Guides reported that all procedures had been fine, as indeed they had been with all her other attunements from other sources.

As I tuned-in to a deeper level I could see the problem lay with thought forms. I could see the Reiki symbols lodged solidly inside this lady's solar plexus chakra. They appeared to me like those little twisted metal puzzles you find in Christmas gift sets for children and adults alike, where you have to untangle their impossible shapes to pull them apart. This was a case of psychic attack with thought forms, driven by the jealousy of a fellow student.

Jealousy is a dangerous green-eyed monster which stalks just as much in the spiritual aspects of our lives as in the material aspects. People can become very jealous of another person's energy or abilities, jealous of the light which they carry. I am sure that the person in this particular case did not want to cause this lady deliberate harm, but not knowing how vulnerable we can be at that moment when our aura is opened for attunement, she had made her jealousy known in a very powerful way and the thought forms had entered the light body of the target of her jealousy and caused this lady five years of heartache and uncertainty.

This lady's auric defences were so delicate that the powerful thought forms had taken a grip inside her and blocked her energy system, so that the attunement could not enter her being in a functional way. The symbols had become lodged and tangled within each other in a chaotic and unusable fashion. They were all stuck in the solar plexus chakra and not present in any of the other chakras, which they should have been.

This is an illustration of how vulnerable our light body can be at the moment of attunement and soon thereafter. It is imperative to have calm conditions for the light body to receive, consolidate and then process the attunement. It is also imperative that the environment be sealed in light and the scene set in love, light and harmony.

## A Classic Healer's Mistake!

When suffering from psychic attack, understandably, you know that something is wrong. Often you can't put your finger on it, but you just 'don't feel right'. Anyone in this situation will try to get some help, either from their healer friends or from their Reiki Master.

Sometimes if the situation persists and all healing help has not relieved their condition, they may even go to the doctor. This can pose other problems altogether, as the medical profession in general does not acknowledge other realms of existence and knows nothing about psychic attack. Consequently, it doesn't appear on their 'list of ailments' and so they can't diagnose it. Even if they could diagnose the problem as psychic attack, they quite probably couldn't repair the damage anyway.

In some cases, the person may not be a healer or have healing friends and so they visit the doctor as the first port of call. This was the case with a nurse who visited me with a serious entity possession. It was only because by chance her husband had seen one of my leaflets at someone's house describing the symptoms of psychic attack that he realised this was what his wife had been complaining of for the past few months.

A doctor will usually suggest a tablet of some sort or other, as was the case with the nurse. There is not a tablet anywhere that will deal with psychic attack. It's as daft as saying take these aspirin and your troublesome neighbours will go away.

What happens if a healer, of any modality of healing, channels hands-on healing energy to someone who is the victim of psychic attack, where entities or spirit attachments are the cause, and are still present in the energy system? The healing energy will certainly boost the energy of the client and bring about a certain amount of balance, whilst providing much needed help. However, this is only whilst the treatment is taking place. These immediate benefits will be short-lived.

Healing energy, or electro-magnetic energy, is just the source of food that entities or spirits require to boost their own energy levels. So, in a very short period of time after the healing, sometimes within hours but certainly within a couple of days, the victim of psychic attack is back in the same position as before the healing, or possibly even worse.

If the victim has entities attached to the aura, these will certainly become stronger. The additional energy they take on board can make them much more powerful. Some will use this additional strength to feed even more voraciously and yet others will, already having been fed, become less active until they again need sustenance.

If the outer envelope of the aura is breached, then this creates a far more dangerous situation for the sufferer. As the light body becomes filled and vibrant with healing energy, or light energy, then the light body shines even brighter. Its luminosity radiates out into space like a beacon, attracting more entities into the energy system of the unsuspecting person to feed from this wondrous banquet which has accidentally been laid on and spread before them.

If spirits are involved, there can be a number of different outcomes. Some spirits will be calm and quiet and not impose much at all on the lives of their hosts, merely taking a little energy now and then, usually while the person sleeps, and then retiring to a regular quiet spot in the house until the following night, when they will again need feeding.

However, if there is a spirit attached to the aura and it is a menacing seeker of energy in order that it might gain enough strength to carry out work pertaining to its own agenda, then this can have serious consequences for the person. Some spirits can become so strong that they try to take over their host and manipulate the host's mental and emotional body, thereby subjugating them to its will, so that the spirit can act out its own desires using the energy of the person.

This is what is meant by spirit possession. When this type of possession is very strong it can completely change a person's personality. Where there is a spirit which is not too strong, the person will often experience doing odd things which are out of character. They will confront themselves, bemused, and say, "why did I do that? It's not like me at all". When this occurs in a home where other people are living and perhaps they are a close family, the others in the household will notice the 'out of character' behaviour and usually remark on it.

Psychic attack involving active beings who have attached themselves to the energy system of a person is a serious business to deal with. We can see here that these beings feed on the very energy most well-meaning healers would use to try to bring relief to a person suffering some discomfort. Our psychiatric wards are full of spirits and entities attached to people and manipulating their personalities in the way mentioned above. The regime of treatment to which the patients are subjected makes for an ideal living environment for spirits and psychic vampires.

I mentioned earlier that some people, not understanding what is happening to them, might visit the doctor for help. The description of the symptoms someone would give a doctor might fit quite nicely into the category of anxiety and so the doctor would usually prescribe a form of tranquilliser. In reality this can also make the problem worse. Firstly the tranquilliser is not going to remove an entity or a spirit, or indeed repair a damaged chakra or aura. Secondly tranquillisers can weaken the electro-magnetic energy within the aura and in some cases may cause actual damage to an aura which is otherwise intact.

We have so far looked at the most common forms of passive negative energies and active negative energies. At the other end of the scale we have demonic possession, a very serious form of manipulative attack capable of extremely destructive work.

## The Realms of Light

It should be understood that all forms of energy work involve opening doorways into other dimensions. We know little or nothing of the nature or number of these dimensions. In these other dimensions, which we call the realms of light, dwell other beings, beings such as spirits, entities, psychic vampires and others. Only with a great deal of psychic protection should anyone venture to place their mind or consciousness into these realms. One should only attempt this when in full knowledge of the intent and collaboration of one's Spirit Guides and in full awareness that the guidance is provided specifically for you to enter this space.

When opening to channel healing energy, it is often the case that intuitive messages are received as to what to do, or where to place the hands. This information may be coming from Spirit Guides or from others. Which, is of no importance. Here the key point is that the information is coming into our conscious mind via another dimension. If the mind is open to receive from another dimension then it can also transmit into that same dimension. Another way of painting this picture is this. When I place my consciousness across distance to see what might be happening in a case of psychic attack on some unfortunate person, I am looking directly at perhaps a spirit or entity. As soon as my consciousness touches that being, not only can I see it, but it can see me.

At the very moment my consciousness touches the being which I am seeking, there is nothing to stop that being transferring its attack from its present host to me and entering my energy system, other that is, than my psychic protection. Spirits, or any other being of light, can move at the speed of thought across any distance. I discovered this when I was looking into a case of serious spirit problems in a house some fifty miles away whilst on the telephone to the very distressed occupant. As I put the phone down, I became aware of a spirit standing next to me, it's energy sending alarming signals up and down my spine, or central nervous system to be precise, as it interacted with my own energy.

The realms of light pervade and pass through everything. We understand that the vibration, or frequency of light which we know as X-ray penetrates and passes through the body. The vibrations which constitute the dimensions of light are even higher than these. How many different dimensions there are, cannot be known in our limited perceptions as humans; there could be millions, each supporting it's own forms of life.

The realms of light pervade every aspect of our being. The physical body is no barrier to the vibrational frequencies of other dimensions or the beings who dwell therein. This is why we see a spirit pass through a solid wall, because the vibration is so high that physical matter cannot prevent its passage. It will pass through the solid wall without disturbing a single molecule. Imagine pushing your hand through bubbles without moving or affecting them at all.

The aura is our protective shield against anything which travels these highways of light, preventing them from gaining access into our core being. The existing realms of these other beings interpenetrate our own dense, physical world. Our light body or aura, of which many of us are unaware until it begins to unfold and we develop the sensitivity to see, feel or perceive it, also parallels these high frequency vibrational levels of existence. This is why the aura of a person can be felt or measured through a solid wall. Our physical body is subject to the governance of the physical laws; our light body, which is the core essence of our being, may be anchored to the physical body while we are alive to protect us, but behaves in accordance with the laws of high frequency light: that is, it can pass through what appears to be solid matter.

Another form of psychic attack is by thoughts projected onto or into us by other people. Voodoo, black magic and many forms of witchcraft are practised around the world and as the world becomes a more cosmopolitan place, the ethnic practices of such forms of psychic interference are becoming more prevalent in western countries. I have had many cases of victims of witchcraft and black magic to deal with within ethnic groups and because the people of these groups are well practised in their craft these are frequently very powerful forms of psychic attack. Also, because this type of attack is common practise in some cultures and acknowledged and accepted within the mind-set of these ethnic groups, their minds are more open to receive the attack than prevent it from gaining a foothold. However, as well as the negative side of these actions, the positive side is that most people know of a medicine man who can help them deal with them.

Entities and spirits are one thing and yet only the beginning. From what I discovered when trying to release a particular energy source from my own being one time, we can come into contact with things which function beyond our limited comprehension, and mine is perhaps expanded more than most by the nature of this work. There are beings which can exist in more than one dimension at the same time and are able to transit through every part of the essence of our being, either harmlessly or resulting in great pain.

When these energy beings are within the aura, they can pass through each different level of energy and also through the physical aspects, unhindered. They are but as a misty essence which is consciousness itself, which can pass through every cell without disturbing it. There is nothing these levels of energy cannot do within our lower vibrational being once they have gained access.

## Entities

The entity is a being much the same as you and me, inasmuch as it is a living being. Just as we have billions of cells in our bodies which have a life force and do a job for us, but which we cannot see, so the entity has a life form which we cannot see, but also exists in a higher frequency dimension. If you imagine existing only as an aura, then this is similar to the existence of an entity. It is an electro-magnetic being without the encumbrance of a physical body.

The entity can take a number of different forms, although we tend to classify them under the one description of just entity. At the lower end of the evolutionary scale is the entity which just feeds. It has a form of consciousness and little else and I usually visualise these as just a ball of energy, quite spiky and harmful, a bit like the little sticky bobs which grow in the fields that we used to throw at each other as children, which then stick with their Velcro-like hooks onto your clothes. Mostly about the size of a tennis ball, they attach themselves to your aura in order to feed from your energy. A general term for these is psychic vampire, for that is exactly what they are, only instead of sucking your blood, they suck your energy.

This energy form is more or less a parasite or scavenger, it has consciousness which tells it that it needs to feed to exist and so that is what it does, not really knowing or caring where, or upon whom it does it and certainly not conscious that it is harming the people which it is feeding upon. Much as a tape worm or liver flukes live within the body, it exists in a parasitic role, feeding and surviving with no real understanding of the damage it does to its host.

The next level of entity has consciousness and awareness, like the consciousness and awareness that we have. They know what they are doing and they know to whom they are doing it. They have a certain level of intellect, that is, they are intelligent and they can play games with us in order to get what they want without being caught. These types of entity can be very powerful beings, cunning and clever. In the case studies you will read about an entity which, knowing that its host was on her way to be cleared of its presence and in order to avoid being dispatched, split itself in half so that the people doing the clearance thought that it had gone, but in fact as soon as the poor victim got back into her car to go home, it jumped straight back onto her with even greater presence than before.

## Auric Fragments

When we die, the energy in our aura can persist for many years in a coherent and semi-coherent state as it slowly disintegrates or is dismantled by light workers. Sometimes, a person can pick up particularly bad and negative energy from this source, which then binds itself into their aura. Dependent upon the level of emotional and mental residual content left in the auric fragment, this can have quite a powerful effect upon the mental stability or emotional balance of the person to whom it becomes attached. Healers practising fundamental hands-on healing can easily loosen this type of energy from a client and absorb it themselves if not sufficiently trained in energy cleansing techniques and psychic protection.

## The Spirit and Trapped Spirits

Spirit attack is a big area and one could write a book on this subject alone, citing case studies in particular. On a good week I have rescued the souls of as many as thirty spirits from different locations. These may have been wandering around peoples' houses or living more closely with their host by following them around as they go about their daily activities, or may even become attached to their aura. In some cases there are many spirits in a single house.

When we incarnate into the physical world, our spirit comes to this dimension to inhabit a physical body in order to undertake a journey from which spiritual advancement is the intended goal or prize, through the lessons we may learn while we are here. Sometimes when we die our spirit or personality structure becomes trapped or stuck in the physical dimension instead of returning to the source in the spiritual realms from whence it came. There can be many reasons for this I am sure, and it is only through many experiences that any of us can construct any hypothesis as to what happens and why the spirits, sometimes referred to as discarnates, are stuck here.

We also need to be clear as to what we mean by spiritual and physical when referring to realms, so that we understand where the trapped spirit is located in relation to other dimensions. It is also necessary to understand that a trapped spirit, or lost soul, is not the same as a Spirit Guide. The physical realm is the place where all things are vibrating in physical form, a relatively slow vibration compared to that of the spiritual realms. The Earth is our physical planet and everything on it, including our bodies, is physical matter. We exist in a physical universe. However, the other dimensions of which we speak, such as the spiritual realms, are places which may or may not exist in parallel with the physical realm but certainly do exist in some form which we cannot identify at this point in our evolution. Although they are there, most of us have distinct trouble in accessing them. The difference between these realms is rather like the difference between sea and air. Birds (or most of them anyway, don't anyone mention penguins!) cannot transfer from the realm of air into the realm of water, any more than a shark can take to the sky (though there are a fair few of them walking the earth). Likewise, we cannot cross into the spiritual realms in our physical form.

When the lost soul becomes trapped in the physical realm, it is merely a case of helping them to move across a boundary, which for one reason or another they cannot do for themselves.

I remember very clearly as a boy wondering what it must be like to be a grown-up. I had the distinct impression that grown-ups were a different type of creature altogether. As I went through my teens and into my early twenties I was fascinated that my thoughts and consciousness, the very essence of who I was, remained the same and did not go through some strange metamorphosis into the other being I had always known to be an adult. As a result of course, I have remained a boy. I am not sure whether this a good or a bad thing. My son, who is now seventeen, said something similar about this phenomenon to me a couple of years ago. I wonder if anyone else has had the same experience? And so, just as the boy becomes the man but maintains the same essential self, the spirit maintains the integrity of the same personality after the physical body passes away. I suppose that means I will be this same boy for a number of incarnations, if this is the nature of the essence of me!

A spirit is just the same as you or me, apart from the fact that it has lost its body. If you were to die, your consciousness and your thoughts would be just the same as they are now. Apart from losing the physical mantle the only other real difference, due to the spirit being eternal, is that of time. Because time has no meaning in the spiritual realms, it is of little importance how long the spirit remains trapped here. One minute or a hundred years, it matters not. Spirit is eternal.

When a spirit remains trapped here it is in a different form to that which we call a Spirit Guide, although trapped spirits can help humans if they can find a way to communicate. The Spirit Guide is a much finer vibration and has not necessarily had an incarnation in an earthbound physical body. Sometimes it is possible that the spirit of a loved one can make it's transition into the astral realms and after a period of 'debriefing' and adjustment, return into the physical realm to accompany a person as a helper or guardian. This is not a trapped spirit, it has returned by choice, or with permission, in a finer vibrational state and it can come and go at will across many different dimensions or worlds.

The entrapped spirit retains a much coarser vibration which can be felt very strongly by anyone who is sensitive to these energies, but also perceived by many others who are not so sensitive. The energy of a spirit reflects that of the human counterpart which once was its representation when it was incarnate. The personality remains the same. The lower mental body and emotional body are still intact and we can pick up information from these, as well as communicate on a telepathic level. The spirit will continue to live out its emotional self as determined by its consciousness.

Telepathic communication is quite easy if the spirit is strong and powerful in terms of the energy it carries, or the person within its vicinity is in a relaxed state of consciousness, or perhaps a meditative state. This is why people are often aware when a presence comes into the bedroom at night. In addition, the yin energy of night-time is much calmer than the yang energy of day-time, due to the earth's changing position within the Van Allen Belts, and corresponding relief from day-time electro-magnetic pressure. This yin energy provides a good background against which to pick out any change or movement of a subtle energy source, such as a spirit.

Spirits, just like people, differ greatly, one from another. If a person was very disturbed and angry in life, then the spirit of that person will be the same, as this was its nature when incarnate. If the person in life was light-hearted and jolly, then the spirit will be the same.

## How and Why Spirits Move In with Us

Spirits arrive in one's life for two main reasons. They are either attracted to the energy of a person or attracted to the energy of a place. Frequently, lost spirits will try to find the energy of something they can identify with and be comfortable with. Therefore they will try to find a person whose energy is similar to that of a partner or close companion while they were alive. The alternative to this is for them to find a house whose energy is similar to that of the home where they used to live.

Spirits often arrive in your home in this way. They may be travelling with or attached to a person who visits your home. While visiting, the spirit may find that it prefers the energy of your home to that of its present host and when your guest leaves, the spirit stays on. Alternatively, the spirit may prefer your energy to that of their present host and this is why it decides to stay. Yet again, the spirit or spirits may well have already been in your house before you moved in.

## The Start of Trouble

Spirits can behave very much like the psychic vampire we discussed earlier. If the spirit is powerful and needs a lot of energy to support it, or to feed it, it will stay close to a host person. It will feed more often and as it does so the energy of the host becomes weaker, the person usually feeling increasingly drained and debilitated, frequently getting up in the morning and feeling as if one has had no sleep at all. If the spirit craves even more energy it actually attaches itself to your aura so that it is in a constant state of communion with its food source, which of course is your own electro-magnetic energy.

If the constant feeding breaches the auric defences and your escaping light becomes visible across other dimensions, you are then exposed to all kinds of psychic attack. As mentioned in the introductory paragraphs to this subject, this initial damage usually initiates panic attacks, which become progressively worse. The stress of living on this knife edge constantly takes one deeper and deeper into psychological trauma and uncertainty whilst at the same time it continues to deplete the resources within the subtle energy system.

As we have already said, but it bears repeating, the energy of spirit and entity acts like a magnet to similar energies. Like attracts like in the case of psychic energy. An entity will first of all be attracted to your energy and usually it will jump from another person into your aura. You will take it home and there it will dwell. Sometimes they will dwell in the house and feed from you at night, when you are asleep, or they may feed from other members of the family. A colleague of mine once saw an entity jump out of a person, run through the house and jump onto a baby, causing the infant immediate distress. At other times, they will cling to your aura all the time, feeding as the need arises. In other situations, they will have jumped right into a chakra and take up lodgings there. In this case little, other than psychic rescue help, will cause them to flee, and they cause quite serious trauma. Who else lives in the house dictates to some degree what the entity will do. If you have pets, they may begin to feed from the pets. Cats and dogs in particular are very sensitive to spirit energy of all kinds. When you have had a Reiki attunement you will find that these creatures will respond to you differently as your energy changes.

Cats are very spooked by energy. I give off a lot of energy through my aura as I use it to sense atmospheres and environments, therefore my senses are probing the atmosphere of a space as I am investigating it. A cat will often jump up, very startled and then run away at first, until the fabled curiosity gets the better of it and then it will slowly come back towards me to investigate, or alternatively it will run a mile, never to be seen again while I am in the house. They sense all energy very keenly and if it is an energy they don't know, which in the case of Reiki it often is, they will react instantly to it. They will either love it or be totally spooked by it.

I went to investigate a house for Geopathic Stress one time. I had been in the house for ten minutes or so, having a cup of tea and discussing the case with the people, when the cat came in. It walked straight over to me and jumped up on my lap, brushing its head under my chin in the cat-like tippy toe stance of affection which they adopt. It then immediately climbed onto my shoulders and lay across the back of my neck, legs stretched out in opposite directions. The owners were astonished, they told me that the cat has never been near a stranger in its life before, preferring to be a solitary creature, hardly even bothering with the family most of the time.

When entities arrive in a home, cats in particular become very unsettled and their behaviour changes dramatically. They will start to spend more time outside and frequently will not want to come back into the house. They will in some cases try to find a hiding place or will spend more time than usual sleeping. It is as if they are trying to hide from the energy by being asleep. When you get spirits in a house, the cats' behaviour changes are even more dramatic.

## More Serious Aspects of Spirit Activity

All spirit activity is draining on your energy. If a spirit is living in your home, then at some level you are supporting it with your energy. Some spirits are very gentle, delicate beings and require only a little energy and others are powerful and require a lot of energy to maintain their existence. Yet again, some spirits are not content just to exist, they have their own agenda. Even though they have passed out of the physical body they have desires of a life which they still wish to live out and they can be very powerful in influencing the lives of their host to bring them what they need. As a drug addict craves a fix, so some spirits are equally caught up in the support structures of mankind's existence. They will take as much energy as they can in order to put pressure on you to respond to their needs.

If the spirit in life was an alcoholic or drug user, sugar junky, chocoholic etc., then it will bring pressure to bear in influencing the personality of it's host to bring it the subject matter of its desires or cravings. Beer and cigarettes for instance.

When a spirit becomes attached to you it influences your personality through its own emotional and mental body, which are still intact and powerful. It overlays your emotional and mental body with its own and or imposes its own energies onto your subtle energy system. At one end of the scale you might find yourself suddenly doing something or saying something off the cuff which is not normally you, or having a craving or desire for something which you have never yearned for before. You will respond quizzically, asking yourself why you did or said that.

You will usually forget it until this mild 'acting out of character' happens more often, to the point where you notice it regularly and you are beginning to feel uncomfortable with it. As the spirit becomes stronger you will begin to notice that you seem to be acting out of character an awful lot and doing things that might have become very uncomfortable for you, but which you cannot resist. These out of character actions are uncontrollable because it is not your character. You are being controlled in a way which will give the spirit what it desires.

Spirit attachment goes through the whole range, from acting mildly out of character as above, through complete personality change or disorder to serious possession. We need to be clear about possession as opposed to attached. True possession is when a being gets inside your aura. Beings can be attached at many different levels. Entities can even get into your chakras, but this is not possession. The aura has a definitive shield or screen which keeps out most major things even though it may become slightly damaged. True possession is much less common than psychic attack, but when it does take place, it is very serious. When a being has actually taken up residence within a person's aura it can play havoc with their life and it usually has a serious agenda. In a case of serious possession the spirit is so strong that it takes over your consciousness almost totally when it so desires, which is not all the time, only when it wants something. Then it will negate any free will you may wish to apply to the subject of its desires.

## Multiple Personality or Spirit Possession?

There are many documented and verified cases of multiple personality disorder, which in some instances are clearly due to spirit possession. One case in particular which comes to mind is that of a young student who was taken into custody and tried on serious charges. On being found guilty he was transferred to a psychiatric hospital for help. He is now the subject of a book entitled *The Many Minds of Billy Milligan*.

In a straightforward case of multiple personality, the person may switch into and out of different personalities without any knowledge of who they are acting out. However, within these personalities they cannot display any skills or abilities outside of their life's experience. In a case of spirit possession they can.

The young man in question underwent detailed investigation by eminent psychiatrists who all agreed that he did indeed display multiple personalities, but what they could not explain or acknowledge because of the limits of their own experience and belief system was that Billy displayed skills and abilities which clearly he could not have knowledge of within his life's experience. One of Billy's personalities was Arthur, who spoke and wrote fluent Arabic, yet Billy had no knowledge of the language. Another was Reagan, a Serbo Croat who spoke with a very broken American accent in a voice different altogether to that of Billy.

If psychiatrists could bring themselves to acknowledge that there are indeed powerful psychic forces at work in the world and that spirit possession is not just in the realms of the Hollywood movie, then we might see many people being greatly helped, cured and released from the torture of having aspects of their lives controlled by other living beings over whom they have little or no knowledge or power.

## Demons

As any healer or subtle energy worker continues to work with subtle energies their stamina, strength and perceptions within the subtle realms will usually increase. The universe then brings forth more and more challenging work to be done. Demons are a step up the energy ladder from spirits. Whenever I have work to do which involves demons I always have a few more Spirit Guides with me. Clearly this work is another step up the energy ladder in the Spirit Guide world also and the heavy brigade are brought in to support the team.

Whilst performing a clearance one day on a house in Essex, I found a number of spirits plus a mischievous demon. I mention it here for a particular reason in relation to hospitals. The creature was a kind of Griffon-featured dog, a sort of brownish, sulphur yellow in colour and about the size of a small whippet. It seemed to be content to prowl around the house and cause as much discomfort to the other spirits as well as the occupants as it could, banging draws and cupboards during the night and thumping the underside of the bed, causing great distress to the occupants. When I was telling this tale to a friend sometime later she asked me for a description of the creature. She told me that a clairvoyant friend of hers had described seeing these same beasts prowling over the occupied beds of patients in hospital.

I have also had cases where the demon has left the scene of the crime, so to speak, perhaps many years earlier, but the energy is still with the person or place. Demonic energy can be a very strong psychic force attracting other negative forces into its dark vortex to bring even more problems to the innocent victim, or unwary healer.

Demons are common and come in many guises and strengths. Most of the demons I have been faced with have been more troublesome rather than demonic, but I am sure now that I have written this, some bad ones will come along. (I wrote this in 1999, and yes they have appeared.) I have encountered the energy of very powerful types of demon which has been left at the scene after a person's energy system has been compromised by its presence. It is much more solid and evil than that of a spirit or entity. One such example was that of a young a lady who had suffered terribly. Understanding that she had been possessed by some force which she could only identify as demonic possession, her doctors couldn't help her and obviously worried, they sectioned her under the mental health act and she was taken into a psychological institution. Many years later her parents' path crossed mine when they asked me to do a Geopathic Stress investigation on their house. During the work on the house, they mentioned their daughter and asked me if my particular type of healing work would help her. At this time, they hadn't told me the story of the demonic possession, only that she had been unwell for many years.

A few days later, when time allowed, I tuned-in to the girl and discovered a number of things, one of which was a terrible demonic energy in the area of her chest, even though the demon had long since departed. The energy was so strong, my Guides advised that I dealt with it at a distance rather than on site. Only after this psychic rescue was I allowed to see her for a healing session.

## Extra-terrestrials

This is a difficult subject to broach with any sane person, for the simple reason that the majority of members of the public immediately draw the line here and others are quick to brand the pronouncer completely barmy. Well, let me assure you, I have my feet firmly on the ground and have not been the subject of alien abduction ... yet!

When you work in the area of investigating subtle energies, as I do, you will come across energies which, for want of a more apt description, are totally unfamiliar to you. Entities have a particular vibration and feel, and when you have done as many clearances as I have, you get to know the vibration. Sprits, likewise, are easy to identify and communicate with on an intuitive and telepathic level. I have experienced some of the energies of demons and seen some of their forms. Of beings from the underworld, I have only encountered a few, but I knew what they were without prior knowledge of them.

Then there are other energies, which have a life force with consciousness and awareness, which do not fit the description, vibration or feel of anything we have so far covered. No matter how I try to identify them via my dowsing or tuning-in, they are not of this world or of any other we have so far looked into. These beings communicate telepathically with great ease and power, the vibration is strong and clear, focused yet gentle, but with intent and knowing that I am aware of their presence. Sometimes they wait in the wings as it were, respecting my free will to remain silent and uncommunicative. They know that I know I am being observed, they know that I have much knowledge and experience of light beings and have deduced quite easily what they are.

I perceive them from within my working place of protection provided by my circle of Spirit Guides and acknowledge their presence with gratitude, love and light and I carve the experience on the hilt of my sword of inner knowing. They are beings, they are not spirits and they communicate. They dwell in other realms. As they do not originate from the Earth they are extra-terrestrial and so that is how I identify them.

The first time I became aware of this type of being was in a healing session when I felt the presence behind me, looking over my shoulder at my client. I knew what it was immediately, even though I had never experienced this energy form. In my mind I said to myself, 'there is an alien here'. Very quickly in a caring and loving energy I received the telepathic words "I am a Brother". To this day I am very careful not to use the term alien as a description of any other life form.

We engaged in conversation, his answers coming almost before my questions had manifested as thoughts. He approached and showed me how he can cloak the aura of a human and expand or contract to fit their physical size. He told me he looked after the girl I was treating and that they had been together in an Earth incarnation some three hundred years before.

Some time later, I asked the woman; "are you aware of any Guides who may be with you?" She said "no, but a lot of people say they can sometimes see an alien in my face". Of course, he had just demonstrated to me how he did this. I asked "is he here now?" She responded, "I don't know, but I have been calling him".

He told me many things in a short space of time and offered his help if ever I needed it. The meeting had been so profound, I often called across the universe to him when praying at night, but to no avail. However, a year or so later, I had a case where I found a light being, or 'a Brother', who was indisposed and needing assistance to regain his own dimension. My Guides told me to call for our friend, which I did, and within minutes he came and helped us resolve the matter.

Most people have the idea that all extra-terrestrials should have physical form and arrive in space ships. Why should this be? If we have so many dimensions that we do not understand or comprehend, why should we not have some that contain other civilisations and beings who are more advanced than we are?

Since that first encounter, I have had a few others. Some I have rescued as I might rescue the soul of a trapped spirit. Others have visited and given me their name and offer of help in my work. I have even called on that help and it has been forthcoming, evidenced by the success of the work in progress.

I could say "you be the judge of my sanity", but preferring to try to remain non-judgmental in all aspects of existence I would say to you, "be open minded, so that you may also have the chance of experience". For it is with an open mind that things can enter into our consciousness and experience and it is with a closed mind that a very limited perception will be the norm.

## My Own Damaged Aura Experience

Ask and you shall receive. We have learned that this biblical message refers to spiritual aspiration. If you chase spiritual advancement with sincerity, you will be guided and given help in the areas which best suit your own energy. Well, as we have previously discussed, sometimes you are given without asking, particularly when those up above think you need a lesson of some sort. I've been dealt out a number of lessons over the years, but as I was writing this chapter I received a personal experience, the like of which I have never had before. It was as if the Guides were saying, you need this experience so that the readers can see that even something as simple as a fundamental absent healing session can open doors that nobody could foresee. This at first seemed like a perfect and classic example of psychic attack. In reality it was much more interesting and revealing.

It was around 11.30pm on a Sunday Evening. Denise and I had just got into bed when she said to me, "Oh, I forgot, I was supposed to send some absent healing to Kate". As Denise was particularly tired I said that I would do it. I settled down and although I don't always use the Reiki symbols for absent healing, I felt an affinity for them for this job. I spent some time tuning-in and bringing energy downward and into the chakra system through my crown chakra and then focused a channel of energy to come down and surround me. When the energy was suitably 'up and running' I used the Reiki symbols to open a direct channel to Kate. It was a wonderful session, my consciousness was right out amongst the stars. Denise said something which brought me back again. I gave some instructions to the energy to continue for as long as it was appropriate for Kate to receive it, and then closed myself down.

It was an absolutely straightforward absent healing session and nothing out of the ordinary was required. Simply open up with the Reiki symbols, send the energy to its target and close down again. I've done it hundreds of times. I turned over to go to sleep and within a few moments began to get extremely restless.

I was tossing and turning and I began to realise that something was not right. I began to detect energies getting into my system which I should not be able to feel if my aura was OK. The pangs of anxiety began to creep in and rapidly increased their intensity leading to powerful panic attacks. In the half-conscious state between sleep and wakefulness, my mind was trying to figure out what was wrong as I slipped in and out of anxiety and hazy dream states.

I then grasped that my aura had been damaged. I dowsed a series of questions in my mind to confirm this and became calmer, knowing that the anxiety state was energy shooting into my central nervous system through the tear or hole which had been blown in the outer sheath of my energy field. I asked the Guides for protection and battened down the hatches to ride out the coming night's storm.

The following morning at breakfast, I told Denise there was something wrong, I was absolutely wrecked. She dowsed and confirmed that my aura was damaged. I called in my Guides and received information as to what crystals to use to repair the damage. I went and lay on the bed and Denise set out the crystals in an appropriate grid and left me to stew while the Guides did the repair work.

That morning I had a client booked in but was in no fit state to do any healing work. Denise 'phoned him and cancelled and told me I had to stay in bed to recover my energies. I am not a great one for staying in bed, I tend to push the boat out against all the odds when ill, but where working with energy is concerned you have to be one hundred percent to practice, and so I did as I was told.

We finished the aura repair and I got undressed again and went back to bed. The event had drained me so much that I slept all day. It took me two more days to recover my strength and energies to the point where I could again carry out energy work. Now when you consider that I identified the problem more or less straightaway and we carried out the repair work within a few hours of the event, this still put me on my back for a whole day and out of action for three days. Imagine what it can be like for someone who doesn't find out what the problem is for maybe weeks or, in some instances, years. It can then take a very long time to recover your psychological balance and overcome the fear which strikes when you think you are about to be hit by a rush of anxiety, or panic attack.

The other very important point to consider, and this is why this lesson was sent to me at this time, is that this was not psychic attack from an entity or spirit, this was aura damage caused by pure energy. In the book so far we have only discussed serious damage from attack by active energy forces, not passive. This illustration shows that merely channelling healing energy can have the same devastating effects, although in this case there were perhaps some unusual, mitigating circumstances.

We did some dowsing work around the whole scenario, because this was a really odd situation, though one with circumstances which were not at all unusual at first sight. During the night, Denise had felt a presence in the room, I tuned-in and I could see it straightaway. I said, "it seems like it was sitting on you and just looking at me". Denise said, "It knew I was aware of it but it seemed to be repressing me, not wanting me to move or disturb you. You were making strange struggling noises, like when the spirit workers have been to visit you in the night previously and entered your body. I wanted to wake you, but the visitor would not let me move to help you."

We dowsed with the Guides and determined that the visitor was a very high being, his name would be known to us as Argon. He was a Reiki Guide. He had actually been working with me since September the 7th 1999, some four months. He had previously had an incarnation on earth some 3600 years ago approximately. I questioned all the Guides for help via my dowsing. Using the dowsing saves my energy. If I tune-in to receive messages directly, it can be quite draining. Using dowsing is like meeting the Guides half way. It can also be a lot quicker sometimes. A sample of the questioning technique follows.

"Did I use the symbols correctly?" "Yes".
"Did I mix any energies with the Reiki which were incompatible?" "No".
"Why did Argon visit us, was he trying to prevent the aura damage?" "No".
"Was he trying to repair it?" "No".
"Was he with me before the damage occurred?" "Yes". "Could he have prevented the damage?" "No".

"Was the problem caused by something that happened with the energy?" "Yes".
"Was it the Reiki energy alone which caused the damage?" "No".
"Was it something which was carried on the energy or within the energy?" "Yes".
"Was it within the energy?" "Yes".

As I become more tuned-in during the process of dowsing, the link with the Guides becomes naturally stronger and messages begin to come through directly, without draining me. They will usually give me a word, a picture or an emotion which I then interpret and confirm via the pendulum, e.g. "Is this picture correct?" or "have I seen this correctly?" As we progress, the connection then becomes stronger and they can give me whole sentences. As it speeds up, they are sometimes giving me the answers before I have formed the questions. Such is the density and slowness of thought. I can sit at a keyboard and type as they are giving me the messages.

"Was there something with a life force involved?" *"Yes".*
"Was it Entities, Spirits or Demons?" *"No".*
"Was it what we consider to be an extra-terrestrial life form?" *"Yes".* (I am already sensing the male energy of our visitor, but I always ask the questions to make sure. Check, double check and check again. You can't have enough checks when working with energy.)
"Does it have a gender?" *"Yes".* "Is it male?" *"Yes. He is called Corman".*

"Does he work with Spirit Guides?" *"Yes".* "Angels?" *"No".*
"Is he working for the forces of Light?" *"Yes. He is trying to help you because he is grateful that you helped one of his friends recently to get back home into his own dimension. You know who this is".*
"Did he do the damage to me?" *"Yes".*
"Was this accidental?" *"Yes. He was trying to do something with the energy. He was trying to accelerate the energy through you".*

"Was this after the energy had passed through me?" *"No. This was before the energy entered you".*
"Did he succeed in accelerating the energy?" *"Yes".*
"Was he trying to increase the volume of energy in terms of it's diameter?" *"No".*

Although from experience I know a lot of the answers to energy questions it is always prudent to ask the very basic of questions. Do not assume you know the answer, because working with energy is not something you can define clearly. We do not know all the universal laws by which energy functions. What appear to be similar situations can often require very different methods to resolve them. There is always an unknown number of variables.

"When I activate the Reiki energy does this automatically bring in other frequencies of spiritual energy?" *"Yes".*
"Is this always the case?" *"Yes".*
"Is this always the case with everyone who channels the Reiki energy?" *"Yes".* They show me a picture of silken strands or strands like in a fibre optic cable. This is the Reiki energy flowing at great speed, very focused, drawn from a great pool of energy, as if being channelled down through a cone or funnel and made into a fine, fixed diameter flow, being drawn into the crown of the person. As it flows at high speed, it gathers up to its sides, through the sheer velocity of its flow, other strands of different frequencies of spiritual energy which are absorbed and join in the rush.

"Is it possible to screen out all other frequencies of spiritual energy?" *"Yes".*
"Does this mean that the Reiki energy will then be channelled excluding all other

The high velocity of Reiki energy gathers up other frequencies of spiritual energy along with clouds of negative matter.

spiritual energies?" "Yes, if you create and use a filter to screen them out".

"If this is so, is it then possible to channel the Reiki energy solely by itself?" "No". "The Reiki energy will **always** gather up other energies as it flows and you must screen the other frequencies out".

(I am double checking here.) "Will the Reiki energy always bring other energies in with it?" "Yes, unless screened".

"What are these energies?" They show me a vision of the high speed Reiki energy as it was before, but this time it is gathering clouds of misty energy and pulling them with it. I see the Reiki flow entering the crown and the clouds are swept away as they hit the aura of the person channelling Reiki. I also see sparks and hear crackling sounds as if their is a great electric storm being created by the high speed passage of the Reiki.

"If the aura is damaged would these clouds pass into the energy system of the person channelling Reiki?" "Yes".

"Would these clouds pass through the channeller and into the target of the energy?" "Yes".

"Would this also be the case in absent healing?" "Yes".

"Are the clouds a representation of negative matter?" "Yes".

"Am I absolutely clear then that these clouds are negative energies which have been drawn into the Reiki flow by its velocity and they can enter the energy system of someone with a damaged aura, but can also pass right through the Reiki channeller into the recipient of the Reiki healing energy?" "Yes".

"If the channeller has an intact aura would these energies pass through to the recipient of the Reiki energy?" "No".

"Is the Reiki creating this storm of energy release you have shown me?" "No". "Tell me what it is". "The great storm which you see is a centre of creation. Not the centre of creation as in the mind of God which is the creator of all things, but a centre where many energies are created. Energies that may be used by mankind. The Reiki energy is just one of many energies which are born in this great place of upheaval. We see your mind and you have seen this correctly, it is literally like a great storm which you *might experience on earth, only it is in another dimension and caused and fused by things you cannot experience, this is why we show you in pictures you will understand. This place is great. It is a great force, likened to the force which would create a universe. This is a universe of energy from which the human race can tap into the Reiki flow".*

*"What you have seen where the Reiki flow is infused with sparks is other forms of energy travelling with the Reiki. These are positive forces, but they are not healing energies and they are not spiritual energies. They are just energy. It will have positive effects upon you when it passes through your being, although it will not help directly with the healing. It is a different kind of energy, it builds power and in an indirect way it will help with healing".*

*"It is this energy which has damaged your aura as the Reiki came through. Your friend Corman tried to push it through you in an attempt to help you unfold. He meant well and we could not prevent his slightly misguided enthusiasm which resulted in the damage to your aura. Argon came and sat with you, to pray over you and observe what had happened. He was powerless to help until you worked out what to do and gave him the tools to help you. You were in good hands and held safely from any form of attack".*

*"Tell me why my protection failed". "Your protection did not fail. Your protection is robust but you are not ready to work with energies as powerful as those Corman pushed through you".*

*"How did it come about that he was allowed to practice with me thus?" "Corman is a high being. In the hierarchy we are his equals, but there happens a time when our forces must be pooled and shared. We acknowledged Corman and his gift to you of unfoldment and although we knew that you were not ready for this we could not prevent him from trying. He was confident, but not well versed in our energy work. He has great knowledge of working powerfully with great energies but not as subtle as the ones we are currently using in our healing work. The energies he is familiar with are great and powerful, capable of moving planets and he wished you to be infused with the lightning of these energies. This is the lightning and sparks which you have seen being gathered up and channelled with the Reiki energy".*

*"Forward to him my gratitude and forgiveness for the little discomfort I suffered in the name of his gift of potential and bid him again to return and observe and help us if he so wishes".*

## What Happened at the Other End?

As a matter of interest, at the other end of this absent healing debacle was an equally intriguing study. When I began to dowse what had happened, I asked my regular first questions to establish who or what was involved. In that first session, I detected a demon; however the demon was nothing to do with the problems I had suffered. The demon was in fact within Kate's being. At first, I had the feeling that the energy which I had sent absently had hit something and bounced back, and this is what had caused me the problems. It felt like back pressure, as if I had sent so much energy that the recipient had not been able to absorb it and it had come flying back at me. In the event of what we found out, that first impression was not far out. It was certainly to do with energy which was too powerful. In the event that I found the demon, I thought that he had sent the energy back at me and my protection had failed me.

When I discovered the demon, I had to change the tack from trying to find out what had happened to me to trying to discover what was happening to Kate. Kate is a lady in her thirties and the demon had apparently been with her from the time she was in the womb. More interesting than that though was the fact that she had carried this possession from a previous incarnation on earth. In this incarnation she had been born in 1876 and died in 1933 and had lived in Belgium. She had not been involved in any occult practice but had become possessed in 1924.

When I first found the demon I knew he was not very active. I say he because I picked up the male energy immediately. I have subsequently seen him and he is a loathsome snake-like serpent which dwelt in the higher bowel region of her light body, across the umbilicus. He didn't move very much and maintained a sort of silent vigil, slowly taking the life force energy for himself. Needless to say, Kate has suffered terrible physical ailments of a wasting type in this lifetime and the demon was certainly responsible for her demise in her past incarnation.

How could it be that she was born into this world with a demon present in her? Could the work to remove this beast from her spiritual essence not have been done after her previous earthly death? The answer was no. I was shown a picture of three spheres of existence similar to the earth. In simplistic terms, on the left was 'hell', in the centre was the earth and on the right was heaven. I was told that hell is where the demon belonged and the earth was the place where it wished to dwell among humans in order to feed. In so called heaven, it was impossible to deal with this demon. I was told that there are certain other dimensions where the demon could be dealt with but for whatever reason it was deemed necessary to send Kate back to earth to have it dealt with here.

It gets still more interesting. It would appear that Kate's mother was pregnant and then three months prior to birth, the soul was removed from the foetus and substituted with the soul which is Kate. I asked how this could happen and was simply told 'by a higher authority the first soul was removed'. Sometimes I am told in great detail and sometimes it seems to be on a need to know basis. This was one such occasion where it is 'need to know'.

You can see that the job of a psychic investigator is not always straightforward. Who could possibly imagine that a simple job of fifteen minutes absent healing could result in such a great deal of work, pain and suffering? There is always something new and very challenging to work out. By my nature I can sometimes be a little lethargic in working out the details of a case. My approach is usually 'what is happening and how do we fix it'. I don't want to know all the details, which take time and energy to find out, but every now and then I get a job which is designed to take me up in my evolution and understanding and I have to work on it. This was one of those jobs.

I have never had a damaged aura before through my work and it seemed appropriate somehow that I should get one whilst writing you this book, just to serve as a proper experience which I could then share with you as my truth. I did have a damaged aura some twenty years or so previously and before I was involved in this type of work, but did not know what the problem was. I suffered for some five or so years before I began to recover, the problem perpetuated by prescribed drugs which were supposed to help. This early experience was brought clearly into view as people with aura damage began to describe to me their symptoms.

The time taken to work all this out was probably around four hours, over several days and with much thinking in-between. The energy needed to tune-in and channel is considerable but this has to be done in order to discover what we can do and thereby increase knowledge.

## Attacked by The Energy of Place

Every place has its own distinctive energy. Every building or piece of land has its own personality signature by the nature of it's energy imprint or by way of the energies which move through it. The very basic nature of a race of people is patterned partly by the energy emanating from the earth in that place. Contrast the difference between the Latin people of South America and the Russian people. Those of you who know or use crystals will see that a quartz crystal from these respective places contains an energy vibration very similar to the people. The Russian quartz has an energy which is dark and powerful and the Brazilian quartz has a light, dancing quality about it.

Recently, Denise and I were looking for a new venue to hold workshops. The energy has to be just right, especially for Reiki training. Denise was full of enthusiasm for a local community venue she had found. It had all the facilities we desired and was on the doorstep.

It was a modern building, perhaps no more than ten years old. Run by committee and manned partly by volunteers, it was used as a community centre and focused its attention on helping people with mental and emotional difficulties. Essentially, it helped those with 'care in the community' needs, some of whom had in the past been in-patients and out-patients of the local psychiatric hospital, a wonderful place doing wonderful work for those in need.

The two healing/massage rooms were decorated beautifully and very individually and were equipped with modern hydraulic couches and aromatherapy oil burners. All over the building there were murals depicting positive attitude and thought. This was clearly a place where help was available for those who needed it, provided in many instances by volunteers who genuinely cared about helping people with psychological disorders.

Everything we desired for our workshops was present: a large open-plan assembly room with sofas to relax on, plus separate dining room facilities; a workshop room, again very nicely decorated with an Egyptian theme; kitchens, bathrooms, healing rooms. It was perfect.

From the moment we walked through the door I was uneasy. We waited to be seen by the duty supervisor for some ten minutes and then we were told that the person who was to interview us for suitability to hire the facilities was going to be late. The lady said we could look round on our own and they would arrange the other details over the telephone with us.

As we walked around, my uneasiness got worse, but I was trying to maintain my interest so as not to hurt Denise's feelings. Denise's enthusiasm was bouncing around as she showed me how perfect the facilities were for our needs. I was retreating further and further within myself, trying hard to be objective and enthusiastic, but my senses were desperately trying to close me down.

We had completed our tour in around ten minutes and we left. Walking back to the car Denise said to me ..."You don't like the place, do you?" She was obviously very disappointed in my reaction, which was hard to disguise, and hurt that I didn't share her enthusiasm for what she had seen as a perfect venue.

I couldn't discuss it. I was still closed down within my shell. We parted company and went about our respective daily duties. By the time I had arrived at the office some half an hour later, I was an emotional wreck. I was almost in tears, my stomach was turning over and my head was in a spin. I felt physically sick.

All this had come from a pleasant, early summer morning visit, walking hand in hand, enthusiastically to view a venue of care, compassion, healing and creativity staffed and operated by caring people for those in need of help.

## Analysis

This is a classic example of how the energy absorbed by the fabric of a building can affect people. I was so distraught, it took me an hour to realise what was going on. Quite often when your emotions get churned up, you are so wrapped up in your inner feelings that you can't rationalise what has caused you to feel this way. This is the right hemisphere of the brain taking over from the left hemisphere and not allowing you to put your analytical processes to work.

Although the building was modern, it had nevertheless picked up many vibrations of the mental and emotional trauma of the people who came there for help. As soon as I walked through the front door, it hit me. Even though I had automatically closed down and receded into myself as a self preservation or protection reaction, a subconscious reaction which we are all endowed with, I still absorbed, through my very sensitive aura, enough of the very powerful psychic energies which had been stored in the fabric of that building.

When my mental faculties had once again resurfaced above the stormy sea of my emotions, I could see that I had picked up the very disturbed patterns of emotional and mental trauma from the atomic fabric of the building.

Even now, with all my experience, I still get caught out by energy affecting me at such a dramatic level. It hits so hard and deeply that I don't realise immediately what is happening. It is at those moments when you are most relaxed, open and happy, drifting along merrily through life without a care, that it always gets you.

When I am prepared and tuned-in for energy sensing, barriers up, armed with my psychic protection, letting just enough energy through to sense what is going on in a place, there is not a problem. I do the job and remain relatively unaffected.

I sat behind my desk and began to generate from my solar plexus chakra an emotionally cleansing energy and projected it from my inner core outwards through my aura, at the same time bringing in energy through my crown chakra to recharge my system. In this way I regained my balance within a few hours.

Later that day, I could rationalise the whole situation and I could see that what the building needed was some very intense psychic cleansing and space clearing and then, yes, it would be perfect for our workshops.

## What About the Workers?

Now spare a thought for the workers in this place. I was in the building for about twenty minutes in total and during that time I was fairly well closed down and protecting myself after the initial onslaught had hit me. The people who work within that space are subjected to those energies on a daily basis for several hours and certainly they will be affected at some level by the very powerful energies which are emanating from the building, not to mention the people!

At a subtle energy level they will absorb that energy and their system will have to cope with processing it. At a certain level it will be draining them, day in, day out. Now think about the consequences at a mental and emotional level.

After I had been knocked sideways and then regained my composure and realised why I felt so bad, I cleared myself of the offending energies. For someone working in this type of environment who is not so sensitive or knowledgeable as me, the scenario is quite different.

They will probably feel very tired quite quickly during the course of the day. They may become irritable or irrational. They may even wonder why they always feel so drained. For women it can be worse than for men, for their endocrine system is very much more delicately balanced and influenced by the energies around them. This is why the woman is nearly always the one who becomes ill first, in a house with Geopathic Stress. Both male and female are particularly susceptible to absorbing energy, although the female energy system is more delicate and she may well become emotionally upset very easily. The male, being more left brained, will usually become tired rather than emotional. If the exposure persists over time they can both become very depressed and psychologically disturbed.

This is a form of psychic attack. They are being attacked by the stored psychic energy within the building. Not only that, but they will also be susceptible to the same energy absorption from the people they are seeing at the centre. In a worse case scenario they may also be attacked by entities, as these are very prevalent amongst those with psychological and emotional problems.

What I describe above is a non-malicious form of psychic attack. It is really a passive absorption of psychic energy, which happens to people regularly. It usually results in headache, general debility and tiredness or feeling nauseous. If you have removed yourself to a positive energy place you will recover via the means of your own inherent energy state quite quickly. In the case above, I have cited the energy of a place which can be the cause. However, merely coming into contact with people in the street, shopping or at work can bring unwanted energies into your aura just the same. People pass them around unconsciously like some unwanted illness, and indeed in some ways that is exactly what it manifests.

## Dangerous Liaisons

We have looked briefly at some of the areas where you can be at risk from interacting with psychic and spiritual forces, so let's finish this section on psychic attack by putting it all into perspective.

Certain places are frequented by spirits and entities more than others. Bearing in mind that the society of trapped spirits parallels our own society, you will find the nastier ones in the nastier places in terms of energy. Pubs are a good place to pick up spirits, (no, not the whisky, gin and vodka type,) who like to feel the effects of alcohol. Put another way, this is the ideal place to pick up an alcoholic trapped spirit or lost soul. Frequently you will find that a person who is addicted to alcohol will carry with them a spirit or entity type attachment which craves the feelings it gets when a person is in drink.

Anywhere where drugs are available is another major hazard spot. Drug users tend to be affected more by entities than spirits and these drug entities can be very powerful and controlling of a person's abilities to break a habit. In the case of drug entities, they can be very malicious and demonic in the way they totally destroy a person's resistance to the addiction. Detox and drug rehabilitation clinics are great places to pick up any unwanted passengers of this sort, which can and do affect people's lives in a powerful negative way.

In both of the above situations, spare a thought for the care workers and the support workers. In all these situations, whether they know it or not, they live life on a knife edge and could become the victim of psychic attack at any time. A friend of mine, a gifted sensitive and healer, who does counselling and support work, speaks to me about colleagues who "don't know what is going on" beneath the surface with their clients. Also, psychic attack is not something you can speak about to everyone because our society doesn't recognise other dimensions of existence. My friend says, "I fight every night with these elements". "Every night I am tackling these problems inside of people". He looks into his client and addresses the entity. The client does not know that he is bypassing a certain level of their consciousness to get to the crux of the problem. So, literally, he is carrying out a type of exorcism on his clients, unbeknown to them, and at the same time carrying out a psychic cleansing of the support centre on behalf of all the other care workers. If only these subjects were brought out into the open more, all manner of people who work in an energetic way with others would be better informed, and as a result protected.

In counselling work in particular, the counsellors are frequently on the front line, fighting an enemy most of them have never heard of, and virtually all of them don't know how to deal with. A counselling centre should have a kind of exorcism room, where the clients are vetted for any entities or negative energy attachments, before the therapists are allowed to face them. Also in counselling, the counsellor and client frequently sit face to face, which is considered to be the most attentive form of communication. This is ideal for chakra to chakra connection, where negative energies can be absorbed and positive energies drained from the counsellor. I have advised many counsellors to sit so that their body is at an angle to the body of the client, so that the chakras are not connecting.

We have briefly mentioned hospitals. Hospitals and clinics are a big problem also. When people are sick, quite often they may be carrying a spirit or entity which can contribute to the symptoms of their illness. As people come and go so quickly in hospital, including those who visit, there is ample opportunity for entities and spirits to hitch a ride into or out of the hospital and jump from one person to another. Of course, where people are ill, their defences are low and they can be an easy target for spirit or entity attack.

We also need to remember that people die in hospitals, so there is a natural process of spirit release from the physical realm taking place here. Many spirits find their way into the astral realms, but many more are left trapped in our physical realm. These beings are left wandering, trying to cling to relatives, or where they have been a solitary person, trying to cling to anyone who feels good to them at an energy level. The trauma of an accident victim who dies soon after the event often leaves the spirit in turmoil, not realising it is dead and failing to make the right connections for transition, desperately trying to regain access into its physical body, but of course, failing as the body's life support mechanisms are now defunct. They all need to find somewhere to go, or somebody to be with.

On top of all these situations, we have the additional problems of passive psychic energy which is passed from aura to aura as the people come and go through these transient places. Hospitals are like a bus stop for energy. Remember also the sensitive gentleman who had seen demon dogs prowling the wards, walking over the people, obviously feeding from the energy of the sick and injured.

In some alternative practises or where staff know and understand about the problems of psychic attack, they will carry out a clearance on a daily basis. Many therapists who are familiar with subtle energies also carry out a clearance after every client has left the premises and a final clearance at the end of the day.

I won't dwell any longer on the individual public places where we might encounter these types of energy. However, let's consider another aspect in society as a whole. Think about the less fortunate members of our society, who may live on very challenging housing estates. I have had occasion to visit houses for psychic and spirit energy release and cleansing and as I have walked down the street, I have been overwhelmed by the number of entities living in each house as I pass by. In this situation, as soon as a clearance is done, it can become re-contaminated by the neighbouring problems within days, unless one understands how to protect the place when the clearance has been done.

The people who have to live in these situations are often unaware of the psychic forces governing their very existence. All they see is the fabric of society breaking down around them and their own tolerance and moral fibre being eroded in the cess pit of psychic misfortune.

There is no doubt in my mind that dark and evil forces are at work to bring humanity to its knees in whatever form they can manage it. We all need to be vigilant and understand what is happening around us at an energy level. It may not be malicious, but it certainly will debilitate you, nevertheless.

When I am out on a case I do as much clearance work as I can identify, but I am only one small glimmer of light working in a sea of darkness. I hope some of my readers become tuned-in enough to see what is happening around them and learn how to tackle the growing negativity amongst us. Again I ask you to recognise that the more light work we do, the more we will be targeted by the forces of darkness. However, understand this: the universe never sends you a job you cannot do. You carry enough light to tackle successfully anything which is thrown at you.

Learn to look, not just at people, but within them and around them for unseen forces, and never let your guard down.

## 08

"Righteous Father, though the world does not know you, I know you, and they know that you have sent me. I have made you known to them, and will continue to make you known in order that the love you have for me may be in them and that I myself may be in them".

**Jesus Prays for all Believers**
**John 17:25-26**

DURING OUR 'JOURNEY THROUGH ENERGY' SO FAR, WE HAVE looked at our energy structure, the chakras in particular and the aura, and what happens when we begin to bring additional energies into it. We have seen what can go wrong and how it affects us. Now let us explore what we can do to minimise the unfortunate situations which may befall us.

When you begin to work with energy you are opening up to channel high frequencies of light, into and through your being. When you are channelling light, as we have previously said, you will attract the attention of Spirit Guides who wish to work with you and help develop you in the healing or energy work which is most appropriate for your particular energy system. Remember, you rarely choose your own path where pure energy work is concerned. The Guides and the universal consciousness as a whole will bring to you the tasks which you are best equipped to perform, provided that you are open enough to allow this to happen. Of course, you always have a choice.

# PSYCHIC PROTECTION

The more you work in the light frequencies the more light you will be able to channel and hold within your being. As you develop, you won't realise how much more light you are channelling or carrying, as the progression is very gentle. As this process unfolds, you will work at an ever increasing depth and progression, for and with the powers of light — the powers of creation. Or, if you prefer, in simplistic terms you are working for and with your God, whoever or whatever the term God may mean to you. As you develop your healing abilities and your intuition begins to unfold, you will need to be aware of forces other than your Spirit Guides, who will also have gained an interest in you.

We inhabit an existence of duality. Where there is Yin, there is also Yang, where there is male, there is also female, where there is light, there is also dark and most importantly, where there is good, there is also evil. Continuing in simplistic terms, you must understand that you cannot work in channelling the light without attracting the attention of the powers of darkness.

When we set off on our wonderful journey as a light worker and the energy begins to flow through us and fills us with excitement at the new sensations and possibilities, we often fail to identify fully with what and who we are becoming, because of the gradual unfoldment. New people will be attracted to us and likewise we will be attracted to new people as our energy changes and the energy around us changes. New frequencies of energy bring forth new perceptions and desires as our lives begin to change in a positive way. As we look back over the months we can see the difference between who we were and who we are now. To put it very simply, we are becoming a member of God's little army of light workers, bringing additional rays of sunshine into the world, shining like a tiny new star in the night's firmament above. As you move up in your power over the months and years, your star will be growing and shining brighter, it will be creating a progressively more powerful magnetic force, which ultimately glows so brightly that it cannot fail to give forth a signal which the powers of darkness can no longer ignore.

The attention you attract is usually directly proportionate to the level at which you are working. If you are working at a level where you are doing hands-on healing and a bit of aura cleansing, you will attract probably nothing more than the occasional entity or spirit, or a cloud of negative energy which sticks to the increased magnetic attraction of your aura. If on the other hand, you are doing serious spirit clearance, psychic energy removal or dealing with demonic energies, the chances are you may be attacked by a force which can completely knock you off your feet, paralyse you or even kill you. The difference between these levels of evolution is that the light workers at the lower end of the spectrum pick things up more or less accidentally, or through a bit of bad luck in the case of an entity or spirit attack. The entity will be looking for a good meal and anyone who comes along with the right energy and a lack of psychic protection will supply that meal for it. In the case of a higher level worker, the dark forces may actually be watching and waiting for you to make a mistake … and then they will pounce.

Don't be confused about lower and higher level light workers. These are merely terms I have used to illustrate the differing levels of light being carried by any one particular person. We all start more or less from the same basic plane as we begin to unfold on our journey of spiritual and energetic evolution. The more we work with the light, the more it brings up issues for us to deal with and the more it strips away old patterns so that we can move forward. I am not belittling anyone who works at what I have termed the lower, or early evolutionary levels. We all start from this point and light work at this level is just as important as light work at a higher level, which can also be construed merely as a different level. The rate of our unfoldment is governed by many factors, some of which are considered by our activities in previous incarnations, others by the amount of work and determination we apply to ourselves in this incarnation. How much karmic debt we need to redeem or how much dross we need to release, whether accumulated in this lifetime or before, are however, two of the main governing factors.

Take this scenario. A hands-on healer gives four people a valuable and powerful treatment in one day. Another person releases half a dozen trapped spirits from an electro-magnetic vortex in the earth and frees someone from possession by a demon. The effort in human terms may be exactly the same and the results of both of these illustrations on a measurable scale of work done, may also be the same. However, the amount of light or energy used may be very different depending on how much light we carry or channel. We are all needed and the universe will send to each of us, the work which we are capable of performing to a satisfactory outcome.

When we listen to the messages from our Guides, which may come as intuition, a voice, a vision or emotion, they tell us exactly what we should be doing and at what level we will work. We are all important. We are all doing the job that the universal consciousness requires of us. You will be guided to do what is best by the present ability of your ever changing energy system.

Returning to the issue of being targeted by the dark side, you may ask is there an equal balance in the power of light and dark forces? I don't know. Does everything balance out in the end? I don't know. What I do know is that you must be aware at all times that you can be seen by both sides, and the more attention that is paid to you from the good guys, the more easily you will be seen by the bad guys.

When you first begin healing work, you are only a tiddler in the great energy pool in the universe, and as such you don't make many ripples on the surface of the water. The forces of darkness don't really take very much notice of you. You can't really do any harm to their soldiers or disturb any of the dark conscious forces they may be operating. However, those of you who may have a long overdue healing gift, usually due to evolution in a previous incarnation, will begin to unfold very quickly and channel increasing volumes of light energy in a very short period of time. This will have the effect of creating many ripples on the water. Energy disturbance at this level, where powerful forces of light are at work, will not go unnoticed by the forces of darkness for very long. In the beginning, they will start to keep an eye out for you. They will watch what is happening and how well connected you are to the forces of light and how many Guides and Angels work with you. Some people will even be working with the energy of Archangels and Jesus. Others may even have Jesus with them as they work. Eventually the dark forces will actively do something to bring you down from your lofty position. After all, this is their reason to exist, it is their job to bring chaos to balance, to bring dark into light.

Now those who have reached these peaks of performance in previous incarnations and are unfolding quickly in this one, can usually get themselves out of these situations, either by insight, as their mind opens the doors of memory and rapidly brings the answers, or by assistance from above, usually from a fairly hefty band of Spirit Guide helpers keeping an eye out for them. Those who force the light into and through themselves by rushing and pushing their unfoldment need to beware, because they usually don't have anything they can call upon to defend them, either in terms of what they achieved in previous incarnations through the evolutionary process or through high connections in this incarnation. Now spare another thought about fast tracking through Reiki! Now, let's have a look at how we can protect ourselves.

## Pre-requisites for Psychic Protection

Psychic protection is not an easy concept to understand or to practise for the beginner who has perhaps not had any contact with the disciplines or mind enhancing techniques of yoga, meditation, visualisation, the energy principles of the martial arts or even just relaxation therapy. Indeed, anything to do with altering one's consciousness, or the principles of subtle energy. There are some fundamental pre-requisites for psychic protection.

These are:    **Visualisation & Intent**
              **Cleansing and Balancing the Subtle Bodies**
              **Building a Power Base**

## Visualisation & Intent

Visualisation and Intent come first in this list of pre-requisites because these powerful techniques are very helpful in the other two main areas of psychic protection. Imagination is a very powerful tool for the healer, spiritual aspirant and energy worker alike, as we discussed in chapter 2. Let me refresh your memory in the present context with regard to the maxim, 'Energy follows Thought'.

We have discussed thought forms and the power these can have on someone at a subtle energy level. Witchcraft, voodoo, ju ju and many other forms of the black arts are practised in various countries around the world. In many of these practises, thought forms are used to attack and break down the subtle energy fields of the intended victim, rendering them weak and usually subject to visions and hallucinations. Once the energy field of the target has been compromised, the attacker can send in visual demonic forms to torture the victim until they go mad. Anyone who has looked into these practises can have no doubt as to their effect. Indeed, there is much documentation to direct the occult practitioner in the black arts. If you use imagination with intent to harm someone, with a little practice and knowledge of occult science you will be successful.

Let us just have a look at the word occult. Most people these days associate it with bad things, devil worship, a witch's coven and that sort of thing. The word occult actually means 'invisible or unseen'. So when I use the term occult knowledge I mean knowledge of the unseen. Unseen forces can be used for both good and evil intent. Whereas we have tomes of work on the dark use or misuse of occult knowledge, as this goes back thousands of years, what is less well documented is the good use which these forces can be put to. Healers and therapists use this same connection to energy and power for our purpose of light work, as do other practitioners for dark work.

As I said earlier, if you imagine you can influence a situation, then you are putting the energy of thought into that situation. What starts with a little imagination, builds a flow of energy via thought. As you practise this over the years, you will become very connected and an adept at creating powerful healing techniques with just the use of thought and the mind.

Using these techniques, I can see chakras and run energy through the whole chakra system of a person to cleanse and balance them. Sometimes, faced with a difficult situation where I may not have my healing tools with me, this can be a very quick and powerful way to rebalance someone who may have their aura out of alignment. Another way I can use this technique to great effect is over distance. I can read a person's chakras the other side of the world via the telephone, just as easily as if they were sitting in front of me. I can also do this without any connection at all with the person, merely by projecting my mind into the universal consciousness and asking for a connection with the individual concerned. To practise this technique, ask a friend to give you the name of someone they know, who is unknown to yourself. Try to tune in and describe their personality. Your friend will be able to tell you if you are near or not. Practice will eventually bring you this connection. Remember, energy follows thought. Think it and you can do it. In many cases of psychic rescue, this is the only method of perfecting a successful outcome. It may be impossible to approach the person projecting the attack for one reason or another; indeed they may even be on another continent. I have done this many times with great success. Visualisation then is imagining a scenario, building a visible picture in your mind, but putting a great deal of intent into the imagination. Once you have got your picture in the mind you can begin to manipulate the energy around it to achieve the desired result. Trust what you see to be the truth.

Before we commence the practice of visualisation it is best to gain some control over our senses. As we discussed in chapter 4, working with the breath is a time honoured way of accessing energy. Firstly find a place that is comfortable and peaceful. Play some gentle music if you wish. Next, you should concentrate on what the breath is doing and then manipulate it very gently into a rhythm. Breathe slightly deeper than normal. Breathe in and hold the breath for 2 seconds and then breathe out and hold the breath for 2 seconds. This technique puts the breath into your control rather than being in the control of the autonomic nervous system. You are learning to focus your consciousness for personal power and growth.

When you feel balanced begin your visualisation. A good one to start with is to visualise a ray of purifying white light entering the body on the in-breath and grey negativity or putrefaction leaving the body on the out-breath. Do this very rhythmically and as the white light enters your body visualise it penetrating first of all the lungs. After several breaths, try to feel the cleansing process beginning to take hold. When you feel ready to move forward, allow the breath to pass beyond the lungs into the organs and, subsequently, in stages, pass into every cell and strand of DNA of the body until you feel totally cleansed and energised. Finally, when cleansed ask for the golden light of the force of all creation to enter into you.

Another visualisation you can do is to work on breathing in the white, golden light through each of the chakras, to cleanse them. Imagine your chakras breathing in and out like lungs, which in fact they do. First they spin one way as they bring the energy inwards and then spin the other way as they spin the energy outwards. Again, visualise cleansing energy being brought in and negative energy being expelled. Begin with the base chakra, purifying your connection to the earth and then move upwards, one at a time until you reach the crown chakra. When you have cleansed the crown chakra, visualise it expanding upwards, connecting firmly with the universal consciousness. When this process of cleansing is complete, return to the base chakra and go through the whole process again, but this time concentrate on revitalising the colours. Visualise bright iridescent light of the appropriate colour to each chakra, infusing it with an almost electric vibrancy. Next, run through them all again, but this time empower them. Visualise them growing stronger and more powerful, imbued with great sensitivity. Finally, ask for universal guidance, or help from Spirit Guides in balancing and adjusting them to the most appropriate functional level for you. Also ask for the base chakra to be strongly connected to the earth so that you are well grounded, and for the crown chakra to be strongly connected with your higher self and the God consciousness to bring you intuition.

Do not underestimate the power of these exercises: over time and with practice they bring you powerfully into focus with energies and beings of a very high source indeed. To digress for a moment, here is an example. As I am sitting here writing to you today, I am recovering from a slipped disc which happened a couple of days ago. The first day, I couldn't get out of bed. The second day, I tried to do some work on this book, but the pain was so intense I could not sit at the keyboard for more than about fifteen minutes at a time without having to lie down again to take the pressure off my body. At this time I decided to ask for help from above. I connected with a high source, an Archangel source, who can provide the perfect physical blueprint of my body. Asking for an exercise to correct my problem, I surrendered unto the consciousness of the source and it took over the movement of my body, putting me through an exercise which moved me forcefully into impossible positions without any pain at all. When this exercise was complete, it had released a lot of the pressure, reduced the muscle spasm and taken away a fair amount of the pain.

The third day I felt much brighter mentally and I again asked for assistance with an exercise to help put my disc back into place. I tuned in and connected to the Archangel source and within seconds my body began to sway to and fro and then twist and turn into impossible shapes. It waved my arms around in Tai Chi type movements and took me down to touch my toes. It twisted me around to my left side so far I was almost facing backwards while my feet were still facing forwards. How can this be, when under my own steam I was severely limited in my movements and in pain? Yet the source knows exactly how to move me without pain and in a very dynamic and flowing way. It is a fascinating thing to experience or indeed to observe.

The exercises last about ten minutes each. After the first one I was much more vertical and had lost a fair degree of the pain. During the second one I felt the disc move back a little towards its correct location and the third exercise was similar to the first in that it improved the condition although the disc didn't appear to move this time. That night I slept undisturbed and the following morning my body, which was previously twisted and contorted was much more aligned. After a few more exercises the following day, the disc was back in place.

This illustration is one of connection to a high source. This connection has been attained from starting out with simple visualisation and chakra exercises such as those described above to motivate and manipulate energy. As a pupil, I was not very good at visualisation for a number of years, so I am sure you will be able to achieve what I can do with a little practice and the help of Spirit Guides.

Meditation is all about reaching other places with your consciousness. Many meditation techniques use breathwork to achieve their aims. Meditation and visualisation are very much close friends in energy work. There is not much to separate them other than different schools of thought. In meditation we try to still the mind to allow the consciousness to rise upwards and move outwards. In visualisation, we try to focus and create a vision that we can use.

Intent is the prime mover in these techniques. Address yourself to the higher source, whatever that may be for you. If you are dedicated and pure of heart in your desire to bring the light into your being, it will be given to you. Make your intent as focused as you can. Bring all the power to it that you can, by breathing in the light and sending it out again with your focused intent. Intent is all. Without intent you are like a powerless and rudderless boat, which drifts around the bay out of control. But with intent you will have a rudder to give direction and a motor to push you forwards through the water.

Now we have looked at visualisation, meditation and intent, what are we going to use it for? We are going to use it for psychic protection!

## Putting it into Practice

When I first tried to visualise protection I couldn't get any picture in my mind at all. I really struggled and was hopeless at it. I tried and tried to see all kinds of things but failed every time, and this went on for a couple of years. The first time I got a proper vision was one Friday evening while working with some friends practising Health Kinesiology. This was a regular meeting in those days and Anne used to make us do a visualisation for protection. Because I was hopeless at it, I used to just sit quietly in a kind of meditation and ask for protection. Then, on the night in question, while we were all practising our protection I got a very powerful vision, but a most unusual one at that. Certainly not one I had ever asked for or practiced.

Those of you who have seen the Batman films of the late 1980s might remember that Batman had a most amazing motor car with the ability to cloak itself in a kind of scaly armour, like some prehistoric reptile which had encountered some modern techno-fashion house. When activated, this suit of armour appeared, as if by magic, and placed itself around the car, one piece at a time in rapid succession, looking like some scaled creature when complete. The visual effect of the car cloaking itself up in this way was very dramatic in the film and I remember being very impressed by the effects at the time.

Well yes, you've guessed it, when my visualisation eventually occurred automatically, it wasn't some golden or violet cloak or silvery white force field surrounding me, it was a suit of armour like that of Batman's car. It began at my feet and moved rapidly upwards, one piece at a time, until I was completely cloaked, except for my face, which was left uncovered so that I could breathe. This visualisation was so powerful because it was not driven by my conscious thought or desire, it was given to me from somewhere in the subconscious or from a higher source as something which I could identify with and relate to in my everyday world. Sometimes, when these things come, the simplicity and direct-ness of the image throws one off balance and even today I get communications in visual form from Guides and I throw them back out of my mind again because they seem so silly. However, if they keep coming back in again, that is how I know it is a message. Often, the message can be so blunt and to the point, that I have to find a diplomatic way to approach the subject with the client. If you like, by throwing the vision out, it is a way of confirmation that the image is not just the imagination playing tricks.

So, when you begin to practice visualisation, what will you get? Well, none of us knows at this moment, but we can use two techniques to find out. As I did in those early days, you can sit quietly in a meditative state and ask for protection and see what eventually comes for you. In this technique we have seen from the illustration above that what does come will be very appropriate for you and be something you can relate to and identify with easily. However, you may wait some time. Time though is not important: achieving your goal of visualisation is. Even so, the actual vision is less important than the intent!

Going back to my suit of armour vision, whether I had received this vision or not, is unimportant. That I sat in meditation with the intent of being protected is the important point. If you do receive a vision, then that is great and it is another step up your spiritual and intuitive ladder, another connection at a subtle level and a new thing you have experienced and achieved. These genuine, powerful experi-ences are something which cannot be taken away from you, and by the same token cannot be shown to anyone else. These are your truths, your experiences, your foundations to build upon.

The second technique is to practice trying to see a particular picture. Imagine a cloak being placed around your shoulders. A cloak of protection. Use the intent that this cloak is specifically to protect you against any psychic forces. Colour is a powerful healing tool and the energy in colour can also be used as a powerful protection tool. It is common for people to visualise their cloak in radiant colours. Purple and gold are powerful colours because purple or violet is associated with the crown chakra and the crown chakra is the entry and exit point of your higher consciousness.

Light is another powerful healing and visualisation tool. Silver and gold light is associated with the radiance of a higher source, the Christ Light or the God Essence. This can be brought down through your crown chakra and into your physical body. Green light is associated with healing energy and you can also use this to wrap yourself in. Therefore, you can visualise a radiant cloak being placed around your shoulders and wrapped around you so nothing can get in at all. You can then visualise a mist of light around the outside of this cloak, cleansing in a swirling motion, like a vortex or whirlpool around you. Next you can bring down the light of the creator into your entire being.

Imagine your consciousness opening up a stream of thought, rising from your crown chakra and penetrating the clouds and sky beyond; going higher, beyond the dark night sky and the stars, into the realms of spiritual consciousness. Ask for a connection to the high spiritual forces, to the Angels, the Archangels, Christ the Healer, the all pervading and omnipotent mind of creation. There is no limit to what you can ask for. Remember, your imagination is your only limiting factor. Without limitation your consciousness can go anywhere.

Your intent is all that matters. If your vision of God is that of an astral road sweeper who cleans up all the mess the human race creates, then you ask for a connection with that image. Look at the words 'image' and 'imagination'. You imagine your image, not someone else's. Imagine what comes easily to you and you will receive a better connection than if you try to imagine or visualise something that feels difficult to hold, alien or uncomfortable to you. I have often seen strange and funny things in difficult situations of suffering. These are reflections of my inner being, my personality which often sees the irony in, or funny side of disaster or trauma, both in my own life and other people's lives. It would be wrong to push these visions away as being inappropriate in the situation, because this is how my mind and imagination work and make their connection so that I can move energy. My Spirit Guides can see my mind and they too give me similar images, which they know I will relate to. This is a lesson in acceptance: acceptance of who and what you are and acceptance that this is the way in which you can make a difference. Embrace the authorship of your own imagination. If you are attuning in love and desiring to help humanity, in truth, then whatever you receive is right for you. Don't hide it or be ashamed of it if it doesn't fit the picture you think it should in terms of what we think to be holy or good. Embrace it as the aspect of God which is working within and through you. And remember, the forces of God are already perfect, they need no adjustment.

When you have made your connection above, ask for the light to be brought down into your being. Imagine the light streaming down through your crown chakra and filling up your lungs as you breathe in. Connect with this source of light and breathe it in with every breath. When your lungs are full, imagine the light bursting out from your lungs to fill every other part of your physical body. When your physical body is full, see the light squirting out of every pore of your skin to fill up your aura, and then go beyond this, so the light projects outward from you as far as you like.

Another technique you can use is to put yourself into an egg or sphere or bubble. Imagine that you are floating inside one of these shapes and that this is a force field which is impenetrable from the outside. When you have constructed the object, be it egg, bubble or whatever, infuse it with light to charge it up. Put electricity into the outer regions, so that if anything should touch the outside it will get such a shock as to throw it to kingdom come. Then deal with the space between you and the outer shell of your bubble and infuse this with coloured light. You can add as many levels of protection as you like and the more you practice it the easier it becomes.

So, just to make sure you've got the point, the intent is what you begin with. Put your heart, the centre of your universe, into your intent and the rest will follow.

## Other Aspects of Psychic Protection

Once again, remembering that we are all individuals and we all relate to energy in our own way, it would be inconsiderate of me to give you my own techniques and guidance without sharing those of others to balance the picture. Therefore, I include a couple of techniques from other sources which you may find of interest or connect with on a personal level.

Firstly from Dr. Lori M. Poe's book *Mystic Wisdom for Richer Living,* I would like to bring to you a visualisation entitled 'The Secret of Your Mystic Light'.

1. Seek a restful place where you may practice undisturbed. Seat yourself comfortably into your easy chair, feet uncrossed and flat on the floor, hands resting in your lap.

2. Close your eyes and envision the Christ-Light in the form of the Celestial Blue Fire in the shape of a large tongue (a tongue of flame), that shines silver-white, descending upon your head. See it now dissolve into a white mist that begins to spiral downward.

3. See it fill your head; every part of your brain. See its crystal light shine brightly from your Soul. Throughout the direction of your will see it passing downward through your being, filling every part of you with Divine Light. And as it reaches you're feet, direct its flow three feet beneath you into the ground. Now see it flowing upward again, enveloping your outer form, wrapping your shoulders in Its Cape.

4. Mentally send this pristine Force swirling, diffusing and encircling your body three times. As it reaches your head the third time, lift it again above your head, see it reshape into the Flame and see Its bluish-white Mist merge back to God from which It emanated.

Dr. Poe says … "This technique should be practised at the same hour for three days, although once is sufficient. Yet I would like you to feel the healing effects it leaves on your body and mind and become accustomed to the strength you will feel in your aura".

The second act of protection comes from the late Dion Fortune in her book *Psychic Self-Defence* and is concerned with making a magic circle. It should be pointed out that it is mainly to protect against a direct and deliberate psychic attack upon you by another person who may be involved in the work of the dark side. This is common practise in many cultures around the world, where people do still practise putting spells and hexes on those they feel threatened by. As healers and energy workers, we are more likely to be attacked by spirits, entities or perhaps just a negative energy of some sort, which would not usually have the same deliberate malice attached to it.

Dion says, *"The formula offered here will be found effectual for all ordinary conditions. Extra ordinary conditions can only be dealt with by a person who has had experience"*.

"In making the magic circle the operator stands upright facing east. He faces east because the magnetic current on which he proposed to operate runs from east to west. His first procedure must be to steady his own vibrations and purify his aura. In order to do this, he makes the Quabalistic Cross on breast and brow".

| | |
|---|---|
| (Touching his forehead) he says, | 'To Thee, Oh God' |
| (touching his solar plexus) | be the Kingdom |
| (touching his right shoulder) | and the Power |
| (touching his left shoulder) | and the Glory |
| (clasping his hand) | unto the ages of the ages. Amen' |

"By this formulae the operator affirms the power of God as sole creator and supreme law of the universe to which all things must bow and he establishes this formula magnetically in his aura by the action of making the sign of the Cross upon himself. This Sign is not exclusively a Christian symbol and can be used as readily by the Jew as the Churchman, for it is the equi-limbed Cross of Nature that is being used, not the Calvary Cross, of which the shaft is double the length of the cross-bar, and which is the symbol of sacrifice. The equi-limbed Cross refers to the four quarters of the globe and the four elements, and the formula associated with it proclaims the dominion of God over these, and thereby occultly formulates His kingdom within the sphere of the operator".

"The operator next imagines himself to be clasping in his right hand a large, cross-handled sword, such as is depicted in pictures of Crusaders. He holds it point upright and says, 'In the Name of God I take in hand the Sword of Power for defence against evil and aggression', and imagines himself to be towering up to twice his natural height, a tremendous armed and mailed figure, vibrating with the force of the Power of God with which he has been charged by his formulation of the Sword of Power".

"He now proceeds to draw the Magic Circle upon the floor with the point of the Sword of Power and he should see in his imagination a line of flame following the point of the Sword, consisting of small flames, such as spring up when methylated spirit is spilt and ignited, but of a pale golden colour. The circle should always be drawn deosil, that is from east, to south, to west, to north, in the same way that the hands of a clock would move were the clock laid face upwards on the floor. The contrary way is widdershins, the way in which the witches danced at the Sabbats. The deosil movement affirms the rule of God's law in Nature because it is the way of the Sun; the widdershins movement repudiates God's rule over Nature by moving against the sun. In resisting an occult attack the whole formula should be tuned to the key-note of asserting God's dominion over all existence, the aim of the operator being to align himself with Cosmic Law and cause the Power of God to deal with the interference."

"The Circle being formulated, the operator ceasing to visualise the sword, but still visualising the circle, clasps his hands in prayer, and raising them above his head towards the east, prays: May the mighty archangel Raphael protect me from all evil approaching from the east. Turning to the south he repeats the same formula in prayer to Gabriel. Turning to the west, he invokes Michael. Turning to the north he invokes Uriel. Facing to the east again, and thus completing the circle, repeats the formula of the Quabalistic Cross."

"This formulation of the magic circle is especially valuable for protecting the sleeping place, the circle being drawn around the bed. It is not necessary to move about the room, or shift the furniture in order to draw the circle, it will be formulated wherever it is visualised to be. It is necessary to reaffirm this circle each time the tides change; that is to say, a circle made after sundown will hold good until sunrise and a circle made after sunrise will maintain its potency until sunset. After the circle has been affirmed a number of times in the same place its influence will persist for a considerable period."

In addition to all these methods, simple prayer, the Lord's Prayer in particular, can be a very powerful ally in times of psychic stress. Again I mention the most important aspect of any form of protection, and that is … intent! If you intend something and your heart is pure in its desire and your intent is for the benefit of anything within the universe, especially human kind, you will be heard and the forces of good will do for you what they can. Persistent use of intent strengthens the connections with those who listen to you from the other realms.

## Cleansing and Balancing

Anyone doing energy work of any sort must have a sound and robust aura. If you don't know whether you have or not, you should seek out the help of an experienced healer who knows about such things. Again, it is worth a reminder of the analogy of the tuned engine. Energy workers tend to need more looking after than non-energy workers, where chakras and aura are concerned. We energy workers are the ones with the tuned-up systems and so we need to maintain that high state of tune. Energy cleansing and balancing is one of the most important parts of looking after your aura and chakras. You must make the effort to keep them in tune, otherwise your edge will become dulled and out of balance, accumulating negative energies and blocking the chakras.

When working as a healer you should regularly receive a healing from another healer who is at least your energy equal. How much you are working with energy will determine how often you should have a treatment, but it should certainly be at least once every three months. It is much better if you can find someone who is more experienced and working at a higher vibration than yourself. When we are working, we often think that we are fully functional and our energy system is fine. In reality we often pick up little bits of this and that which lodge firmly in our system, namely the aura and chakras, reducing our vibrational perfection and inhibiting our effectiveness. Moreover, we can unknowingly pass on these negative energies to our clients if we are unaware of our condition. A good counsellor receives constant monitoring by a control or another counsellor to make sure they are keeping to the right track and are not being consumed or drawn in by the depth at which they are working with their client. By the same token, a good healer visits another healer to have a cleansing and balancing treatment. A good healer knows that they cannot always see what is happening in their own energy system. This is how we find out the truth about our energy. A good healer will cleanse your aura thoroughly, far better than you can do yourself without a great deal of practice and knowledge. And besides, it is wonderful to relax and get some work done on yourself. Let's have a look at a few things which help in a big way to keep you cleansed and balanced.

**Trees:** Walking in the woods and being with trees is a very powerful cleansing process. The aura of a tree is usually many feet wide and being within this space and tuning into the tree can do wonders for your energy. Many of us today understand the power of aromatherapy and homeopathy. Both of these very effective therapies use the power locked in the subtle essence of plants and trees. One method of exchanging energy and receiving a cleansing and healing from a tree is as follows:

Stand about 4 or 5 feet from the tree with your arms by your side, but held slightly out from your body to allow a free flow of energy, elbows bent with the palms facing the tree. Close your eyes and take some deep breaths, concentrating on breathing white light and healing energy inwards through the crown chakra. Stand with your legs slightly bent to avoid energy blockages in the knees, make contact with the energy of the earth and allow this to be drawn upwards through your legs and base chakra. Bring both of these sources of energy firmly into your being, linking you with heaven and earth at your heart centre. Visualise your aura expanding with this influx of energy. Allow this healing energy to flow towards the tree through your aura and the palms of your hands. Be aware of your breath and be calm, meditative and contemplative. Try to reach a calm or spiritual place in your mind.

When you feel ready and connected, ask permission to speak with the nature spirit of the tree. It doesn't matter whether you can perceive the spirit or not, your intent will open a channel of communication. Tell the spirit of the tree that you bring an offering of healing energy for its benefit and acknowledge and thank it for the work it does unceasingly for the world and mankind. Allow the healing energy to flow towards the tree for a few moments and then ask the spirit of the tree for help in healing and cleansing yourself. Ask to be absorbed into the great healing power of its energy, ask to be one with the tree for a few moments. You may notice an increase in energy flow as the tree responds to your gift and your request. Often you can feel the energy building up from the earth as the tree draws energy through you. Stay with the tree until you feel the process is complete and be sure to thank it before you break the connection. When breaking the connection, do this as you would with any healing situation, that is slowly and with thanks and respect to the forces that have joined you for your purpose.

Be sure to do this exchange during the hours of sunlight, as later in the afternoon, the tree changes it's polarity as it changes its task. Remember, trees are the lungs of the earth, converting carbon dioxide into oxygen. Without them we would not be able to breathe. The tree is magnificent and stately and like all nature spirits, it can respond to our communication efforts if we attempt to find a link to interact. As a matter of interest, one of the tree spirits I encountered while making the Devic Essences on the Isle of Tresco was over 80 feet tall. On this planet of over 6 billion souls, only a tiny fraction of the population spares any time at all to communicate with the trees, yet without them we would all die.

**Cleansing:** Nature in all its forms is very powerful at cleansing and balancing. We already know this, although we may not really acknowledge the things we say on a conscious level. A friend some thirty years ago used to have on her wall one of those pre-war posters advertising holidays at the seaside. From memory, it said something like 'Visit Skegness … it's so bracing', with a picture of a man being blown along the sea front by the strong, fresh breeze. The seaside has always been an absolutely perfect place for cleansing, albeit a little too cold for most of us in the British Isles for most of the year.

The element of salt has always been a powerful weapon against psychic attack in occult practice. It absorbs foul and negative magnetism and emanations from objects, people and places. It literally soaks up vibrations like a sponge soaks up water. Salt is often employed in the cleansing of crystals. The element of water can take negativity out of a person or object. By immersing the object in a stream of running water, the energy will totally change. Try putting your hands under running water, a mountain stream, a tap or a hosepipe. You will feel the uplifting effect as it changes the positive ions in your body into negative ions, bringing about a vibrant effect on your consciousness. Put water and salt together and you have got the sea. Salt water is one of the most powerful forces against negativity. Mix this salt water energy with a walk in a strong wind close to the edge of the sea and you've got nature's very best process to cleanse and then blow away the cobwebs.

**Salt Baths:** If it is too cold or inconvenient to get into the sea, which it is for most of us unless you live on Malibu Beach, then we can create our own sea at home in the bath. The salt bath is very healing and very cleansing. The best salt to use is rock salt from deep underground. Unfortunately, the seas of our beautiful blue planet are so contaminated these days with heavy metals and other substances that sea salt should not be considered. However, there are a few good sources of rock salt, some of which you can buy from your local supermarket.

As you run the bath, sprinkle the salt into the water and dissolve as much of it as you can. Some rock salts are quite chunky and it can be difficult to achieve total solution. The worst part of this is having to lie on salt crystals, which, believe me, can be as sharp as lying on a bed of nails. Use at least a cupful if you can spare it and soak yourself in the water for a good half hour. The salt will draw negative energies from deep within the physical body as well as from your aura.

**Skin Brushing:** The skin is the biggest organ of the body and in many cases skin problems are merely the process of the body trying to eliminate toxins which do not resonate within the vibrational fields of the body. If we stimulate the skin, it begins a process of detoxification, which can only be a good thing.

Taking a soft but firm brush, with bristles of a consistency which will not scratch the skin, begin brushing from the extremities towards the heart. Start with the feet, moving upwards through ankles, calves, knees and thighs up to the torso. Then do the hands, arms and shoulders. Finally brush the torso, from groin area to heart, moving upwards, and from shoulders to heart moving downwards. Get someone to help you do your back.

If you do this a couple of time a week, the skin becomes stimulated and begins to release locked-in toxins. If you wipe over the skin afterwards with a clean flannel you will soon begin to smell the debris which has been released. Find yourself a good exfoliant or body scrub product, available at beauty salons, and give it a go. Your skin will begin to glow and have a wonderful satin like feel to it.

Remember that bringing about a detox situation at any level of your being may have side effects, so be ready to identify these and proceed slowly until you know how skin brushing affects you.

**Run to the Hills:** Mountains are another great natural cleansing place. Here you can find the fantastic energy of crystal-rich vibrating rock, mixed with pure high altitude air with fresh, cool temperatures and a breeze which blows you inside out in the spring months. Exhilarating! In the summer months the energies are very different. The vibrant rock bakes in the charging energy of the sun, and at the same time we benefit from the sun's essence as it beams down directly onto us, enriching our physical system, cleansing our aura and boosting our defences.

**Sunlight:** I once went to a house which was full of negative psychic vibes and earth radiation. The poor woman who lived there was in a terrible state and very confused as to why she felt so bad. Not long after being in this house, even though I was well protected, I could feel the effects of the psychic energy draining me. I felt a great need to go outside and stand in the sun, which I did. Within a few moments of tuning in to its powerful cleansing resonance, the sun's energy total- ly transformed my energy state. I then went back into the house to complete my work. I eventually convinced this lady she had to move and her own transforma- tion has been wonderful to see since she left that place. It was not just the house, which of course could have been cleansed of all Geopathic and psychic energies. But the whole neighbouring environment was negative and of course, many of the local people around her were affected likewise.

Use the same techniques to breathe in the sun as you would to breath in the white light in a visualisation. Bring it powerfully into all the chakras and feel how the rays burst upon every cell in your body and cleanse them. If you live in a country where the sun is a little shy of appearing, never fail to take the opportunity to stand in its brilliance for a few moments if it comes out to play.

**Diet:** One of the most important cleansing processes of all is considering what we put into ourselves in terms of food and drink. Many thousands of books have been written on diet and so I don't intend to lay down any laws here, but rather give some guidance from a spiritual and vibrational medicine viewpoint.

We are what we eat as the saying goes, and to a large extent this is true. Therefore we should give great consideration to what we want to be. Our food in the last 50 years has undergone more change than in the last 50,000 years. These days we mostly buy food from super-markets and a great deal of this food has been processed in some way prior to our receiving it. The humble vegetable has been subjected to a whole host of toxic, man-made chemicals to preserve it from marauding insects and in some cases to make it look better and last longer on the shelves.

What we need to understand about this process is that during the past 50 years or so science has created new substances, consisting of molecules which previously did not exist on planet earth. In the great energy pattern picture of life on earth, these chemicals are new energy patterns and as such are not recognised by the coding in our present energy structure, namely our genetic coding, DNA, cellular mechanisms and subtle energy systems. Many of these chemicals are highly toxic. In fact the majority of them are specifically designed to kill, albeit to kill insects or diseases. However, in the right quantity, and this is usually extremely small, they will also kill humans.

These energy patterns can lodge within the human energy system and prevent energy flowing in the way it is designed to do, according to the grand plan. This is what is meant by a blockage. This is what vibrational medicine aims to remove from people. I will give a quick example. For some months Denise has suffered recurring bouts of a serious skin rash which appeared on her face. We sat down and dowsed it once and came up with the answer that she was drinking too much water. I dowsed the maximum she could have per day and she cut back and the problem cleared up. However, it returned again some weeks later and, being very busy, we didn't tune in and dowse it, but thought there must be something else and tried to work it out over a few weeks in a logical manner. However, after being on holiday for a week, Denise's skin cleared up perfectly. Within a couple of days of being at home again, the problem returned. Denise dowsed out it was the water again. It was not the quantity though, but the content, which was causing the problem. She switched to bottled water and the problem cleared up within two days. Of course, when I dowsed it the first time, the answer was correct to the question I had asked. 'Is she drinking too much water?' Yes. However, it was not the water aspect which was causing the problem, but the chemicals which were suspended in the water. If I had asked was it something within the water, we would have had the answer totally correct the first time. The next stage is to write to the water board and find out what chemicals are in the water and then dowse these to discover which is the offending toxic chemical.

Water is the basis of our whole being. If our water is contaminated with chemicals what chance do we stand. In Denise's case the symptoms were clearly visible, but the cause took some working out as, naturally, we do not expect the drinking water to be so contaminated as to cause such a serious problem. Consider though how many people may have problems with other organs as they try to secrete the toxins from their bodies, where perhaps the symptoms are more difficult to perceive — bladder, kidney, liver etc. Quite simply this is chemical poisoning and the body reacts more or less instantly to rid itself of these toxins. In Denise's case, it tried to eliminate them through the skin. When we know the cause the answer is easy, but imagine going to the doctor to try and sort out this problem. The only answer in our current medical model would be to try to treat the skin with E45 cream, hydrocortisone or similar. You can see straight away the problem this brings. Not only do we still have the toxic water-borne chemicals in our system, but we are now also putting other toxins into the system, namely the creams, to try to correct the imbalance. The body will also want to be rid of these as quickly as possible. Result; toxic overload.

Many farmed animals these days are kept permanently on a cocktail of growth hormone and antibiotics to prevent disease developing. Milk for instance is not meant for human consumption, but for calf consumption. Milking cows are kept artificially pregnant on a permanent basis in order to give milk. Milk is often contaminated with antibiotic, blood and septic matter from mastitis. Government information has always led us to believe that milk is necessary for our calcium needs, when in fact calcium from green-leafed vegetables is far more easily absorbed into our system.

It doesn't take a great deal of thought to realise that if animals are held for any length of time on antibiotics and growth hormone, it is going to prevail through the whole of their bio-system. Therefore when the meat is consumed or the milk drunk we consume everything that the beast has processed in its system.

Where meat is concerned, all of the above holds true, but in addition we have all kinds of hormonal release at the time the animal is killed. As a young man, when working in a hotel, I was often sent to the slaughterhouse to collect meat for the kitchens. I have seen how animals die in these places and for anyone to say they do not suffer or have feelings is completely wrong. They can sense the fear and death of their fellow beasts and that fear permeates the whole of their living tissue. When a person consumes meat, they also consume a tremendous amount of anxiety, fear and trauma.

Soft drinks are a cocktail of chemicals. There is much evidence to show that children brought up drinking cans of soft drinks are very likely to develop weight problems. One of the most dangerous chemicals in food stuffs is aspartame, used for sweetening. Aspartame is, by far, the most dangerous substance on the market that is added to foods. Aspartame accounts for over 75 percent of the adverse reactions to food additives reported to the US Food and Drug Administration (FDA). Many of these reactions are very serious, including seizures and death, as disclosed in a February 1994 Department of Health and Human Services report (USA). A few of the 90 different documented symptoms listed in the report as being caused by aspartame include: seizures, nausea, muscle spasms, weight gain, rashes, depression, fatigue, tachycardia, vision problems, heart palpitations, anxiety attacks and memory loss.

According to researchers and physicians studying the adverse effects of aspartame, the following chronic illnesses can be triggered or worsened by ingesting aspartame: Brain tumours, multiple sclerosis, epilepsy, chronic fatigue syndrome, Parkinson's disease, Alzheimer's, mental retardation, lymphoma, birth defects, fibromyalgia and diabetes.

Aspartame is made up of three chemicals: aspartic acid, phenylalanine and methanol. It is listed in the book *Prescription for Nutritional Healing*, by James and Phyllis Balch under the category of 'chemical poison'.

There are mountains of research on aspartame if one wishes to pursue it. This is a small example of only one chemical additive in food. There are thousands more that we know little or nothing about. This gives you an idea of how vigilant one has to be when trying to cleanse the body of toxins.

Whatever we put into ourselves gives the body a job to do. Anyone serious about spiritual evolution should look very carefully at what they eat from an energy and toxin view point. The cleaner you keep your system the better it will function at a high vibratory level and the greater the sensitivity it will develop to subtle vibrations. There is lots of information around today about food and food additives and it will help you greatly to become informed.

Today I bought a newspaper, a rare occurrence, but I was attracted by the front page headline *The Independent*, 2nd September, 2000. The British Government's new Food Standards Agency reports ... **Organic food 'is a waste of money'**. The head of the Agency, Professor Sir John Krebs said that "Organic food is neither safer nor more nutritious than conventionally grown food" ... and it went on, etc. etc.

I would point out that I have no particular political affiliations, being neutral and fairly sceptical that any government actually has the interests of its subjects at heart. The above statement in *The Independent* is from a Government which is desperately trying to promote genetically modified foods and push chemical farming. The point that is missing in the article is that the people are not buying organic because it might be more nutritious, but because they don't want to ingest chemical pesticides or other genetically modified molecular structures. This is the main reason informed people buy organic food.

There are two main points to consider. The first is that virtually all farming areas have been fed the most amazing amount and variety of chemicals over the last 50 years. It takes a long time for the earth to heal itself from such a deluge. Therefore organic food is bound to contain a little pesticide residue from past farming methods. However, it is important we give support to those who are trying to improve the methods of food production against great odds. It is interesting to note that in the United Kingdom, there are virtually no subsidies available to organic farmers, whereas their chemical farming counterparts have a wealth of financial incentives to support them. As an aside, professional water dowsers who find water for people, consider that there is nothing worth dowsing for at less than three hundred feet because the earth is so contaminated with chemicals.

In my own practice of Geopathic Stress Investigation, I find major earth currents, or ley lines, which carry toxic vibrations as a result of the surface of the earth becoming contaminated. If a line such as this is passing through a dwelling, what should be a wonderful and harmonious vibration of nature, supporting life in its many diverse forms, has turned into a vibration which stresses the bio-system of many living things, including people.

The second point is nutrition, which is a big and growing issue. Many people do think that organic food is more nutritious. This is often not the case, because the land has been so drained of its natural nutrients through intensive farming methods over the past hundred years, that the food grown on this land is nutritionally deficient. Therefore, we need to seriously consider supplements in our diet today. If you learn to dowse and get a list of vitamins and minerals, you can find what you are deficient in and correct the balance.

In *Positive Health Magazine* issue 54, July 2000, there is an article entitled 'Toxic Chemical Overload'. The opening paragraph states that "A recent case cited in the daily papers showed that 500 dangerous man-made chemicals were present in a single fat cell of a seemingly healthy 30 year old female living in Britain today. By comparison, a single cell of an Egyptian mummy contained none".

I'm not going to labour the points about our food any longer because it is a massive issue. I think you get the drift. The main point to consider is that you open your eyes and see what is being served up to you and look behind the disguise. You know the rules by now, Governments are directed by those with financial muscle. If the financial muscle wants to push its latest chemical or genetically modified product into the market place, then it has that power to manipulate the whole focus. We quite naturally believe what our leading representatives tell us. After all they are supposed to be looking after our best interests, aren't they? By the same token, if food producers want to sell their latest creation to the public, they employ a marketing company to tell us of it's features and benefits. Often they create some spurious scientific link to impress us or manufacture a scientific sounding name to give the product credibility, whether in reality it has any or not. Once you know what you are eating there is only one further thing to consider, and that is the life force energy content. If you eat egg and chips every day your energy will be dull.

One final tale. My old hero John Lennon was on a macrobiotic diet when he died … my friend Malcolm insists it was the bullets that caused his untimely demise. I'm not so sure? (joke)

**Flower Remedies:** Dr. Edward Bach (pronounced batch) was one of the few historical figures who revolutionised the way we look at the human condition. Hippocrates, Paracelsus, Hahnemann etc., had all brought original thinking to bear and Bach is amongst these great figures.

Highly qualified, Dr. Bach was a greatly respected physician and surgeon, holding positions in several London hospitals. He carried out much research both in orthodox medicine and homeopathy, but he is remembered today primarily for the simple and completely natural flower remedies he created through his sensitivity to nature and his observation of people and his 'Theory of Types' of people.

Dr. Bach burned all his research before he died and left only a handful of notes on the preparation and use of his flower remedies. He believed that people within their own communities should be able to treat and heal without resort to the knowledge and complexities of medicine. He thought that if he left his research, science would take it and try to formulate it into something too complicated.

The Bach remedy philosophy is simple. By balancing any negative emotion, the body will heal itself from the stress which has subsequently been relieved from the person's energy system. Bach wrote ... "The action of these Remedies is to raise our vibrations and open up our channels for the reception of our Spiritual Self, to flood our natures with the particular virtue we need and wash out from us the fault which is causing harm".

These remedies are wonderfully simple to use. It is a condition of a registered Bach Remedy Practitioner, that they teach the client how to select and use the remedies themselves, therefore putting the power of healing back in the community. These remedies can be very cleansing on many levels for the aspiring energy worker and should be considered as a 'must have' in your kit of 'self-improvement' and 'self-empowerment' tools.

Throughout our world today there are a number of vibrational essence producers creating wonderful and original essences for use by therapists in their practises, or at home by anyone who understands the simple benefits of these energy tools for health and well-being. Some of these producers make their essences by the sun infusion method of Dr. Bach and others have developed their own individual methods of harnessing an energy signature from nature. Details of these producers are available from BAFEP—The British Association of Flower Essence Producers. Flower essence practitioners and therapists are also represented through the BFVEA—The British Flower and Vibrational Essence Association. Details of these two organisations are at the back of the book.

My own vibrational essences are called The Devic Essences. These consist of thirty-eight essences collected from sacred sites such as stone circles, standing stones, cromlechs and dolmens with the occasional tree and flower. They have been selected by spirit guidance and the energy patterns or signatures have been offered up by the nature spirits or Devas of these places. I specifically ask for energies which mankind needs at this time and energies which would help the people who come to me for help with healing or spiritual evolution. The range consists of Geomantic essences for Earth healing, (Geomancy is the ability to communicate with nature), Healing, Cleansing and Detox, Psychic Protection, Spiritual Transformation and finally Communication on many different levels within nature and the universe. Further information can be found at the back of the book and at www.davidashworth.com.

## Building a Power Base

The previous two pre-requisites of psychic protection, namely Visualisation and Intent, and Cleansing and Balancing are all part of building a power base. Without these disciplines, anything else we do is only going part way to achieving safety and effectiveness in energy work. It is no good thinking that things will take care of themselves, because they won't. We have to consciously make an effort to bring energy into our system to support us in the work we do. There are a number of techniques to help us do this, and building a power base is all about building up the energy within the aura so as to provide as much natural protection as is possible.

**Crystals:** Carrying and working with crystals is a powerful way to bring energy into the aura and boost our defences. We have touched on crystals in chapter 3 and the techniques mentioned there are relevant to this process of building a power base. In addition to these methods, carrying and wearing stones at all times should be considered.

There are many excellent crystal books available for you to consult and I don't wish to produce an in-depth treatise here, although I will point out the essence of a few fundamental but important stones, which you should consider having in your armoury.

A selection of various crystals and stones is a must for any energy worker but there are some stones which are very powerful energy transmitters and others which have excellent properties for avoiding the accumulation of negative energy. In her book *The Crystalline Transmission* Katrina Raphaell cites the following as the predominant power stones and I can confirm and agree with her that this is so.

Selenite

Kyanite

Calcite

Hematite

In addition to these, all the types of quartz are very powerful, especially Russian Quartz from the Sub-Polar Urals, where excellent natural citrines and smoky citrines are available. These are called tea crystals by the local mineralogists and miners due to the colour being a deep brownish yellow, like tea. The Russian quartz is not easy to come by due to the difficulty of getting it out of the country. Quartz from Madagascar has a beautiful calm purity to it and Brazilian quartz dances the fandango permanently. The final power stone I would mention here is Apophylite from India, a vastly underrated energy transmitter and healing stone.

## The Power Stones

**Selenite:** This is what I call a self activating crystal. The energy is readily apparent — you do not need to activate it using your consciousness. The energy positively floods out and is tremendous for moving energy in the area of the spine and central nervous system.

**Kyanite:** This crystal won't store negative energy. I have worn it for some years since receiving a powerful spirit message one night in my sleep. Katrina says that it "connects the lines of energy from the light body into the causal realm of the etheric mind". This brings forth all kinds of possibilities as the energy connects you to the highest frequencies.

**Calcite:** This stone, in my own experience, is an energy doubler. Whenever it is used with another crystal or stone it increases the energy at least two-fold. It is a powerful energy transmitter.

**Hematite:** This has a powerful grounding effect, instantly bringing the energy in the aura to earth. When anyone has suffered a temporary energy loss or has taken on some energy that has thrown them off balance, hematite will root their energy back to earth and often bring them back into a centred state.

**Citrine:** Natural citrine as opposed to heated amethyst which turns yellow during the process and is often sold as citrine, is another powerful crystal, like kyanite, it does not store negative energy. If you can obtain a natural smoky citrine, this is even better as it brings power, cleansing and grounding effects. One of the best crystals you can have.

**Blue Obsidian:** This stone is tremendous. When I use it in healing work it behaves like the veritable chain saw. It literally unzips the aura to allow the healing energies to penetrate. Used in combination with other crystals it drives their energies deep into the levels of consciousness which need attention. Brilliant!

**Apophylite:** Vastly underrated, apophylite (part of the Zeolites group) is also known as the Reiki Stone and works in many wonderful ways. When used in healing or with the Reiki energies it activates by beaming a green ray into the heart chakra of the healer and the client simultaneously. It has the effect of taking the client into a deeper state whereby they can receive the healing energy at a deeper level. It acts on the healer by removing them further from their conscious actions of healing, allowing the energy to flow in a way less encumbered by human consciousness. When used as a vibrational energy transmitter to bring energy to an environment such as a living room, apophylite gives off thousands of bright sparks, like those of a firework sparkler, penetrating the atmosphere to keep the energy bright and vibrant.

## The Chakra Stones

Wherever you go and whatever you read, you will find different stones are attributed to a particular chakra. This is not wrong in most cases, as the vibration of many different crystals and minerals will resonate with a particular chakra. For instance Carnelian, Tiger's Eye, Red Tiger's Eye, Hematite, Black Obsidian and Herkimer Diamond, along with a few others could all be used for the base chakra. In addition, a particular chakra may need a particular vibration to allow energy to be released and bring about changes. Only yesterday I dowsed some Kyanite for the heart chakra of a young lady. I could see clearly into her chakra and perceive the energy blockages that were there, even though I have never met her and she was over two hundred miles away. She will only need this energy for about two weeks and then the problem should have cleared. It would then be possible to dowse something else so that she may continue with her healing. My choice of fundamental chakra stones below is based on my own experiences and information provided by my Spirit Guides.

| Chakra | Mantra | Property | Stone | Colour |
|---|---|---|---|---|
| Crown | I Am | Spiritual | Amethyst | Purple |
| Brow | I Perceive | Intuition | Sodalite | Indigo |
| Throat | I Speak | Communication | Blue Topaz | Blue |
| Heart | I Love | Love | Serpentine | Green |
| Solar Plexus | I Know | Knowledge | Citrine | Yellow |
| Navel | I Create | Creation | Calcite | Orange |
| Base | I Live | Life Force | Red Tigers Eye | Red |

## Using Chakra Stones

Using chakra stones is very simple. First of all familiarise yourself with the position of the chakras in your physical body. Remember they can actually extend outwards into the aura by several feet, dependent upon your energy state, but this does not affect what we are going to do.

Take a little time out to listen to some relaxing music or a meditation tape. Find a comfortable place to lie down on the floor, select each of the chakra stones and identify what colour or stone goes with which chakra. Place the stones on your physical body for the duration of your relaxation or meditation. The base chakra stone can be placed on the body or between the legs about six inches from the base of the spine. The crown chakra stone should be placed on the floor about six inches from the top of the head.

Just one word of caution here. The brow and crown chakra can be very sensitive and you must take great care with these chakras. If you are using azurite for the brow chakra for instance, which is a very powerful stone, this can cause a great deal of discomfort if placed directly upon the chakra. So experiment and see how things feel. If it is uncomfortable, leave that particular stone off and place it on the floor with the crown chakra stone, or use it after the meditation just for a few moments, held by hand over the chakra. If ever there is discomfort, discontinue, for this means that either you are too sensitive at that time, or there may be a small chakra problem which can often clear up by itself. If the sensitivity continues or you are unsure, consult a healer who can tell you whether you have a problem or you are just very sensitive to these particular frequencies.

There are no hard and fast rules with chakra stones, so don't be afraid and don't be rigid. Use your intuition and see how things feel. When you can dowse, you will find that you can select many different stones which will resonate with a particular chakra. Remember that your energy system is fluid and dynamic, it is changing all the time. This means that what is needed one day might be obsolete the next, having provided the energy which was needed at a particular moment and therefore done its job.

When you have collected a selection of other stones together, you can dowse what you need to carry with you each day for specific purposes. For instance, what energy do I need today for self development? What energy do I need today for balance or protection, etc.? It is a good habit to get into. Doing a little work every day like this keeps everything in motion, moving in the right direction and avoiding stagnation.

Cleansing and Empowering your stones is important too. Cleansing should be done regularly, at least once a week if you are using them all the time, or after each session if using them in a proper working or intense manner. Running them under cold water for a few minutes while holding the intent that they should be psychically cleansed, is sufficient. To charge them up or empower them, standing them on a large quartz cluster for an hour or so is very effective. Alternatively, you can create a crystal grid consisting of various crystals arranged like the spokes of a wheel, all pointing inwards, and place your working stones at the centre of this wheel. Another method is utilising Pyramid Power. Many books have been written on the power generated beneath a pyramid and many documented experiments attest to the amazing results obtained from this source. Finally, one of the best methods is to allow your crystals to charge in pure sunlight. Although this takes longer, there is nothing finer than sunlight to empower anything. You can also couple the sun's energy and pyramid power with a device called the Pyramids of Light. These are wonderful pyramids created with coloured glass by a lady called Pauline Knight. The information and dimensions to make these pyramids was channelled to Pauline. A crystal placed in one of these pyramids becomes radiant in a very short time. You can also use the pyramids to charge anything else too, including essences (details at the back of the book). Remember, the sun is the giver of life to the whole planet.

The effect crystals have on the aura is dramatic. If you can see auras, or when you learn to sense or feel auras, which is relatively simple, you can appreciate the powerful and immediate effect crystals have in the subtle energy field.

If you follow these instructions carefully, you will be able to feel auras.

1. Working with a partner, bring your consciousness into your finger tips and sensitise them by rubbing your hands together. Now stimulate your palm chakra by rubbing in a circular motion with the thumb of one hand in the centre of the palm of the other hand.

2. Stand at right angles to your partner, with one hand held out, with your palm over their solar plexus chakra. We usually have one hand which is dominant or more sensitive, so if you are struggling to feel anything once you begin, try sensing with your other hand.

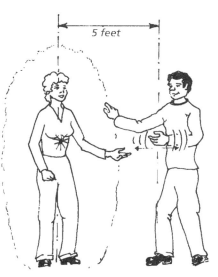

3. Keeping the hand at this level and in line with the solar plexus chakra, move directly away from your partner to a distance of about five feet.

4. From this position start to scan, by moving your hand slowly and gently back and forth a few inches in a constant motion. As you perform this scanning technique, begin to move closer to your partner a few inches at a time. Somewhere around three feet

Scanning to sense the aura over the solar plexus chakra.

from their physical body you will begin to sense a change as you detect the energy in the energy barrier known as the etheric aura.

We are trying to detect different levels or intensities of our electro-magnetic field, which is what an aura is. Because we are all different, we perceive energy differently. Most people will feel energy in one of three ways. The first way of perceiving the energy is a tingling sensation like electricity. The second is like a pressure sensation, as if you are pushing up against something, and the third is temperature change, feeling a distinct difference in temperature between one level and another. So keep these options in your mind until you discover the way in which you perceive energy: tingling, pressure or temperature. Some people can feel all three sensations.

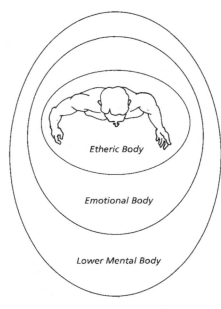

*Etheric Body*

*Emotional Body*

*Lower Mental Body*

The bands of the Aura in the lower self.

The different levels of the aura, between etheric, emotional and lower mental body, are separated by bands of energy which are more intense or thicker than the surrounding energy. The bands can be anything between an inch or two thick to a foot or more. Everyone's aura is distinctive and individual, just as a fingerprint is unique to each person. Practice this technique and you will be able to perceive these energies very easily. I can usually teach anyone to sense auras in about ten minutes. Once you have been shown how to do it, you have the skill for life, all you then need is the practice to perfect it.

The energy band which is the outer limit of the etheric aura from the physical body is usually around 18 to 24 inches. The emotional body is usually some 6 to 8 feet further out than this and the limit of the lower mental body is around another 2 to 4 feet from the emotional body. Within each energy body or space between the thicker bands, you can often find other narrow bands of high energy, but the difference between these and the outer limit of a particular body is usually very tangible.

Another way you can do this is by dowsing with a pair of 'L' shaped dowsing rods. Using this method approach the person face to face from a distance of about 6 feet and ask the rods to cross when the tips touch the etheric aura.

## Crystal Power

Now that you have mastered the aura detection technique, ... you have, haven't you?, let's try an experiment. Have a partner stand on a spot and dowse or feel where the etheric aura projects to. Mark the spot of the outer limit of the etheric aura on the floor with a piece of paper. Now give the person a small piece of crystal to hold. Almost any crystal will do, but quartz or calcite are very good for this purpose. Now, once again repeat the aura detection process and you will find that the etheric boundary has moved approximately twice as far out as it was before. Mark it on the floor to confirm this.

Bringing a crystal into the energy field has a more or less instant effect on the aura. Under the influence of crystal energy, especially quartz, the aura usually expands to twice its size or double the distance from the physical body. It is like suddenly and instantly inflating a football to twice its size. Such is the power brought to bear from something as innocent as a piece of crystal.

Essentially, when placed in the aura, either in a pouch around the neck or in the pocket, the crystal energy gives the subtle energies of the aura an enormous boost and the aura responds by expanding to accommodate this influx of positive energy. If you now monitor the expanded situation which has occurred in the aura, for anything up to an hour, you will find that the aura slowly returns to its original position. This does not mean that the aura has lost the energy which it absorbed from the crystal. The aura is now assimilating the crystal energy and at the same time returning to its normal functioning position. However, it is now much more energised than it was previously and it will continue to hold this energy as long as the crystal is carried on the person. This is one of the most effective ways to protect yourself from computer radiation. As you cannot screen this form of radiation, the way to combat the problem is to boost the energy in the aura. This is also the effect we wish to accomplish for our psychic protection.

**Salt Baths:** In cleansing and balancing above, we looked at the power of salt and water to cleanse negativity from the aura. Salt baths are a way in which we can also empower the aura. Run a bath and dissolve the salt as previously detailed. Get into the bath and spend a few moments with your eyes closed and focusing your mind on the cleansing and empowering aspects of the salt and water. Take a few deep breaths and then focus on the breath for a while, noting every in breath and out breath until the breath is completely balanced and calm. Now visualise your physical body absorbing the essence of the energies of the salt water going deep within you. When the body has fully absorbed the white, cleansing energy of the salt, visualise this essence now moving outwards into the aura and permeating every last atom of the outer subtle energies.

In chapter three we discussed the empowering nature of crystal baths. If you couple a crystal bath and a salt bath together you get an extremely powerful way of both cleansing and empowering all in one. Remember, visualisation and intent can move mountains in the realms of subtle energy.

Bathing is one of the most relaxing things we can do. Anything you can bring to this situation which will enhance the desired result should be considered and experimented with: aromatherapy oils in the water, or on a burner; candles to set a soft light scene. Sometimes I also take a guided meditation tape into the bathroom with me. Breathing exercises, chakra meditation or guided visualisation works wonders in this situation. Working in this way, can bring about tremendous healing and empowering shifts throughout your whole being. (Do Not take a live, mains operated tape player near water).

**Diet:** We have looked at many aspects of diet from a cleansing point of view, but let us now consider it from the building of a power base.

A meat free diet is desired from an energy point of view. The large intestine has great difficulty in processing meat. Meat may contain minerals and proteins, but has absolutely no life force energy in it because it is a dead substance. Eating a dead substance is energetically not good for you. You may as well eat cardboard with a sprinkling of vitamins and minerals on it. If you desire spiritual attainment and evolution or great faculty as a healer, then you must seriously consider a mainly vegetarian diet.

Dr. Edmond Bordeaux Szekely was a great scholar who translated many ancient Aramaic texts. Some of these predated the Bible by many years and others were from the time of Jesus' ministry on Earth. In *The Essene Gospel of Peace, Book One*, Jesus says:

"But I do say to you kill neither men nor beasts, nor yet the food which goes into your mouth. For if you eat living food, the same will quicken you, but if you kill your food, the dead food will kill you also. For life comes only from life, and from death comes always death. For everything which kills your foods, kills your bodies also. And everything which kills your bodies kills your souls also".

With reference to the word 'quicken', this means to attain spiritual transformation. When one is quickened, the subtle energy system functions at a higher or faster vibrational rate, bringing one closer to the realms of the higher beings or to a point where one can receive information and guidance directly from a higher source, be that Angels, Guides, etc. However, the subtle body can only quicken if the physical body is not holding it back. Therefore, what you put into the old boiler determines what you get out of it!

*The Essene Gospel of Peace, Book One* is a short but marvellous study in how we should live if we want to attain spiritual progression in this lifetime. It teaches much which is common sense, but has been lost in the teachings of the church, most of it being excluded from the Bible at the time of the Council of Nicea in AD 325 under the governance of the Emperor Constantine. The reason we only have four Gospels in the Bible today is an acknowledgement of paganism by the Emperor. Constantine ruled that there should be one Gospel for each of the cardinal points, north, south, east and west. At the same time, Jesus' teachings were too difficult for most ordinary people to come to terms with and adhere to. For instance, living on a vegetarian diet, and so the teachings were changed. With the discovery of many early texts, the Dead Sea Scrolls amongst them, the original truth of Jesus' teachings is now coming forth for those who see the value and are ready to walk this path, although in the case of the scrolls, these truths have been closely guarded (or repressed) now for over half a century. Clearly they speak of 'False Prophets'. It is also important to be clear about Jesus. He did not start Christianity, he was a teacher and came to teach us the way back home, the way to God, or indeed how we could contact God who dwells within us all. To Jesus, we are all God's children, no matter what religion we follow. His truth excluded no-one and was freely given, that we all could drink from the truth of his knowledgeable cup.

What we are looking for in our diet is food with a high vibrational content. This is found in 'live' food, that is, food which has a life force, such as vegetables and fruit. Live food has an energy field which will show strongly on a Kirlian photograph. When vegetables are picked, the life force continues to radiate for some considerable time. Obviously it is important to consume the food as soon as possible after it is harvested to get the best from it, but it is good to know that it does not die immediately. Apples, for instance, properly prepared and stored, will maintain their energy for months.

Life force energy is the absolute prime mover in building your power base. It gives to us on many levels, not just the physical. I would like to refer the reader once again to the book by Dr. Gabriel Cousens, *Spiritual Vision and the Rainbow Diet*. An excellent introduction to the colours and energies of food and their relationship to the chakras and vibrational value to the whole being.

When you start to experiment with auras, once you have mastered the techniques, you will find a great difference between the levels of energy in different people's auras. Those who live on processed food and burgers, pizzas etc., usually have totally flat energy in the aura. In some cases it is barely there. This is very similar to a person with Chronic Fatigue Syndrome or M.E. There is virtually no energy in the aura, because they can't store it.

Food preparation is also important. To keep the highest content of Life Force Energy, the food should be eaten raw. Steaming and pressure cooking is the next best. Avoid boiling if you can, as most of the nutrition goes out with the water. However, a word of warning here. Anyone who suffers from low energy such as M.E. should be careful with raw food. This sometimes needs a great deal of energy to break down and process which will deplete the energy system of the person too much, causing their fatigue to become worse.

Microwaving food is to be avoided at all costs. Apart from the electro-magnetic radiation danger from these devices permeating your living space, the irradiating of food at this frequency kills the Life Force Energy stone dead. The radiation also alters the molecular structure of the food, which brings about other problems for our bodies to deal with too. There is much information coming forth now from physicians and scientists to show that micro-waved food is changing the blood chemistry of the poor unsuspecting public. One Doctor commented that "this is a new range of diseases waiting to befall us".

## One Final Aspect of Psychic Protection

Through my own journey of spiritual advancement, I was not very good initially at protection. I used to pick up energies from people all the time. This taught me some valuable lessons and gave me experiences which otherwise I would not have had. However, the answer to my protection came via a different route to most.

As I started to get an increasing amount of psychic rescue and spirit clearance work, I was under great pressure for time and I have to admit to being too eager on many occasions to 'get in there and sort it out', without taking time to think of the protection issues. It's my nature unfortunately, I'm a bit excitable and impulsive. Eventually, I think my Spirit Guides got together and said something like, "we can't wait for this guy to get his act together with protection or we'll never get any work done, so we better provide it for him". So it came to pass that my protection was provided for me by my Guides. However, in my experience this has only been the case for the very few and not the many.

The Guides can only do so much though, and the time eventually comes when they want to bring you more and more powerful problems to solve; at the same time they can only provide protection up to a certain level. In my work now I am regularly dealing with demonic energies, whether in possession cases or in clearance from buildings. The problems which are brought to be solved constantly challenge you to push back the barriers and learn new techniques. What is the point in staying where you are, when all this help and guidance is available to push you onwards through your spiritual evolution?

We never stop learning and there is great truth in the saying that the more we learn, the more we realise we know nothing; or relatively little anyway.

## Dancing with the Devil

This would seem a good point in the book to explain the title. *Dancing with the Devil as you channel in the light!* The reality is that many healers come to their work in great ignorance of the dangers in healing. They naively open themselves up and connect with Guides and Angels without ever thinking that it is just as easy for other beings and sources of energy to connect with them while they are open.

My Guides showed me a vision of a group of healers, chatting amongst themselves as they worked with the energies, bringing in ever-greater streams of light while their Guides and Angels danced amongst them. And there in the background, dancing too, were the demons and dark forces; watching and gaining strength from the energy as they all danced together in the light.

Many people objected to the title, but it was given to me and therefore I knew it was right. The title is a gateway. Those who are ready will pass through it and move up in their evolution and those who are not will be repelled by it.

## 09

What we do in this life echoes in eternity.

**Russell Crowe as Maximus,
from the film Gladiator.**

## Overview

I SEE MANY CASES OF PSYCHIC ATTACK. NO CASE IS EVER the same, although the mild forms can be fairly similar. A mild attack would normally produce symptoms of general tiredness, through varying degrees of energy depletion to being worn out all of the time, especially extremely drained in the mornings upon waking up. Quite often there is mild anxiety and a fear that something is wrong. In many cases the person has visited the doctor and in some of these instances tranquillisers have been prescribed. In all cases the person knows there is definitely something wrong, but cannot describe what is happening adequately.

I usually find an accumulation of negative energies within the aura and occasionally slight damage to the fabric of the aura. Perhaps there are even a few entities gorging themselves within one or more levels of the energy fields within the aura. This can also be within the chakras or on the exterior of the aura. Sometimes there may be a spirit with the person, actually attached to the aura, or the spirit may have waited outside or at home to avoid detection whilst

# CASE STUDIES

the person has come for consultation. All spirits and demons and certain levels of entity can read the mind, both the mind of their host and mine. They know from the very point in time that the person decides to contact me, that they are seeking help to rid themselves of their problems. Hence why the more intelligent beings wait in their perceived place of safety to avoid detection.

On average, the treatment of mild forms of psychic attack usually takes up to a couple of hours. This includes removal of the offending parties; soul rescue where spirits are concerned; transportation where demons are concerned and dismantling or energy transmutation for entities; repair to the aura and balancing up the person to a point where they can again function normally from an energetic perspective. However, sometimes more work is needed in the case of a badly damaged energy system.

This is the common picture and it would not be very interesting or informative to relay a number of these 'ordinary' case studies to you. Therefore, below I have listed for your delectation some of the more unusual and challenging cases, to give you an idea of what one comes across when peering into the fascinating worlds of the light realms. When I am unravelling the picture for the troubled client, I never cease to be amazed by some of the things I discover. I hope you will find them interesting too.

## Entity Attack

This very straightforward case, which was early in my psychic attack career, shows how an entity can hide behind what most people would diagnose as a severe case of flu or lung infection.

Anne was an experienced therapist and had been ill for several weeks and could not move the symptoms of her terrible cold, which had been getting worse, particularly on her chest. She looked especially frail and weighed down by her infection. I was quite worried for her when I first saw her condition. I said I would give her some hands-on healing and see what else I could detect which we might be able to deal with.

As I approached and placed my hands on her shoulders and began to channel energy, I became aware immediately that her energy system felt strange. I backed off and closed down my energy system very quickly, until I had looked into the matter further. I began to dowse with a pendulum, without using my consciousness to 'view' what might be inside her and discovered that she had an entity which was taking up residence in both lungs. This is unusual, as most entities, if they breach the auric defences, usually take up residence in a major energy area such as the chakras, but this guy was quite smart in a way. What he was doing was feeding from the healing energy which this lady's body was sending to the affected area, namely the lungs. As she was a Reiki practitioner, she had also been doing some hands-on work on herself, which was feeding her system in general, but she had been specifically targeting her lungs because her infection was so bad. So our little friend, who was very dark and grisly, was in the best place he could possibly be to access this energy and feed himself.

With the help of my Guides, I removed the entity and then applied some hands on healing to the lungs first and then generally to the rest of her body. I used a few vibrational tools to assist in clearing blockages and re-balancing her, which took about three quarters of an hour. The difference was amazing. It was as if ninety percent of the lung problem had disappeared. She had been on an inhaler for a week because her breathing had been so difficult, but now she could breathe quite freely and easily. Her poor lungs had been so deprived of healing energy by the entity that I think she would have been in hospital within days with a very serious condition had we not found the cause. From that point it was plain sailing and she recovered fully very quickly.

This demonstrates how much damage these beings can do. One would think that because a person is ill and therefore in a run down condition, that an entity would not attack them because the food supply, namely energy would be in short supply. However, the body will try its best with all available resources to heal itself, and if the energy is all going to the same place, such as lungs or throat etc., then this would be an ideal feeding place for an entity. In this case the lady herself was applying additional healing energy to supplement the body's own, which of course was benefiting the entity in the lungs. The lungs were not getting the slightest help from the healing energy, but deteriorating even further.

## A case of Psychic Attack

5th November 1997

I was called by a very experienced healer to help a lady who had been psychically attacked. The lady in question had noticed that a colleague in the office where she worked was probably suffering from some kind of energy depletion and she had tried to help her during her lunch hour using Reiki. Later that day she began to feel unwell and realised that she may have picked something up from her colleague. She hadn't been the victim of psychic attack previously, but due to her thorough training, she quickly recognised it for what it was.

Once she realised what was happening she called her teacher and Reiki Master for help and this was arranged for that same evening. As the day wore on, the attack became worse with the invading entity becoming stronger as it fed from her energy. The result was that she was becoming progressively more depleted and was beginning to get frightened. Fear is a great energy powerhouse to an entity or a spirit: when we become frightened by something, we release a lot of energy from our core being, which is an emotional response to a stimulus. This emotional energy can quite literally charge up an entity, spirit or demon, giving them very great strength.

As the lady was on the journey to her Reiki Master's house for help, the consciousness of the entity knew where it was going and why. It drew all the energy it could from her and became so strong she was almost paralysed. She described the feeling as like being electrocuted. The result was that she could not continue to drive and had to telephone her Reiki Master to say that the entity was taking control of her and resisting all her attempts to make progress to the house.

The Reiki Master performed some temporary help at a distance so that she could continue her journey. When she arrived she could barely walk and was in such a state that she was physically sick. It took the Reiki Master, with the assistance of some of her other student healers, some three hours to bring the lady round and balance her energy to somewhere near normal.

Unfortunately, when she left to return home, it transpired that the entity had remained in the car, lying in wait for her. This, of course, was not immediately apparent, as she travelled home and went straight to bed. However, the following morning she was quite ill again and realised that things were again, very wrong. She called her Reiki Master again and the Reiki Master realised what had happened and managed this time to do a complete clearance of the entity and also of a spirit in the lady's house. This she did at a distance with the help of Spirit Guides. However, the lady was still very poorly and the Reiki Master called me and asked if I would check the work she had done. I duly tuned-in over the 'phone and confirmed that everything the Reiki Master had seen and done was correct and the entity had finally been dispatched and transmuted as was required.

However, as I was dowsing and viewing, I could see that there was also auric damage from this attack and that the entity, which had been a clever and powerful being, had also affected the energies of the lady's house, leaving a nasty magnetic energy pattern which would certainly attract other unwanted visitors to the premises. This would also need some clearing, plus resetting the energy of the house. The Reiki Master asked if I would take over the case, which I did.

I did some more specific dowsing next and discovered that the lady had suffered damage to the emotional elements of her etheric body and also damage to the emotional body itself and the lower mental body. The dowsing showed that the house was clear of entities, but a little further investigation would be needed. I also dowsed that the lady could not remain in that house until I had corrected and reset the energies. I arranged to visit the following day.

Before leaving for her house, I spent time attaining a deep state of attunement with the place and the work to be done and called in my Guides. I dowsed out all the energy tools I would need to do the job and then double checked my analysis of the day before. Always check, double check and check again. This can be a very dangerous business and you can't afford to make mistakes. I took out the A to Z map book and focused in on the area to see whether it was safe for me to go there. As I was in a trance-like state, very tuned-in, my pendulum, which was still in my hand began spinning like mad, it was almost at the horizontal it was going so fast. It certainly drew my attention. I asked was their another element to look at and the answer was yes.

I checked quickly through my notes and it was something to do with the house. I dowsed that it was not safe for me to go there immediately. I also dowsed that the house was at present still clear of active spirits and entities. I worked out that I had to send some Reiki energy by the absent method to the house before I left on my journey. This took about ten minutes before I received the all clear and I then set off.

When I arrived at the house, I approached cautiously. It is not my practice to enter the premises until I know I am definitely safe. I announced my arrival and told the lady that I had to do some work outside before I could enter the house. By this time I was very closed off and protected. It is difficult for me to communicate with another person while in this altered consciousness state.

I worked out what needed to be done, a few little rituals, and then I was guided to walk through the front garden gate and back out again. I can only wonder at some of the things I am told to do. I can't help thinking sometimes that the Guides are just having a laugh at my expense. More likely though, it was to open an energy door of some sort.

I was now clear to enter the house. I dowsed the house and found that there was a spirit present in the kitchen. I checked my earlier dowsing which told me that there weren't any *active* spirits present and found this to be correct. What had happened was that the distant work which I had performed prior to leaving the office had woken and energised a dormant spirit, so that I could find it more easily when I arrived.

The spirit which was not malevolent, was that of a woman, I didn't ask how old she was when she died but I dowsed that she died in around 1782. I checked when the house was built and the lady told me it was about three hundred years old. I like to ask some basic questions of the spirit because I can address my help to them in a more personal way. The spirit was in the kitchen and the lady told me later that she had noticed something different in the kitchen just before I arrived. I explained the situation to the spirit lady and opened a doorway into the astral realms for her. She understood what she needed to do and was not frightened. She went quickly and quietly into the arms of those who had waited for her for so long.

I now had permission to do the work on the lady which was so desperately needed. It was a straightforward case of aura damage from entity attack, if you can say there is any such thing as straightforward. As previously mentioned, much of the damage was in the emotional elements, an area in the aura which is a real powerhouse. Using vibrational essences and crystals, the Guides told me what to use and where to place them on and around the lady. The process took around an hour. Most of the damage was down her left hand side. At last, after the terrifying ordeal this lady had suffered, she began to feel better as the open aura was once more sealed and the high frequency signals, which cause so much anxiety, were screened out. She began to look a lot better in the face and soon said she was feeling more relaxed and balanced.

Clearing the house was more or less straightforward, using crystal grids in some rooms to raise energy and then channelling light into the house to use as a power tool to release the magnetic forces and vibrational patterns left by the entity. In other rooms I used vials of essences to provide the vibrational power, and the Guides used this via my energy system to do the clearance. Eventually, after some three hours, the job was complete: house cleansed and balanced, with lots of light brought in to raise its vibration and one human energy system repaired and balanced. Result: a great deal of relief. Bear in mind, all this suffering resulted from offering ten minutes of help to a work colleague. Make sure you are protected!

You will notice in this case above that I display a great deal of caution. Again, I was very much still learning the ropes with powerful entities at this time. Nowadays, I carry a lot more protection than I did then, as my 'energy stamina' has increased vastly through working with ever increasing levels of psychic energy. These abilities have been introduced to me one step at a time by ever more challenging cases coming my way. Although I would probably just 'wade right in' to a case like this these days because of my experience and knowledge, although I am still very cautious with other cases. One gets a feel for how dangerous a situation might be and I have to say some of them are very frightening indeed and I probably practise even more caution today than I did back then. Essentially the stakes are much higher with a case of demonic possession, than from entity attack and one doesn't leave anything to chance.

## A Troublesome Gang

This case involves a lady I have helped a couple of times previously, who seems to be a little susceptible to psychic attack. She had 'phoned me with a serious problem in the afternoon of New Year's Eve. She told me she had picked something up and it felt very bad. I detected an entity, but no aura damage and I cleared it at a distance for her. I called her on the telephone later that night and told her that everything seemed to be clear.

A couple of days later she called me again to say that something really terrible was happening to her. I put the telephone down in order to have a look into her energy system. I tuned-in and saw it straight away. The first job of the new century and it is a Demon! I tuned-in to it and the Guides went over and opened channels for me. I checked and double checked my protection and the protection of all my family and those around the lady. It was a good connection and he appeared at first sight to be more of a mischief maker than totally evil. I didn't want to tune-in too much and get lots of information, just the necessary amount so that I could find out what he was doing and how to deal with him. Also, the Guides will let me know when I have enough information. In some cases they make me tune-in to a deeper level so that I learn new lessons about what I am dealing with. Other times we just get what we need.

He was jumping around saying "I am a fire cracker", showing me this was his personality and energy, hot stuff, lively, fast moving; but then I saw his character. I then saw him in action, acting out his particular facet of possession, which was very different from the mischief maker I had first thought him to be. I was probably deluded by his lively personality, for in reality he was much deeper and darker than I first perceived.

I could see him now, crawling all over her, sucking her energy, draining her a bit at a time. Gaining energy which made her weak and gave him the strength to play his evil games. The being is controlling … it is sexual … it is crawling all over her body in a lustful and loathsome way. There was demonic laughter as it looked at me, demonstrating its power and ability, whilst beginning to possess her in an ever deeper way. It wants to possess and control her as a sexual plaything. Domination is his key purpose. I didn't need to see any more.

I asked the Guides, could I clear it at a distance or do I need to go over? Yes, I needed to go over. The Guides also showed me that we needed the traditional sorts of things associated with exorcising a demon, like we see in the movies. I thought it was quite corny really, salt, garlic and basil. I double checked that the Guides were not having a bit of fun with me, but they confirmed the list.

The Guides said, "you have to place a clove of garlic at each corner of the house, both inside and outside, also one clove in the centre of each of the external doorways. Next, the salt has to be sprinkled across the external doorways liberally. She then needs to bathe in a salt bath and finally a sprig of fresh basil should be crushed to release the aromatics and wafted around the living room in a final cleansing ceremony". These are essentially the energies which the Guides will work with, coupled with my own as a driving force, to access and remove the demon from her energy system.

Once I had worked out all the details, I called the lady back. There is no easy way to break this sort of news to people. I have to tell them exactly what I have found so that firstly I can judge the accuracy of my findings and secondly, they will have confidence in me as I describe to them exactly what they are experiencing.

I told the lady precisely what I had seen and experienced of the demon crawling all over her in a lustful way. She confirmed that was exactly what it felt like. By now she was quite drained and desperate. I gave her the shopping list of things I needed and made arrangements to go over as soon as she called me back to say that she had the salt, garlic and basil.

In the meantime, I was asking the Guides how they were going to deal with this demon. Usually I assess whether they can be turned to the light and re-programmed or rehabilitated, or if I have to send them back to where they came from. However, as I tuned-in I was surprised to hear "we are going to extinguish him ...", and as they could see my questioning and puzzled mind, they added, "totally". They showed me a scene which clearly described crushing the life out of him, as if crushing a potato crisp packet. Of course, while I am connected to the demon, he can read me like I can read him. He knows exactly what is in store for him and he knows that he can't escape.

The lady called me an hour later to say that she had the items we needed. She also said that she thought the demon was having a final fling as she could feel his activity becoming stronger and she had become very weak to the point where she could hardly stand up. She asked would I come out and pick her up from her son's house and take her back home.

I left the office within ten minutes, collected her from her son's house and took her home. On the way in the car, the demon had a little go at me a couple of times, creating great pain in my left arm, as he had a nibble at my energy. As we approached her house on foot, the lady could hardly walk or keep her balance and had great difficulty getting up the step and into the house itself. Her son had given me the garlic, basil and salt and I set to work immediately, keeping my focus very tuned-in and keeping the demon out of my system. Firstly I put the salt at the doors and then split the garlic into cloves and asked where to put it within the house. Then I began the outside of the house. As I came to place the last two cloves, an enormous, howling, freezing gale blew up, almost pushing me over and so bitterly cold as to virtually freeze my hands instantly. As soon as I got back in to the house, the wind subsided completely. I have seen this happen with the weather before when working at a high level with energies in the landscape. In this instance it was difficult to tell whether dark forces were conjured up to hinder me or not, although the wind didn't blow again that day, but in some cases there is no doubt at all.

Once I had everything in position I sat across the room from the lady and tuned-in to the demon. He was not happy and was struggling and in denial of us and our ability to rid her of him. As soon as I made a strong connection and held him with my mind, the Guides took hold of him and were restraining him. It was quite a performance, but somehow they seemed to be holding back a little at the same time. Nervous of the possible outcome, I had asked several times about the way they were going to dispatch the demon and I have to admit to a little trepidation to being party to what appeared to be murder. However, every time I questioned their method, they told me that it had to be done this way and that I would see why. I was told to bring lots of light into the house. I began to channel as much as I could. They kept saying "more, more. More energy, more light". I was opening an ever increasing channel of pure light from above. I could feel the room changing as it flooded in. I was guided to fill up the external walls so that the fabric of the stone and brick was completely saturated with light. They wanted a fortress of light. The intensity of energy coming in was incredible, the walls felt white hot with energy and at this appropriate moment I felt him go.

I asked the Guides where the body was and they told me he was outside, "Did you kill him?" "Yes … you will see why, tune-in". I now saw why I had to bring so much light into the walls of the house and why we needed so much protection from the salt in the doorways and the garlic placed at the four corners. As I tuned-in I became aware of a whole host of these same demons outside the building, a great energy of anger being projected at us. It was becoming clear that this demon-type creature was a strange little thing in some ways. It was very much like the gremlins of cinema fame and quite different from any others which I had encountered up until that time. They were up at the windows looking in and snarling at us, but couldn't get through the force field of light. The energy in the house was improving already since the demise of our friend. I faced them in their anger and told them there was nothing they could do to us, we carry too much light for them. There were sixty eight of them and I asked the Guides could they do something to rid the world of all the rest of them, to which they replied that they could. I instructed the Guides to go to it then, and the rowdiness outside began to die down.

They began to leave in a gaggle, carrying the body of their comrade. The Guides eventually herded them together in a somewhat dejected and quietened state, putting them into a kind of holding pen. I was told that they were to be moved into another dimension and would undergo a little re-programming, as they were not, generally speaking, a bad sort but had gone off the rails somewhat. The death of their comrade had been necessary for two reasons. Firstly to show them that they cannot interfere in such a negative and harmful way with other beings and not expect to accumulate some karmic debt. The second was that the Guides knew that there were others of his kind wreaking havoc all over the local town and in order to capture them all, they had to 'extinguish' this one so that his comrades would 'feel' his trauma and come running to his aid.

I established that this gang of marauders were not all working together or for the same agenda, but had all slipped into the present time/space area at the same time. They were all up to some sort of fairly serious mischief and the Guides saw this as an opportunity to put an end to a lot of psychic problems for humanity in one fell swoop. So we probably rescued quite a number of other people on this occasion, who may have been suffering from a range of different symptoms, but not knowing what was the cause.

The energy which attracted the demon had been with this lady for about three and a half weeks and we tracked it down to an imported car she had recently purchased. The car, a VW Beetle, had come from California and was some twelve months old. I could see the energy of a very large man, who had not been the previous owner of the car, but had at some time sat in it. Something within his energy had imprinted itself into the fabric of the seats and it was this energy which had attracted the demon into her life.

This lady is a well versed healer and knows quite a lot about psychic protection and clearance techniques. For the past few days she had been asking for help from Guides etc. and trying various techniques to rid herself of her problems. At one point she said to me, "make sure your family are protected because I think this is a full blown possession". Although she did not know it, she had cleared the energy from the car by herself and she was right about it being a possession. The rest, as they say, including the demon, is now history.

## The Case Continues

However, the case continues. Subsequent to clearing the problem with the strange gremlin type creatures on Monday, She called me again on the following Friday to say she had been feeling totally spaced out and lacking energy since the day after the work had been completed.

I checked all aspects of the investigation from Monday and my Guides told me that the house was still secure and absolutely locked in light. There was not a single problem with the house at all. Yet I dowsed that she had picked up seven entities. She reported being almost in a state of hallucination and said that if she wasn't such a strong person who had the knowledge of how psychic attack could affect one, she considered that she would probably be in a psychiatric hospital by now and totally unable to cope.

Knowing that her energy system was intact and aura repaired, I checked to see whether a portal had opened up into the house, with the possibility that this was where the entities were getting in. This was also negative, but as I continued to dowse, the picture was given to me a little more clearly as I reached a deeper state of tune.

After we had finished the work earlier in the week, I had checked the lady's aura and it was OK, completely intact. Since picking up the seven entities, she now once more had a damaged aura. I immediately set up a distant clearance with the Guides, to be accomplished during the night while she was resting and her energy system free from waking consciousness. When I checked in the morning, the Guides told me that they had cleared the seven entities but she now had four more! Guides will usually only do what you ask of them for a variety of reasons.

Also, sometimes things have to happen in a certain way to lead you to the problem. If the Guides continued to clear the entities every time she picked one up, then I wouldn't be able to find the problem, because essentially she wouldn't have a problem. So they do what I ask them, in this case remove the seven entities, and then they let things alone to run their natural course. Therefore, as soon as she was clear, she picked up four more entities. This number of entities in one night, without going out of the house is quite dramatic and unusual.

I went over the next day to see her and, as I tuned-in again, I thought the problem was with the crown chakra. There had been a similar problem with another client, which had caused him untold trouble for years until I unravelled it. I think what is happening with this lady is that her crown chakra is stuck wide open and is putting out a signal cutting across different dimensions of light. This would explain why the force field of light around the house is still intact and secure, but that the entities are passing directly from the outside into her being by some direct energy channel. She is literally shining like a beacon, with a very powerful energy beam which reaches outside of the house from her core being, and this is acting like a signal for entities to lock onto and be drawn into her energy system. A crown chakra wide open would also be a good indicator of why she is in a hallucinatory state. When the crown is wide open it is bringing in energy at an enormous rate and disturbing the whole balance of the subtle energy system, but particularly in the mental body area. It is also bringing in very high frequency signals which we as humans are not equipped to process easily, similar to when there is a damaged aura. This causes all kinds of panic attack situations to arise.

It appeared that the crown chakra had undergone some sort of energy overload due to some blockages which were deeply rooted in her system. I repaired the crown chakra and closed it down to normal functioning level. This repair work complete, I began to check her over, in particular all her healing energy channels. The attunements seemed to be OK and chakras were now functioning in a clean and balanced state, but there was something wrong with the energy flow. It took me a few moments to work out that what seemed to be happening was a blockage in the head area which disturbed the flow of energy down to the heart chakra.

The Guides showed me diagrammatic pictures of how the energy should flow in this particular case. It should enter the crown and move down into the heart chakra in a spear-like pointed fashion, arriving in the centre of the heart in a point. It would then spiral out like a Catherine wheel, clockwise and anti-clockwise equally to both sides of the body. What was happening in the head was that the blockage caught some of the light energy as it entered the crown chakra and bounced it back out before it had chance to move down to the heart. The blockage stopped about 34% of the energy from passing down to the heart. However, now I had the picture of what was wrong, the Guides said that we could not do this work for at least two weeks, as they would be continuing the work we had initiated today for about another ten days and then the energy system must settle. Then we could remove this blockage.

This is an illustration of a complex series of problems, which could not all be shown to me at once. Also, due to the fact that this work needs to be done in a certain order of priority, coupled with the time it takes for repair work to become robust in some cases, which in turn depends to some extent upon the level of damage, one can see why it is impossible to complete all the work in one go. Subsequently, we removed the blockage and at last this lady's problems were over.

## Does this House want us?

I was called to this house by the lady occupant. She had been brought up in the house as a child, but had lived away for almost thirty years. Several months earlier, her Mother had died in the house. She and her husband moved in with her Father until he too joined his wife on the other side about a month later. There had been a number of small instances which she could not ignore which led her to believe that perhaps the house did not want them to stay after the parents had died. In particular, she was worried about earth radiation and underground streams, especially as they had an old well in the garden.

The house was an old farmhouse and her parents had died more or less of natural causes, after a long life. This in itself usually tells a tale of the house being a healthy place to live and as I walked around and took notes while in conversation with the lady, indeed I did not detect any real problems with the house.

However, there were other aspects to consider. The lady had a sister who was not very amenable to her now living in the house and was pushing for 'her half of the estate'. After taking the brief, I tuned-in to the house and wandered around alone for about ten minutes, confirming my original sensory skirmish, that there was no real problem from earth or water radiations, only a little psychic energy build up in various parts of the house, but none of this was very debilitating. As I tuned-in to a deeper level, my Guides told me to 'look to the woman and her sister'.

I went downstairs and said, "I'm told I have to start with you, can you spare the time?" And so we sat across the table and I began to tune-in. I had established that this lady was quite sensitive and was on her own spiritual path of evolution. She had also done Reiki to second degree. I asked about her sister as I tuned-in to her. She had always felt that her sister really hated her and that she was convinced that she had actually hated her before she was even born. She said she could not reason why, it was just a feeling. Well, feelings usually tell a truth in my experience, if only we would believe them more. She said that she could feel her sister's presence in her solar plexus if ever the sister was on the way to visit. It had been a difficult relationship, but she had always responded positively and with kindness. However, with the passing of her parents and now the added pressure from her sister to divide up the estate, she was finding things difficult, particularly as her added sensitivity from emotional upset at the loss of her parents, was working overtime and giving her many messages. But unless we are capable of decoding them, the pressure just builds up and confuses us even more.

I was first shown her crown chakra, with a wonderful shaft of spiritual energy entering her being. However, this was blocked at the brow chakra level. The message was clear here, that she was on the right path but had a lot of work to do in trusting her intuition. The brow chakra is the centre of intuition and trusting is the only way it will develop. I was shown that she must absolutely give this her attention and the more she trusted, the more the spiritual energy would come through the rest of her being to enlighten her. Mistakes or errors of judgement will be made, but when learning anything we will make mistakes. In some cases I can help people move forward spiritually by removing blockages such as this with Guided Vibrational Healing, but in this case, I was told that she must do the work herself. Although she meditated, I was also told that she should connect more through prayer. Specifically, I was told that in meditation, we tend to focus on the still space so that other forms can come in to us. However, with prayer, we are actually building a conscious connection directly to those who can help us. Therefore, as an example, if one prays to one's Guides or to Jesus for guidance, one is assembling thought forms in a positive way to make a connection and ultimately we will succeed.

I was also shown the heart centre, which needed some attention in order to progress her evolution, but whose doesn't? As a planetary race, humanity is only just beginning to open at this centre and those who realise this and are working on and from this centre are in the vanguard in human evolutionary terms.

This out of the way, I was then shown her sister and a powerful psychic link which came into her crown chakra from her sister. I could sense her sister's harmful and powerful energy. We talked again about the hatred aspect and she told me that someone had once told her in a reading that her sister had hanged her in a past life. In fact this lady had previously told me that she had always had a problem with her neck. I had seen by this time that the connection between them both certainly did go back prior to this lifetime and I asked my Guides to show me the story. They took me back to a Victorian life and I sensed the energy there, but then they took me back to a Greek life where it had all begun. There may have been other incarnations in the intervening period where one or other had incarnated but where this present pattern was not acted out. These I did not pursue. However, this Greek life was the key to understanding what was happening.

In the present life, my client was the younger of the two sisters. In both the Victorian and Greek incarnations the status was the same. In the Greek life, the lady was shown to me in her early twenties, very beautiful, intelligent and popular. It was at this point I first felt the hatred and as I focused more I could detect the energy of jealousy. Her sister was jealous of her beauty and popularity. Although I was not shown the scene, I was told that her sister murdered her in this Greek life and at this time the power of her hatred was such that it made a very powerful connection with her. Moving forward to the Victorian life, the connection had been reinforced through a link to her crown chakra and the energy of jealousy and hatred was displayed with great force. The sister's hatred was so deep and powerful and all consuming by this time, that dark forces had been alerted by the magnetic attraction of her emotional intensity. Again, the sister was jealous of her intelligence and popularity. I was shown a very typical Victorian scene: social gatherings where her conversation was very bright and her knowledge of different subjects very broad. People were very fond of her and she brightened their lives. I was not shown the murder scene, but it was confirmed to me that she was indeed hanged.

I changed tack at this point, because I wanted to see what was happening around her sister and her sister's husband in terms of entities and spirits. I had picked up the energy of the husband and this was a very self centred vortex, where he took whatever he needed for himself and gave nothing in return. He had two entities with him, which I found surprising, as he was a gardener by way of employment and working in nature usually keeps the light body very cleansed and free of this type of attachment, However, given that he was very 'self focused' and domiciled with someone of very powerful negative energy, perhaps this was understandable.

The sister had seven entities and one spirit in attendance, but I knew there was another aspect to this case which I was about to look into. During the Victorian life, she had attracted dark forces around her and I began to focus on these, detecting four elements which were feeding and driving her emotions of hatred. First of all she was psychically attached to two other people who were strangers to her. I then unearthed a little red demon, not too bad as demons go, but his energy was enough to attract more of his kind. My consciousness then hit the fourth element and I immediately stopped our conversation and the reading, as I had to deal with this one before I went any further. He was a nasty black demon, full of hatred. He saw me the second my consciousness touched him and he was ready to fight to keep his position. After a stand off of a few moments I felt his resolve weaken and the Guides were able to go in and remove him. I asked could we take him back through time to the point where he had been turned from the light and I was told that we could do that with both of the demons, which we duly did. I asked for the connections between the sister and the two strangers to be broken and this was done. After this, the entities and spirit were removed from both the sister and her husband.

Clearly, this lady's sister has a great karmic lesson to learn with regard to jealousy. Nobody can teach her this lesson, she must learn it for herself in her own time, and then she can move on. Perhaps we have relieved some of the tension around her in this lifetime through removing the entities and spirit and breaking her connections with the dark forces which had been in place since her Victorian incarnation. Am I interfering in karma? No. I always ask "can we do this"? If for some reason we are not allowed, I then establish what the reason is. Sometimes we can do it later, or there might be other things we have to do first, or yes, it can be karmic, in which case I see if there is something we can do to help the person work out the karma. I can't read the future for this woman, but one hopes with the lightening up of her energy system, she may become more loving towards her sister and in time may begin to see the error in her life and change herself.

The connection between the lady and her sister at crown chakra level was still intact at this point and the Guides told me that this would be dismantled during the next twenty four hour period, as they wanted to do this at night while carrying out other helpful adjustments to the lady's energy system.

When this work was finished, I was very clear that this was the main problem area in this case. I returned to the house cleansing and removed the build-up of psychic energy, mainly from the upstairs. In essence this was a cleansing of her parents' vibrations more than anything else. I tuned-in to the spirit of the house and that of her deceased parents. I had earlier had some contact with the energy of her mother, which had told me that she and the lady's father had quite literally stepped outside, so the lady and her husband could take over the home. There was a strong energy of love which I found quite overwhelming to my emotions. The spirit of the house confirmed this to me in its own way. I was told that the lady and her husband were very welcome in this house and it was meant for them to be here. As soon as they accepted this was now their space, and adopted it as such, then they would both move forward in life.

Adopting one's parents' home is not easy for most people. There are memories and memorabilia of other peoples' lives all around you. Other peoples possessions are not your possessions and unless you love these objects yourself, you should cleanse them and get rid of them. Other peoples possessions hold their energy and if you are only keeping them for sentimental reasons or reasons of guilt, then they will add to your baggage and weigh you down. It's no good saying "Oh I can't get rid of this because Mum loved it so much", because Mum has moved on and does not need the attachment to physical objects any longer. To a certain degree, one has to be brutal and remove as much as you can, even though it can be painful in the case of parents. The house now has new inhabitants and in order to be totally at home, the essence of their individuality must be washed through this space. The spirit of the house understands this and it can be difficult to get an energy balance right without this 'energy spring clean' of sweeping out the old and bringing in the new.

To sum up this case, we see that I was brought in because the lady thought the house didn't want them, but in reality it was a case of psychic attack from an external source. Not just one source, but five sources, by virtue of the connections which had been built up. This was the very essence of this lady's discomfort in the house and the root cause of all her problems. In the matter of the house itself, the work I did was minimal in comparison to the level of psychic energy which had been targeted at the lady throughout her present life through psychic attack. Although in terms of vibrational cleansing, I did remove and change a large amount of energy in the house, allowing it to now breathe a little more easily, thus enabling the spirit of the house to get on with welcoming its new inhabitants.

## The Beech Woodland

This is not a case of psychic attack, however it is similar in some ways to the case above. This lady also called me in because she thought the house did not want the family in it. Although this investigation reveals a very different outcome to the one above, both cases show how sensitive the occupants were to the energies around them and the fact that indeed things were 'not right' in their environments. However, in both of these cases the house was not the problem.

I had a higher number of Guides present this day, which tells me something unusual, special or new is about to be revealed to me. The additional Guides present always seem to have skills in areas that I have not experienced before and wish to pass this knowledge on to me.

I arrived at the house, and had not been sitting in conversation with the lady for more than a few minutes when I had to say that I found it difficult to look at her. The energy coming across the table was too much for me, it was knocking me over. I immediately thought it was her energy. I tried to look her in the eyes and found it too difficult, all my senses were being saturated with energy. It was like trying to look directly into a bright winter sky and being unable to keep your eyes open against the glare. My immediate thought was that the energy was so powerful she must be a Scorpio and so I asked her what her sign was. She said Scorpio and then we had an interesting little conversation in which she told me that her husband was also a Scorpio and that they were both born on Halloween, but one year apart.

What was actually happening with the energy was somewhat different from my initial perceptions. The lady certainly did have that powerful, piercing Scorpionic energy but a great part of the energy which was knocking me over was coming from behind her, from outside across the drive in a beech woodland opposite. It was pure coincidence that she had positioned herself exactly between me and this woodland energy. Whatever was in that woodland was coming straight through her and overwhelming my perceptions. I remember sitting there as we talked and constantly glancing to my left, at the back door, my Guides saying to me "you have to go outside", and eventually we did.

Quite often a person is not really sure why they want me to 'have a look' at a house or a perceived problem, because they are not sure whether it might be their imagination, but I have always found a reason for what has been seen or perceived and it is usually something which can be dealt with. After some initial chatting around the things she felt were not right, she told me of a vision she had seen in the woodland. She had been working at the kitchen sink and gazing out of the window, when all of a sudden she saw something looking back at her, something gross, horrible and very dark natured! She was so shocked, she dropped her work and ran from the spot through the house. Whatever it was had been very frightening, unnerving her in an uncontrollable way and making her act completely out of character, for she is indeed a very grounded person with a strong constitution. As we approached the area in question, I could feel the energy of the place. It was pulling my solar plexus chakra right out. She told me that she was a photographer and had experienced many wonderful ethereal places around the world when composing pictures, but that she had never seen a place quite like this woodland for the strange light which seemed to emanate from it at sunset. There is a powerful reason why this is so.

There are a number of very powerful energy phenomena at this place. I pointed out to her the way the grass did not grow here. There is first of all a 'geo-spiral'. I could see the energy curving away from me. Tremendous power. I knew immediately that this was very special. A geo-spiral is also known as a water dome in America and this is the energy structure which is used by the Native Americans for their medicine wheel. It is the place used in many ancient cultures for their temple, just like Stonehenge. All true, original stone circles or rings are built on a geo-spiral, of which there are some 2000 or so in the British Isles alone.

The second phenomenon is a planetary gateway known as a Mars square or Mars Gate. The Devas of the plant kingdom have shown me the Saturn gates on a number of occasions and how to create and use them. The Mars gate is similar, but this is the first time I had been privileged to be shown how humans can use it to their advantage. The lady of the house had discovered its secret accidentally when she was gazing out of the window in a casual day dreamy state, probably something close to a meditational state. Her consciousness will have been in alpha state at that moment when her higher vision entered that other world through the Mars gate, where for an instant she saw a being, not of the physical realm.

## Later that Day:

The energy in this place was powerful. I had seen some special things here, but I knew that there was also something dark or unpleasant. I also knew I could not deal with it at that moment in time. The energy was too strong for my sensitivity. Not in a way which told me I couldn't deal with it, but in an awe inspiring way which was turning my intuition and perceptions inside out. It was spinning my focus and pulling me in all directions. This place is also mysterious but magical. I did not tell the lady about everything that was there, or that I couldn't deal with it right at that moment. I didn't want her to feel unsure or frightened. My Guides were so excited to share the secrets of this place with me but at the same time were telling me I was not allowed to tune-in here and now. It was as if I had to put a barrier or filter of time or space between myself and the energies before I was allowed to look in with my consciousness.

We left that area and spent a couple of hours looking at the rest of the house, detecting a few things here and there, but nothing too serious. I explained many things about how energy affects us and I think the lady was reassured when I departed. On the way back to the office, I was totally consumed by what I did not yet know about that beech woodland, but was certain to find out that evening.

I left the office early. I couldn't bear the suspense any longer and tuning in at the level which was required must be done in isolation, with no interruptions. After dinner, I found space and began to communicate with my Guides and dowse the beech woodland in question. I began by dowsing with my pendulum to tune my intuition and vision in. After a few initial questions the information began to channel through quite quickly. It began to flow so strongly that I abandoned the pendulum and typed it as it came through. Here is the story as it unfolds.

## Dowsing with Pendulum:

There are three spirits in this place (the woodland). The energy is all male. They are the spirits of three men. The most recent of the three has been here 462 years.

(I am beginning to receive the visual images now) I see they are Priests of some sort. They are practising dark magic. They are still active after all these years, still practising their work in this place.

When I was in the woodland I saw a planetary gate, the Guides tell me the planetary gate has nothing to do with the Priests. I check the family who live here to see are there are any influences upon them from the spirits of the Priests.

Of the two children, a girl and boy, the boy is influenced indirectly by the Priest's energy work. I see this will affect him on a subconscious level. All other members of the family are unaffected. The work of the priests is not aimed at the family or any people who occupy this space in the woodland or the house. The boy picks up these frequencies of energy because he is sensitive, quite intuitive and also deep. He probably picks it up mainly when sleeping or day dreaming. He may even see fleeting glimpses of faery-like things.

The Priests are locked in a time warp, making pacts and mixing concoctions and potions, working in league with the underworld. They have a connection with the underworld. This is not a demonic kingdom, but a place of underworld spirits and changelings. The time warp is such that they are unaffected by the changes of time. They do not notice that material things in the outside physical world have changed, they only see people as states of energy. However, it was their task to target people with their magic in their own lifetimes and so they continue targeting people in the present day. They are very active in their work.

**Channelled Information:**
The Priests were aware of my prying conscious presence amongst them. I was viewing them quite easily by now but still receiving the information from my Guides. A little bit of telepathic communication let me know that they had been content to allow me to see them and watch their labours from a distance, but now they broke through to speak directly to me.

*"This is a sacred spot. We have used it for thousands of years, as have our fathers and fore-fathers. We have a shaft to the underworld where there is dark power. We have been initiated into the 'Brethren', our colour is brown* (I see them in brown habits) — *brown for the earth which gives us our power, brown for the earthlings who confide in us."*

*"We are the performers of dark deeds. We work for the masters. We work for the masters both on earth and in the underworld. We have the keys to both doors. It is within our power to affect the lives of people, to bring to our masters the fruits of our labours. We bring to our masters power over their subjects, so that the subjects will bend to the will of our masters."*

*"This brings our masters great power, great energy over the people. We speak of our work in what you will call the medieval times, where carts were the transport. We influenced the crop in the field so that it was abundant, so that our master could take much tax from the land and grow wealthy."*

*"We are like the witches in your MacBeth. We do incantate and weave spells. You, David, had this knowledge once, you knew the dark side, you will know it again, you are deep, deeper than the ocean. The knowledge was yours and will be yours again, we will seduce you with the power. You will not be able to resist the tentacles of power."*

At this point I broke the connection and dowsed-in my Guides to check what I had channelled. These Priests were getting too close to me and I was experiencing their energy as if they were in my house. There was a menacing feel of increasing seductive power in their words to me. The energy of their transmission was building to a crescendo as I cut them off. It was very frightening to receive the force and power of their energy this close. These spirits indeed had great knowledge and power and were connected without doubt to forces which I had hitherto not experienced. Although I was disturbed, yet I had an inner knowing that my Guides would not have brought me to a situation that I could not deal with. As I have said many times before, the universe often sends a real challenge, but never something that is insurmountable.

My Guides confirmed that all the channelling so far was correct and told me that the Priests were just having a bit of fun at my expense and trying to frighten me. I can assure you, they did a good job.

Again I checked my protection with the Guides, who confirmed that it was adequate. I couldn't help feeling that they were having a bit of a laugh at my disquiet, knowing that their light was much more than a match for the Priests and their obvious abilities in the dark dance in which they participated. However, I was still a bit shaky, so I called on a few other friends just to make sure … "Lord Jesus Christ, Lord Sai Baba, Lord Buddha, Maitreya, Quan Yin protect me. Archangel Gabriel, put your shroud around me. My Guides, huddle close, gird up my loins, stand four square behind me and I will go forth in your name into the darkness to rid this place of peril".

"I am fortified by your presence and I give myself freely unto your care without fear for my own safety. Walk with me and guide me in our work of healing. Healing the planet and healing the people and healing across the boundaries of time and space. Walk closely by my side and I will do your work". (In hindsight these words seemed a bit over the top, but they did come automatically and so I left them here. At the time this was a very fearful place to be sitting, with my consciousness out on a limb in another dimension.)

"Priests, you may continue to tell your tale".

The communication resumed and the voice and energy of the channelled speaker changed completely, now to one of warm friendliness, very level tones but with the air of a caring tutor, very humane and almost with a fatherly kind of loving patience. Very safe and comforting.

*"For a thousand years and more, we have dwelt upon this place;* (speaking of his forebears) *it gives us access to the underworld. There is power here. There is your good power, which you have seen* (the earth energy radiations) *and there is also power we can use for our work".*

*"Your charge, the girl* (the lady of the house) *has seen things in this place. This was not of our making. We have no interest in these people. She only saw what is truth,* (the reflection of her sub-conscious self). *We see your thoughts and perceptions David as you send your mind into our space and we confirm that you are correct in your perceptions. This is a place of great power, for the visionquest as your people call it.* (This is

of course a reference to the Native American use of the water dome. Whether they read this through my consciousness or knew it otherwise I do not know for sure, but expect it was read through my consciousness. One cannot hide anything at this level of connection.) *This has been here many years, in your hundreds, some five hundred. It was placed here by the beings of the forest, the nature spirits as you say. The girl saw one, the brown dwarf. She was made afraid by his appearance, but he is only a spirit of the earth and brown is his colour. It is their place of power, it is their doorway, a doorway between worlds. They have used this doorway or portal to come and go from your world into their own. You call it a planetary square. It is Mars. It is the power of man, the male energy".*

*"You may gaze upon this place* (the planetary gate) *and it will show you who you are, it will reflect your personality. It will reveal all to those who have the courage to face themselves. You felt it pull at your heart when you were there. It takes your insides and shows them to you. Your subconscious mind, your deep secrets, your very essence, your spirit and soul. This is good power for those who would use it for themselves. It is not of a dark nature such as the energy with which we work. It is coincidence that it is here, near to us, but not coincidence for the other reasons which you know of David, for the things you saw and showed the girl".* (This is a reference to the geo-spiral).

*"We work in a different dimension to the beings who have created this portal. They built it here because of the other energy you found. Again you are right, you have seen it correctly for what it is, you will have great abilities to come. Your Guides had to switch off your perception to some degree, for you would have been overwhelmed by the power. The energy is what you call 'geo-spiral'. It is of great power. Your vision of standing stones here is good. The old ones would have used this place for stones,* (if they had known about it) *they knew this type of power was good and it helped their people in many ways. The seasons came and went and the energy was always there to guide them. It was their temple in other places, like the Henge of which you speak* (Stonehenge). *This power point was never used but it is significant. It is as powerful as the great Henge* (Stonehenge)".

*"The girl is opening,* (becoming more attuned to spiritual energy) *she perceives the energy but does not know it. Of course you know how it affects the light, you can see it with your gift of vision, it is the vertical columns of energy rising from the ground which you have seen. The energy works its magic and she perceives it as it affects the light. It is the living energy of the mother earth. Mother to Mother. The man* (the lady's husband, who at this time I had not met) *too is ready, they will be happy here, they are ready to feel the energies and live".*

At this point the Priests stopped speaking.

I now dowsed in the Guides again and asked what to do about the priests, whether to move them or leave them and was told to move them on. I was told that their work here was done, they had had their time and it is time for things to change.

I now set up with my Guides a process to take the priests from the physical realms into the astral. I decided to check this the next day and then see what needs to be done about the shaft to the underworld.

**The Following Day:**

I checked everything. The Priests had left, all influences over the boy had been negated. The Guides told me to leave the shaft open so that we could investigate it later, saying, "it will not be a problem to anyone. It was only operable by the Priests. Nothing can be brought through without the knowledge and power to connect and communicate".

**Later:**

The lady had invited me to come back any time to have another look at this spot and after a few weeks had passed I furnished her with the information I had found. I hadn't known how to approach the matter initially, but felt it was important that she know exactly what was happening outside her house. Furthermore, my Guides told me that it was appropriate to share these findings and assured me that she would not be frightened of the outcome, but would understand the process which was taking place. Therefore I sent a typescript of the above details and then later spent time with her and her husband showing them some of the energies. I explained what was happening through the Mars gate and how it had affected her.

Alpha state is the key to the door, so to speak, to enter the Mars gate with your mind. It is a portal that reflects your inner self, your subconscious mind. As the priest said, the very essence of your inner self, the self we usually never know. If you approach the gate in a meditative state, it will show you things about yourself which you might not want to see, but all it shows is the truth. The lady had a difficult issue to deal with and she had seen it reflected back to her through the Mars gate. At the same time she had seen the brown dwarf which had so frightened her. However, truth is knowledge and knowledge is power. We can use truth about ourselves to free us from things which hold us back. I believe the knowledge revealed to me of how to use the Mars gate is not currently known. I have been told that such things will be shown to me as the time is right for this information to be shared with those who will use it for spiritual evolution.

Finally, we have the shaft to the underworld. I have found many portals to different places, but not one such as this. I have peered into it but left it undisturbed for now until the time comes to investigate it further. It is not a place of demons but of a type of underworld being that in itself is not harmful, but possesses a knowledge of energies which can be used against mankind by those who have the ability to manipulate them through communication with these beings. All energy is just energy, it can always be utilised for positive as well as negative results.

I don't know whether there is anything else to be found here, but the potential of what has been found so far is great. The earth spirits and nature spirits would work in co-creation with people to develop this place as an energy centre to use for meditation, healing, purification, raising intuition, spiritual work and sharing some of the hidden secrets of the magic of the earth. Perhaps in the future the custodians of this magic place may develop its potential for themselves, as they develop spiritually.

The reader will note that I usually disguise the identities of my clients, as all responsible professionals would do. However, in a recent conversation with the 'Lord of this Manor', he pointed out the extremely important and necessary facet of his personality, which we call ego and its importance in regard to his professional status. An old soul without a doubt and very intuitive and tuned-in, he is bringing through his past life knowledge and evolving spiritually very quickly. Leaning supportively towards his ego's desires, while maintaining a reasonable confidence, I would say he is one Healer everybody should make an effort to see! Will this do Johnny?

## A Complexity of Problems, plus The Sleeping Sickness!

This is the interesting case of a gentleman who first came to see me a number of years ago. He had been attacked by something in the night when he was six years old which had dragged him out of bed and damaged his energy system enormously. He had suffered ever since and when grown up he had been to see many healers and spiritual workers over the years to get help, but always his condition seemed to revert to one of desperation soon after receiving treatment. He found it very difficult to venture out of his home and got very little sleep at night. His condition was so bad that he had retired from work some eighteen years previously, in his early thirties, and spent most of his time looking for help and trying to develop spiritually through prayer and other means.

At first I thought his case was straightforward. It looked like a case of entity attack, entities certainly being present the first time I saw him, plus a severely damaged aura. On the first session, we removed the entities and repaired the aura. The Guides told me there was more work to do and he should return in a week.

When he arrived he told me that his condition was much improved but that he was again having problems. When I looked into him, indeed he had suffered more entity attack, although the aura was still intact. I removed the entities again and also found an extra-terrestrial lodged in his arm. I removed this. We did some more vibrational healing and tuned up the chakras a little. Again, the Guides told me to bring him back again the following week. This was very unusual, as at this time, I rarely saw people more than once for energy system work, unless they were very badly damaged.

On the next visit, again he had picked up more entities, yet the aura was still intact and I couldn't find any place where he might be leaking light which would attract them, or allow them to gain entry to his system. However, clearly there was something very wrong with this man's energy system. Entities don't keep attacking, in my experience, unless they can detect light energy escaping from a person's energy system. So, I had to work harder to find out what was happening, not knowing where to begin.

I tuned-in to his chakras in a clairvoyant sense as opposed to clairscentient mode, and began dowsing, asking questions and asking for guidance to solve the riddle of why he was continually attacked. After some half hour or so, I was getting a picture that there was an energy control system malfunction. I was being shown that the base chakra was receiving a programmed signal every night at about 2.00 am which opened it up automatically and sent a beam of light out through the crown chakra, literally into space. I had never seen anything like this before and so didn't know what to do about it. We spent about another hour looking into the problem and I asked for guidance to remove the program which was causing this automatic chakra opening. We did some guided vibrational work and I was told that this particular problem was now repaired. Again, the Guides told me that the gentleman needed to come back again the following week. I had never seen a client this many times before, and wondered what difficult task was in store for us later. These days I would have probably solved this problem much quicker, as I can now see into chakras more easily.

When he arrived the following week, he told me that he had been much improved and had slept quite well for the first time in years. I looked into his condition, and for the first time there were no entities and the aura was still intact. He had seen many other healers over the years who I am sure all cleared him of the entity problem. But without detecting the chakra problem, all their good work was being undone almost immediately. Real progress at last. However, that morning my Guides had been giving me the same message over and over again that what I had to do today was just sit opposite him on a chair and do nothing.

I told him this and said I didn't know what we were to do but this is what I was told. We duly got ourselves comfortable and I began to tune myself in with a pendulum, but all my signals were blocked. I became tremendously tired, to the point where I couldn't fight my awakened state any longer. I felt the vibrations of active Spirit Guides and noticed that my client could not keep his eyes open either. We both lost consciousness within minutes and did not come round for almost an hour and a half. Clearly, the Guides had taken control of this situation and 'put us out'. Very unusual and quite disturbing in a way. We were both completely wiped out and it took us a good twenty minutes to come round. I said, "I don't know what that was all about, do you?" He answered that he did not know either, but that it felt as if a lot of work had been done on him. I said that I also felt that I had been worked upon and I dowsed that this was correct. This became a regular thing and for the most part during these sessions, the Guides tell us nothing, although over a period of time they have given us pieces of the jigsaw, which overall, make an interesting picture.

Firstly, this man had been a powerful energy worker in a previous, extra-terrestrial existence. This was mainly the reason for the attack upon him as a child. He was a member of a team of three and each of them had individual skills in harnessing and balancing energy on an inter-planetary scale.

After some weeks of treatment I was told that it was almost time for the other two of his companions to re-establish contact, as we had achieved so much repair on many levels. I always dowsed to see at what level of his being we had been working and it was often at a very high spiritual level, but at the same time upon most of the lower self and higher self too. This day arrived about two weeks later and we were introduced to two beings called Dar and Simeon, his previous partners. It was an emotional time.

During these healing sessions of sitting opposite each other, a pattern developed. We sat down and usually within four to five minutes we were both completely unconscious in a very deep place. On some occasions we knew for certain that out of body experiences had taken place, often with the result that we were unbalanced within our auras on return. It usually lasted between an hour and an hour and a half. I usually came round about five minutes before him and it was nearly always the case that he was still being worked upon, but the Guides were winding down from whatever they had been doing on me. The vibrations in the healing room were nearly always very tangible. Sometimes the vibrations were so strong, the whole room would feel as if it was in motion, but for the most part the only information we got was that we were both being worked upon and we should continue the sessions.

Over the months he developed very good dowsing ability through energy pattern transference from myself and a number of Spirit Guides had joined him to help his progress. Also, other members of his family became very tuned-in and developed good dowsing skills also.

On one occasion I received the following information ... "48 Guides present. Jesus and some other beings". I had never had the presence of Jesus with me at a healing session to my knowledge. In fact, I suppose I had never seen myself worthy of asking for such a high authority. Although when working with demons I have asked for the protection of the 'energy of Jesus' sometimes. The message was very forthright and candid and so I mentioned to my client that I had been told that Jesus was here working with us today. To my amazement, he replied, "He was here last week too. Ask and you will see". I did ask and was told that this was so. Since this time I have had Jesus with me on a number of occasions. I never ask for his assistance and I never tell my clients if he has been with us, for it feels a little pretentious to me.

The forthright and authoritarian voice continued. "Today's healing will be extra-terrestrial work. We may not be working on Dave, depending on how much we achieve. Dar and Simeon are here. Today: rebuilding connections with Dar and Simeon".

After an hour or so of the usual 'sleeping sickness', my client was still deeply unconscious and I received a lot of vibrations telling me to tune-in for a message for him. The message was from Dar and Simeon.

*"We know you have not been well. At last you have found someone who can help you. Many things will begin to change for you now."* (Indeed many things had changed for him already and for me also.)

*"Of course, we cannot work together as we used to do, but you will learn and be able to do many things with your dowsing. David is a good teacher. He is patterning you with his abilities through you being in the presence of his energy field. As he progresses, so will you. This is why you are both being worked on. David will develop new skills, mainly in healing and spiritual connections, and these vibrations will pass to you through him, to unfold your own abilities. We cannot do this directly with you, it has to go through David as you come for the healing sessions".*

*"We are helping both of you. David's skills are in healing, but you will develop different skills, skills in communication across the boundaries of worlds. This is what we have been helping you to achieve today: reconnecting you. You had to undergo much repair until you reached a stage where we could help and this has been taking place now for a few of your visits to David".*

*"We visit you at home and check on you, but we cannot do much to help you directly at this time. The time will come when this will be so. You still have a long way to go. There is more healing to take place, and as the healing progresses your skills will develop. You will be able to speak with us directly when this is done and we will be able to tell you more about who you are".*

*"It is not for us to tell you through David, but he is a key element in your advancement and repair. He has done you much good, if only he knew".*

*Dar and Simeon*

Since this time, he has developed regular communication with Dar and Simeon through his dowsing. Other parts of his previous life in that other dimension have also become clear. His family tell me the changes in him have been dramatic and for the most part now he can lead a more balanced sort of life. The sessions of our 'Sleeping Sickness' continued weekly for the best part of two years. My client made much progress during this time and eventually reached a point where he and his family were contacted by an extremely high being. Referred to as 'Sir', this being has brought much guidance to my client and his family and has also helped me on a couple of occasions when I have needed some answers to difficult cases. It is good to know that confirmation can be obtained from another source when needed.

## Another Case of The Sleeping Sickness

When doing distance clearance work on spirits and entities, I may lose consciousness for up to half an hour, the energy drain is so great. During the clearance of particularly heavy Geopathic energies in houses can have a similar effect on me. Frequently, when working with a client in vibrational healing for either spiritual advancement or deep healing of the subtle energy system, the energy exchange and interaction becomes so great that I can lose consciousness for five or ten minutes as very powerful change takes place within the client at the peak of the session. In Geopathic Stress work, when working with nature spirits and earth consciousness and releasing the earth of toxic vibrations, I sometimes lose consciousness for a half hour or so at the crucial energy release stage. However, on a one to one basis, when not actually using energy tools or in the process of any form of healing, 'the sleeping sickness' has only happened on one other occasion, when a very good friend and healer was visiting us one day.

Alan is a very powerful and talented healer who is unfolding very quickly. He also does quite a bit of work in the psychic rescue field. We first got to know each other after I had done the *Housebusters* TV Series on Channel 5, when he contacted me to say that he thought they had problems in the house with spirits. From the time I first went to visit Alan and his partner Ann, they have both developed in spiritual and intuitive terms. After Alan had visited us one afternoon at our home, I received a message to teach him to dowse. I introduced him to the pendulum and gave him instruction in the basics of dowsing. As we were engaged in this work, I received a message that there was a Spirit Guide waiting to communicate with Alan. I channelled a short message through and introduced Alan to Ronaldo, an Italian Spirit Guide. The whole process took about a half hour.

Alan took to the dowsing like the proverbial duck to water. Within a few weeks he was communicating with a good handful of Guides, most of whom were Italian. I joked with him that it seemed that he had landed himself a Mafia family with powerful connections, one of his Guides being an ex-banker. It wasn't long before Alan had dozens of Guides working with him and he was tackling very powerful entities in his work. In fact, all this evolutionary progress had unfolded for him in a little over a year. Alan is a natural born healer, he was just waiting for that catalyst to switch his energy system on.

Coming back to the open day at the studio, the guests had by this time all gone and there were only Ann and Denise, Alan and myself left. Alan and I were sat on the sofa chatting, when all of a sudden I saw a tremendous amount of energy, like blue and yellow flames, shooting out of a large Russian quartz crystal point. I interrupted Alan to point it out, saying "look at that Alan, can you see the energy shooting out of that crystal?" At the same time I reached out and picked it up to pass to him. As I was passing it across, I was being completely knocked out, I couldn't keep my eyes open at all and by the time he had taken it from me, which was perhaps no more than four or five seconds from me picking it up, I was almost unconscious. I remember hearing his voice as he took it, but could not make out the words.

The next thing I knew, it was about forty minutes later and I was coming round again. Alan was coming round at the same time. The girls joked with us about snoring our heads off and said we'd been asleep for ages. Alan told me that as I passed him the crystal, he had said to me that he couldn't keep his eyes open and within seconds had lost consciousness. By this time, I had recognised the symptoms of the Guides taking us out of our consciousness so that work could be done on us, and I explained this to Alan.

It worries many people when I tell them about this kind of process, because one does not have control; but I have to say that I've got used to it and suffer no ill effects other than the usual tiredness which occurs when working with the energies of powerful spiritual forces. People think that it can't be right that there are forces out there that can take control of you at will without one's ability to stop it. Well, I'm not sure that I couldn't stop it if I wanted to, I probably could. The way I look at it is this: I pray constantly for guidance and help in my healing work and I know that help is given me in many different ways. If this is one way my prayers are being answered then I am very grateful for the assistance I am receiving. It certainly has the desired effects.

This has happened so many times, and I have analysed the situation and details so many times, that I know for sure that I am being worked upon at many levels of my being in a positive way. I know that the Guides take the opportunities to help as they arise. On this particular occasion, there was clearly an opportunity for them to help both of us, while we sat in conversation together. Different people have different energies and these energies can act as catalysts to help others. In this instance Alan probably holds energies which can be used by the Guides to help me, and vice versa. The same applies to my client mentioned previously. He has progressed immeasurably during our sessions and I know that I continue to unfold at the same time. Shortly after this incident, Alan developed an ability for spirit to communicate directly through him on a verbal level. They come in through his ear and speak through his mouth, bypassing his mind and brain consciousness. I'm not saying that this one session brought this about directly, as there are many things taking place which help us, but I am certain that he was helped in a powerful way by the process.

I know from experience that I am very much a catalyst for many peoples' spiritual or healing change, merely by them being in my energy field. Was it that I was called by Alan in the first place to check out his house merely to clear it of entities, or were there other universal forces in work that brought us together so that my energies could begin his unfolding process? It may seem egotistical to think this, but as I say, from many experiences, I have seen people begin to open on many different levels after being in my energy. In the same way, it would appear that when I am within the energy field of certain other people and the timing and conditions are right, then the Guides take that opportunity to help us both by whatever means are at their disposal. In this instance putting us both into a state of unconsciousness and either connecting something which was ready or fine tuning some connection which was already functioning at a lower level. Who can say what they did with any certainty, because we don't understand the many ways communication and energy work in the realms of light.

If you think this is unusual, I refer you to Edgar Cayce, who spent the last twenty-three years of his life giving readings from a sleeping or unconscious state. Nobody has done more to advance the understanding of reincarnation and the karmic consequences of past life behaviour, as well as many other aspects of the healing process, than Cayce in his readings. It is interesting to note that this state of trance, or unconsciousness also drained Cayce, and almost certainly shortened his life.

## Serpent-like Demon

This lady had been suffering from general energy depletion and was going through a difficult time emotionally. I began to tune-in to her and could see that there was a great deal of stress which manifested in the upper torso, particularly in the lungs. She had been suffering from a lung infection for several weeks which she couldn't shake off, and was currently taking anti-biotics. I could see within her energy that her emotional state was contributing to the stress in her system.

I asked to be shown the aura and was denied permission. Strange, I thought, why am I not allowed to see into the aura? There must be something I've not seen yet or something hiding. I didn't expect to find anything unusual with this lady, as I thought her problems were just energy system blockages. However, upon tuning in very carefully I discovered a demon. It was hiding in the solar plexus chakra. I checked for entities, spirit attachments etc., and found nothing else hiding in her. I checked for damage to the aura, and this was intact. So far, so good.

Things had taken a slow start to this case and I was being quite cautious. Perhaps my subconscious was telling me something which I was not entirely picking up.

Serpent-like demon over 3ft long dwelling in solar plexus chakra.

When I began to concentrate on the demon, slowly, but deliberately, it pushed upwards into her heart chakra. The lady could feel it moving. I picked up a few of his motives and discussed these with her. I asked was she having thoughts which didn't quite seem to be hers, which she was. The demon seemed to prey on her fears. If she had the tiniest doubt about anything, the demon would pick up on this negative energy and amplify it, so that her slightest fear became a powerful force of negativity, undermining her confidence in everything she did. It was also very manipulative in many other aspects of her life.

As I tuned-in a bit at a time, trying to get the measure of it without putting myself in danger or opening myself too much, I could see that it was not evil, although it did have a darkish side. I could detect that it could be reasoned with and thought there was a good possibility it could be turned back to the light and re-programmed to respect other beings.

As my vision became more attuned, I could see it in the heart chakra, but became aware that it was also still occupying the solar plexus. I concentrated a little more and could see that it had a large round head and a long, fat tail. It wasn't putting up a fight, but at the same time, it wasn't ready to vacate her body either. I felt that we might be in for a long and tedious sit in.

In a situation like this, the only thing one can do is make contact with the consciousness of the being and maintain this link in a kind of tug-o-war stance. Holding the conscious space of the demon, so that it can't move, but not giving any of your own ground. It's a bit of a head to head to see who gives up first. So I take the position of 'you can't stay in here, you have to leave' and they are usually taking the stance of 'I'm not going anywhere'. The pressure on the mind can become quite stressful, but I can't let go as ground may be lost and I may have to start all over again.

It had begun to slither and slide a little. She could now see it in her mind's eye, which of course is reality, and asked was it green and slimy. "Yes", I replied, it was a kind of dark greeny black with what appeared to be a mid-green coloured slime surrounding it. This looked like a lubricant for it to slither on. I first thought that it was going to exit through the heart chakra, but it had merely taken up residence there and seemed to be keeping its head down, hoping I would go away.

I kept the mind pressure on it, and its body, which was still in the solar plexus chakra, started to squirm. It was then that I could see that it was a long, very fat tail, coiled like a snake. It looked too big to be accommodated within the chakra. I continued the telepathic communication of encouraging it to relinquish its hold. As the pressure continued, the Lady began to smell a foul odour of cooking. I couldn't smell it as it was probably only accessible within her being. As the work progressed, she told me that the odour increased in intensity.

The movement in the solar plexus increased and I thought that perhaps it was going to leave her system through this chakra now, rather than the heart. Its tail began to unfurl and it pushed it downwards, through the sacral chakra and then the base chakra. It felt to me as it must feel when one is giving birth. It was a very fat energy pushing down. It unfolded and extended as far downwards as her knees. I asked her could she feel where it was and she could feel it exactly where I could see it. I now thought that maybe he was going to leave through the base chakra.

She was becoming very nauseous and I could feel it too. It was like a thick coating of slime in the throat, and the demon was making both of us salivate a lot as it squirmed around. She still had the obnoxious smell in her nostrils too.

The demon was beginning to feel a little uncomfortable as I held my ground. It maintained this new position for around twenty minutes and then the centre of his body/tail began to lift out of the solar plexus chakra, dragging his head backwards out from the heart chakra and the rest of his tail back up through the base and sacral chakras. It seemed that once it had become uncoiled, it had lost its ability to hang on in there.

Once the demon was removed, there was much more work to do to repair this lady's energy system. She told me that the foul odour had left her about the time the demon left. However, as the energy drain on both of us had been fairly heavy, my guides would only let me use a few essences to help dissolve the energy of the slimy mess left by the demon. They advised that her energy system needed time to process the changes and recover its natural balance and then we could work again in a couple of months time.

Demonic beings come in all shapes and sizes. This was the first time I had seen this serpent-type of being. It had a large round head which appeared to have sticky fins on the sides which helped it to move through energy fields. The body was around three and half feet in length and about three to four inches in diameter all the way to its tail. All in all, this was quite a large being to have living inside you. No wonder this lady was feeling depleted of her energy.

## Psychic Attack and Possession

This is a classic case of a very proficient and experienced energy worker, who did nothing careless whilst practising her healing work, but who was not sufficiently informed to know what was happening when things began to go wrong.

She is a Reiki Master with advanced intuitive and mediumistic skills, has created some very powerful energy tools for dispelling negative earth forces and also possesses dowsing skills. She had called me in because she had experienced a number of problems with her work and her energy. Most recently she had felt she had become possessed by some force, probably a spirit.

I began by assessing what was inside her energy system. I found eight entities and one spirit, a male. At first sight this case looked straightforward, but often things are not as they seem. She was actually possessed by the spirit. This is important knowledge, because often spirits are only in attendance near the person, or occasionally attached to the outside of the aura of the person. To be possessed, the spirit must be inside the aura. At this level it can do much more harm and also influence the personality of the person. For the spirit to enter the aura, there must be fairly severe damage to the outer fabric. The next question we must ask is, how did the aura get damaged and when?

I established, with the help of my Guides that this girl's problems began about five years previously, some time after taking a Second Degree Reiki attunement. I could not find anything wrong with any of her attunements or indeed with any work she had subsequently done which may have caused the problem. This was a case which began very simplistically with the picking up of a single entity. Because the start of this problem goes back so far in time, it is fairly pointless trying to pin down whether the entity came from a client, or whether it just attached itself to her energy because she may have been a little too open and therefore shining too brightly or 'leaking light'. It doesn't really matter which at this stage. It is noteworthy, though, that she subsequently took her Reiki Third Degree attunement without her Reiki Master detecting the problem, which could have been devastating for either this lady or anyone else present during the attunement process, because at the moment of attunement the energy transference is tremendous and the auras of all the participants are fully opened up. This amount of energy can provide tremendous power to an entity in an instant and give them the strength to do much damage. Fortunately it would appear that this chap was only small fry.

Any form of 'light being' possesses a magnetic force of attraction, and once an entity attaches to you, whether within the chakra system or on the outside of the aura, this magnetic force can attract similar beings towards itself. It is the thin end of the wedge, so to speak. If the entity is not removed, then the problem will not go away but will escalate as other entities join in the feeding from the person's energy system. Sometimes this escalation is very quick and sometimes, as in this case, it can take a considerable length of time, dependent upon the circumstances, nature and power of the entity present. The important thing to note is that the girl's energy system has been compromised for almost five years.

During the years following on from the time she picked up the first entity, one at a time she accumulated more, until she reached a point where the outer fabric of the aura became damaged. By this stage, her energy system would have been causing her a lot of problems, in particular causing her to be unbalanced, too open to a certain degree and unable to hold energy. The increasing damage situation began to accelerate about four months prior to my seeing her. Approximately five weeks prior to my seeing her she picked up the spirit, which possessed her.

I began work by creating an energy grid around her and, working with my Guides, we began to remove the entities. Once this process had begun and my Guides continued with the work, I started to concentrate on the spirit which was possessing her. I identified the damage point within the aura and then began tuning my consciousness into the spirit. At this point things took an unusual turn. The deeper my consciousness probed, the more I was picking up the emotions of anger and fear, simultaneously. Emotions were being driven at me directly, with some force. I pushed in deeper and the resistance grew stronger. It didn't feel 'right' at all. I had never experienced emotions with so much energy behind them before, certainly not contradictory ones such as anger and fear together.

I checked my protection and carried on. At this point I received a name for the spirit. He was called Harald and at the same time the girl told me he was from Austria, which I then confirmed. Harald had been a murderer and was very confused. It was as if he had been fed information which was in opposition to what I was telling him, which essentially was that he would not be punished for his crime. I could feel via his emotions that whatever I told him about what was awaiting him if he came out from within this lady's aura, he did not believe. I just couldn't move him out of the aura at all. I had spent some 15 to 20 minutes trying to persuade him to come out and at this point, my Guides brought in two other spirits, who I established, had also been murderers. This was done to help convince Harald that everything was as I had said and that these other spirits had not suffered retribution for their acts of malice.

I left the situation in abeyance for a time whilst I attended to the energy grid and added a few more crystals and essences. I checked on the progress of the entities, the removal of which was now about half completed and I looked into the hole in the aura and made some assessments. Something was not right with this case, I thought yet again, there is something I'm not seeing. Something which does not want to be found.

I tuned-in again to Harald and he was still not for moving. I pushed my consciousness inside the aura again very carefully, with my full awareness on alert, when I received what can only be described as a kick in the abdomen. It came with such force as to lift me off the chair a little way as I let out a startled groan. This was a bolt of energy which had hit me in the sacral chakra and had been directed very specifically at me by some being inside this girl's aura. As I tried to perceive what was happening, the emotions of fear and anger which were coming from within her aura became really strong and I was kicked again a number of times. A new experience this, and so I pulled back my consciousness again and checked my protection. I left things on this front for a moment and again went back into the consciousness of the entities, who were by now all removed.

The Guides often don't give me information until I ask, because this is how they train me to be vigilant and inquisitive, but by now I was getting very suspicious. It doesn't take a great deal of effort to convince a spirit who is trapped in the physical realm, that there is a better place for them to be. I don't force them out, I let them decide for themselves, based on the information I give them, and in this case the Guides had also brought additional help to convince Harald that things were fine. So I started asking a few questions.

It didn't take me long to find the answer. The girl was not only possessed by Harald, but hiding behind his personality was a demon. As soon as I discovered him the whole energy picture changed. Harald, who was being held hostage and manipulated by the demon, was released immediately. It became abundantly clear that the emotion of fear being displayed was Harald's, as he was being threatened by the demon should he so much as move an inch towards his freedom. The emotion of anger was from the demon, as he defiantly tried to avoid my intervention. The kicking I had received in my energy system was of course the demon trying everything within his power to put me off the trail. To release this amount of energy in several bursts must have depleted him a fair amount I thought, but also showed how much power he had to spare, while still holding a hostage.

Once the game was up and I had seen the demon, it was not too difficult to deal with him, although I did have to bring about a new level of energetic power to show our little friend that he was no match for the forces of light. However, in this kind of situation, one has to maintain a very calm but powerful energy. Once contact has been made directly, then there is usually a stand-off between myself and the opposing party, whilst they try to show me how powerful they are, make various threats against me and generally try to undermine my position by whatever means is at their disposal. At the moment my consciousness saw the demon, I closed down part of my energy so he could not feed from me, but maintained my focus upon him, unmoved behind an energy shield of total calm. If, at this point, there was the slightest display of doubt or fear on my part, the demon's energy would prevail over my own and he would gain energy from me, which would put him in a more commanding position. However, in this case, he soon realised that the game was up, and my Guides wrested him from this situation and he was duly dispatched to where he belonged. This scenario raised a lot of questions and if one does not get answers to these, then one does not learn and hence move forward.

I have mentioned the forces of darkness and the forces of light and how, when we are little tiddlers in the great pool of energy, we don't make many waves and hence don't draw attention to ourselves. In this case, the girl was a powerful energy worker with a lot of esoteric knowledge. She had been deliberately targeted by the dark side and as soon as those entities had created a little hole in her aura, the demon was in there like a shot.

The next thing he had to do was get some other guys to do his dirty work, so he kidnapped the spirit of the murderer, Harald. The demon was clever and good at concealment and disguise. I hadn't spotted him when I started the job and the girl hadn't known he was there either. However, when he brought in Harald, she had detected this presence immediately. The job of this demon was to bring in as many harmful energies as he could to bring a living hell to this girl. In this case, the demon seemed to have the power to neutralise any protection she tried to create. All over her flat she had drawn Reiki symbols on paper for protection. All of these had been completely neutralised. His main objective was to bring in spirits which were powerful enough to affect her personality. One at a time these would have made her weaker, to the point where she would succumb to their every desire. These desires ultimately would be to deliberately undermine her light work and to bring her into a position of submission, culminating in the use of her skills and energy in acts that would serve the dark side more than the light.

## Attack from Various Sources

In this next case, the lady had suffered for more than 20 years from many energy system problems. It had begun when she was 18 years old with a mystery illness which doctors could not diagnose. She had also more recently been diagnosed with M.E., which was incorrect, although her energy was very low; but this was due to being drained from a number of different sources.

When I first spoke to the lady on the telephone, my Guides had told me that this case would be a real challenge and far from straightforward. I would only see the real picture as I cleared some of the energies. There would be a number of hidden aspects to be discovered.

Attempting this kind of job is like trying to climb an unfamiliar mountain. It can be tremendously hard work, every time you crest an almost insurmountable peak, another peak appears on the horizon, with the summit forever out of reach. It is very draining and sometimes strains me to the limit of total exhaustion.

In the days before the lady come for treatment, as is often the case after someone contacts me with this type of problem, things around her home got much worse, culminating in her husband phoning to ask for protection for her. She was very nervous and frightened. As soon as my consciousness is sensed by the invading parties, they know that things are about to change. Of course, fear makes them react and so they take as much energy in as they can find and use it to make as much mischief as possible. In this case, amongst other things, the ignition failed on two cars, a very effective way of making sure that people don't arrive for treatment. Fortunately, her husband was able to take another vehicle from the car pound at his place of work.

The lady duly arrived with her husband and I began by taking some notes. I knew we were dealing with 7 entities and at least one demon, if not more, to start with. I allowed my consciousness to tune-in at different levels while she was talking to me. There were three particular aspects which were very disturbing to her. Firstly, she had been suffering from outbursts of terrible anger and foul language for years, over which she appeared to have no control. The second aspect was that she had been hearing crying and wailing voices very clearly in her head, which fortunately she could switch off before they drove her mad. Thirdly, there was a very specific voice which came through and tormented her.

As I began to work, I was guided to deal with a demon first of all, so that we could eliminate this energy connection from the picture completely. I found him without too much trouble and it was interesting to note that I had ten more Guides working than usual. The little demon had decided to move in with the lady's mother for the day, rather than accompany her to see me. This is not unusual, as they will try anything to avoid capture. I sensed that he was more mischievous than evil and as soon as I had made a strong link with him the Guides took over and despatched him to where he could do no more harm.

In the meantime, the voice was having plenty to say to her, including "he'll never find us". Using the word us, he had given me another clue that we were looking for more than one demon! This type of challenge is to be expected, for they will do anything to undermine the confidence in one's ability and therefore remain free. However, this challenge was accompanied by a large bolt of energy which was hurled into me and upset the balance of my solar plexus and sacral chakra and knocked me off balance for about five minutes. Unmoved, I held my ground and reminded them that their darkness was no match for the powers of light which were in attendance.

As I tuned-in to focus on the next obstacle, I discovered a whole raft of lost souls which were being controlled by a very nasty and powerful entity, all black legs and claws, with gnashing teeth. The whole of this group seemed to be assembled within a tube or tunnel like structure which held them captive. This was linked into the lady's aura at the back of the head. The tube had one end sealed, with the other end at the head opened into her consciousness, so that the wailing of these poor souls could be heard more or less constantly. The entity was situated close to the head end of the structure, acting as gate keeper and making sure that the wailing could be heard.

There were 63 lost souls here, and as I perceived them in more detail I saw that they were in a terrible state of despair. The emotion from them was very tangible and I explained to the lady what I could feel from them, asking did she ever feel this type of despair, and the answer was yes. If you can imagine a ship going down with the souls trapped within the ship's structure, unable to escape, wailing and crying out in their desperation and misery, being able to see out, but not be seen, then this was the picture which was being constantly channelled into this lady's mind. It was enough to send anyone over the edge, which speaks volumes for her strength.

We dealt with the entity and left the souls alone to observe us for a while. Soon it became clear that they were indeed very traumatised and needed help to make their transition into the astral realms. The Guides undertook this work, and even with much encouragement and love, they were still very unsure of their future. Eventually all souls were saved and transported through the veil to safety.

At this point I put the lady on the couch to deal with the seven entities and carry out some energy system repair work. This took about an hour, and in between attending to essences and energy tools I was trying to locate the next stage in this jigsaw puzzle. Eventually we cut this session short as the lady began to feel very sick from the entity removal and also very cold from the energy pattern detox. Being clairsentient, I was also feeling the sickness too. However, I had received enough information to tackle the next stage and so she sat up for a while as I foraged once more into the unknown with my mind.

The next little chap we met up with was in the classification of extra-terrestrial. This is always an emotive subject and you cannot be sure what you are dealing with at certain levels of existence or reality. Therefore, I have to put a label on it so that I can identify with something a little more tangible. If it is not an entity, spirit or demon and it doesn't come from any dimension where I know these energy forms to associate, and I ask does it originate from a dimension outside of the physical realm and the answer is yes, then I call it extra-terrestrial. Extra-terrestrial just means outside the realm of the earth of course. This little chap was quite firmly rooted in the physical dimension, but was a trans-dimensional being, that is, he can exist in more than one dimension at once, although in this instance he was only really in the physical, but only visible at a light level.

I called mentally across time and space for my friend Jahl, who also comes under the classification of E.T., to help with the clearance of this little chap. He didn't seem to be too rooted in the here and now and put up no resistance to being moved back into his own dimension. I asked Jahl was he from his dimension, to which the answer was no. I asked was Jahl familiar with this type of being, and the answer was yes. I asked was there something I could do for Jahl in return, to which the answer was yes. Could I telephone a mutual friend as she was in need of some help. And so I had another job to fit into the busy schedule, but I didn't mind in the least as Jahl's help and friendship are most valuable to me.

Once the E.T. was out of the way, I looked into what he had been doing. It appeared that he was acting according to his own agenda and was not linked at all with any of the other goings on we had discovered. It seemed that he was channelling off energy into a kind of power store or power station to be used for some purpose which I did not explore, my own level of energy reserves becoming of some concern by this time. At this point I put the lady back onto the couch and powered up the energy tools again to where we had left off and the Guides dismantled energy attachments from the area of her left shoulder blade, which had been created by the extra-terrestrial chap.

Now it was time for a review of where we were up to and what we could now see. All the seven entities had been removed, plus the extra one who was controlling the lost souls, the last of which had now been saved. The original demon had been despatched and the E.T. had also been removed from the scene. The energy picture was changing dramatically. I assessed that we only had one more aspect to find and deal with, if things were what they seemed, which frequently with energy work they are not. At this point, I thought we should discontinue the work for today. We had taken around three and half hours and clearly the lady was very drained from the experience, as well as being nauseous and cold. Coldness is usually a sign that many energy blockages have been removed. I was pretty worn out too. As I told her my thoughts, she confirmed that she still had the same old voice in her head, laughing and persisting that I would never find it. We concluded the session and after her husband had taken the lady home, my Guides considered that we should tackle the next aspect now, while I was still in tune, even though my energy was very low.

The Guides were telling me to look carefully now, into the woman's energy system as she was travelling home with her husband, a trip of some two hours. I soon located the demon and I could see why he was so adamant that I would not be able to find him. He was jumping between the emotional body within the lower self, through the mind bridge and into the higher mental body, which is outside the physical dimension. Again, this demon was quite small and very mischievous, but active enough to cause some real problems to anyone who was his host. I spent some time in conscious connection with him, surrounding him in energy. He put up enough of a struggle to render me unconscious for a half hour or so, but upon regaining consciousness my Guides had me create a box out of light into which they placed him, most unceremoniously, and shipped him off to wherever they thought fit.

The final part of the puzzle for the day was to dismantle the energy structure which held the lost souls and this was a straightforward exercise which the Guides performed that same evening with the help of my energy and conscious focus. All in all this job had taken about five hours. However, I was not convinced that all was restored to its natural state. I knew this final demon was not the one who was communicating with the lady, he was more mischievous than dangerous and the demon who was so confident of avoiding detection was very controlling. This was confirmed when I contacted the lady a couple of days later. She told me that she was much better, but that she still had a demon present who was taunting her with "David thinks he's so clever, but he'll never find me".

Let's address that statement. Firstly, I don't think I'm 'so clever', because this would be a display of ego and anyone who knows anything about energy work will tell you that ego only deludes and undermines one's position. Secondly, ego both contains and releases energy which will only provide a feast for the entity which one is dealing with and will make it's subsequent efforts of resistance stronger. Thirdly, ego is claiming power for oneself, but when one understands where the 'power' or 'help' comes from, one also knows that it can be taken away again very quickly. Rule number one: don't ever think you are clever or powerful doing this type of work because you are not; and more importantly, you don't do it alone.

In a case of demonic possession, we are dealing with beings who will lie, cheat, hide wherever they can to avoid being seen, and even do their best to attack you and damage your energy system. This was one such case. Every time I thought I had the final measure, there was always another demon ready to cause the lady problems.

A few weeks passed before we could continue the work, and in the intervening period the remaining demon had taunted her and caused her to succumb to a state of extreme fear and anxiety. In desperation she had telephoned me. I checked all our previous work, which I confirmed had remained robust and intact. My Guides told me that she had not picked up anything else in the intervening period, which also showed that her aura was strong. Everything the demon was telling her was completely untrue. He was merely trying to undermine her confidence and recovery, which of course served his agenda.

When the lady arrived for the next session, we sat down to review the situation. I had been very concerned about the outcome of this case, as the Guides had told me in the beginning that it would be tough, and so far it had been. However, they also told me I could do it and so I did my best to remain confident if a little unsure of what lay ahead. I prayed fervently for many nights, asking for help and guidance. I told the lady that I felt I just had to spend time in silence, looking with my consciousness until I found exactly what was happening and where the demon was in her system. Meanwhile he was still full of bravado, laughing and insisting that I would never find him. Indeed, he was nowhere to be found in her aura or chakras or even physical body. I looked several times in all places. I asked the Guides the same questions, "is he inside her or within her energy system?" "*No*" was the answer! "Is he here, present, with us?" "*Yes*"! Well, I better keep looking then. The Guides will not always tell me where to look, as this is how they train me to work harder and learn new things.

I found him about two feet above her head, in the beam of energy entering her crown chakra, but actually outside of her energy system, where he thought we would not find him. He was glowing silver, but this was probably the energy coming into the lady which was illuminating him. I focused strongly on him to make a good connection. There was no anger or threat there, he just maintained his silence and stillness in denial that I had seen him. In fact, I checked with the Guides a couple of times that I was definitely looking at him and not deluding myself. As the connection became stronger he began to have a bit of a childish tantrum and began saying he didn't want to go, a good sign we were getting somewhere.

I asked the Guides could this one be turned back to the light and they said that he could. So I began to talk to him in encouraging and pleasant tones. The Guides told me what to say. A bit at a time I broke down the barrier and got the name Charlie for him. Once I got the name it seemed to get a little easier, he was being persuaded. Eventually he came out and the Guides took him to one side. I breathed a tentative sigh of relief while continuing to check all the aspects and make sure that he was absolutely out of her and could not jump back in. Once I had done this I looked into her system again and asked the Guides a series of questions to establish whether she was now clear of all forms of beings. The answer was no!

I knew we had him, and I knew the Guides had taken him out of her and yet I could only detect one demon in there before we started. I now had another one to deal with. Where had he come from? I focused in again and could see what had been going on, something I had never seen before. There had been two demons, but posing as one single being or personality. The chap I had removed, Charlie, was the lighter of the two, in fact he used to sing to the lady, "We're all going on a summer holiday," by Cliff Richard would you believe, enough to drive anyone mad. But now we had a very different presence. As soon as I had removed Charlie, the second demon had descended into the lady's heart chakra, a place where she carries a lot of energy. I asked how it felt now. "Much quieter", she said. I asked her could she feel things happening in her heart and she said she was burning in the centre of her chest. This was good confirmation that the second demon was where I had seen him and that the total energy change was due to the first part of the personality, namely Charlie, being removed.

After a little chat and explanations with the lady, I renewed my focus. This guy would not look at me. He sat firmly in her heart chakra with his back to me, unspeaking and covering his head with his hands, trying to be as invisible as possible. I spent about 20 minutes talking to him but I couldn't get him to co-operate or even move, so I asked the Guides could they go in and get him and they confirmed that they could do this. I spent a little more time on him and then called all the troops together and confirmed a set of instructions with them. I let the energy settle a moment and then sanctioned the Guides to go in. They removed him without too much trouble, although he expelled a burst of energy as he was being removed, which left a kind of burn mark in her chakra. It was a final act of deliberate defiance to defile her body, but it was nothing we could not clean up later. I spent quite some time making absolutely sure that he was well removed from her before saying anything.

Eventually I said, "I think he is out". The lady asked me had my Guides spoken to her, or was it the demon trying to trick her. I asked the Guides and they said yes, they had spoken to her and I asked her what they had said. She said a very gentle voice with great love had spoken to her which had said, don't be fright-ened, we are coming inside you to remove him. Then she experienced a swathe of golden light permeate her head.

After this there was one more item to deal with and this was psychic links which entered her rear heart chakra. I saw that these had been placed there in this life time and they were links of jealousy and I worked out that it was a female rela-tive. We soon found who it was. The lady was then put on the couch for some guided vibrational work, where the psychic links could be removed along with the burns from the heart chakra and some other blockages. This was intense work, taking around an hour and a half. She suffered sickness and headaches as energy patterns were dissolved and removed. I smelled vodka being released through the aura, and when I asked her where this fitted into her life, she told me that many years earlier, she used to drink a lot of vodka. In fact the headache I then realised was that of a hangover, as the locked in poisonous energy pattern was evaporat-ing from her body.

The Guides will continue to work on this lady for twenty nights to complete what we have started today. She needs some more work to rebuild the total integrity of her energy system, but the Guides say we cannot do any more work for at least four months. She needs to go through a natural process of balancing out from what we have already done, and gain more energy.

This lady had a multiplicity of problems caused by living beings within her energy system. Again, I have learned new things and had to work very hard at a mental and emotional level with my consciousness to find the answers amid the great trickery which has been afoot in this case.

## Summary

It is interesting to note that most of the practices I used in these cases have changed dramatically as time has passed and my abilities have developed. When I look back and see how I did things only a couple of years ago, it seemed such a struggle. Where sometimes it would take me a half hour to perceive what was happening in a chakra or aura, I would see it in a moment or two today and much more clearly than in the past.

Of course that doesn't mean it is easier than before, because the universe sends more difficult cases to solve. Quite simply, the universal consciousness will always send you what you are capable of doing and it will, not always, but mostly, push you to a point where you have to dig very deep to find the answers for your client. How else would any of us develop, if we were not pushed? The universal mind knows everything about you and knows what you can do and what you can't. It knows whether you want to be pushed or whether you are content to work at a steady level. Again, open yourself and ask for what you need and you shall receive.

I have said many times, in this work, one continually changes. The important point to note about this is not to hold on to a particular way of doing something because this is what brings in limitation. Always be open to change your ways, no matter how drastic that change seems to be. This is a lesson in letting go of fear. This is another reason always to use manuals as guidance only and not law. For what might be law to one person is not law to another and law in this sense, again, is only limitation to the intuitive worker.

It is the intuitive worker who will soar from their open mindedness, and the healer or therapist who works by the book, who will always be limited by those words of instruction, often fearing to be adventurous or fearing reprisals from their tutors or colleagues. If you are guided or find something which works for you, then use it. Spirit Guides cannot help those who are not open to receive them. You won't find them in the pages of a book; you will find them by relaxing your consciousness into your work.

## 10

"Jon, you were Outcast once. Why do you think that any of the gulls in your old time would listen to you now? You know the proverb, and it's true: *The gull sees farthest who flies highest*".

Jonathan Livingstone Seagull

WELL, JUST FOR THE PRESENT, THERE IT IS!

For those who were ready for it, I hope I have shared things which will help enrich your journey, but mainly shown you things to be aware of from a general understanding that there are many things which we cannot see, due to the limitations of our undeveloped faculties. Things which are ready to take every opportunity to avail themselves of our energy, either accidentally or deliberately and maliciously.

To those of you who are unsure or even alienated by my work, please let me bring you back to those immortal and important words of pleading, as addressed to that most blessed of birds, Jonathan Livingstone Seagull, from his friend and mentor Sullivan.

*"Those gulls where you came from are standing on the ground squawking and fighting amongst themselves. They're a thousand miles from heaven — and you say you want to show them heaven from where they stand! Jon, they can't see their own wingtips! Stay here. Help the new gulls here, the ones who are high enough to see what you have to tell them".*

Jonathan Livingstone Seagull

# AFTERWORD

Quite often, the alienated and disaffected are those who are *"standing on the ground squawking and fighting amongst themselves"*. In itself, this is not a bad thing, or anything to decry. It is all just as it is, at this moment in time. Every moment in time is temporary. It is merely a point on the evolutionary path at which one stands, and the pathway travels for many lifetimes. The realisations of this place in time, right at this moment, are all that matter to many people. They are not in a position to see a higher reality yet, for they have not evolved to a point where it can be seen. They are where they are. We are all where we are, and this we cannot change in an instant. When one has travelled from one particular *'heaven'* or place of realisation to another heaven, then you can, not only see the realisations where once you stood, but also appreciate the realisations of your higher heaven, your new present place. You know you have travelled, you know you have made evolutionary progress, for now you feast with new eyes upon the place you now inhabit, the place which once you could not perceive.

Not being able to see your *'wingtips'* is merely a place upon your journey. You won't see those wingtips until you have evolved. What Sullivan was saying was that Jon could not teach those others or *"show them heaven from where they stand,"* because they have not reached a point where they can see what he can see, or a place where they are ready to receive his wisdom. This is a very frustrating place to be from the teacher's view point. The teacher can see the possibilities for those *'birds on the ground,'* but until they can perceive at the same vibratory level as he, then they cannot understand the truths and realities of his place of observation.

Firstly, the teacher sees these wonderful beings and knows that they must walk their own path, through perhaps more than one lifetime, before they have been able to dissolve their fear of the unknown and embrace it. Dissolve their fear of holding on to their own perceptions as being the absolute truth. When we meet something which challenges our own truth, we recoil from it. We display anger as a defence mechanism or state that it is rubbish. This is a natural reaction to save us from having to work hard at perceiving the meaning and value in something. It is safer and much less work to stay where we are, *'standing on the ground,'* than to push back the barriers and constantly try to move forward.

Not only this, but sometimes, we *do* try hard to move forwards and are frustrated because we seem to stay where we are, still locked into the same old patterns. But the truth is, we will only evolve at the rate our own weights can be removed. The dross we carry from previous lives, the mental and emotional patterns which we need to change, essentially the often complex patterns we choose to incarnate with, in order to heal them within our present lifetime's experience. When, as a soul, we choose to project a personality structure into human form, or incarnate, we usually don't choose an easy path. We choose a challenge which will take us as far up the path to home as we can get in one lifetime. Sometimes this is a struggle. If you are reaching a Master vibration, then you will get Master type problems to solve. They are not easy, but the rewards are great when you get through. Therefore, as much as we may want to understand another's truth or point of perception, we cannot do this until we arrive at a point where our consciousness is operating on the same frequencies or wave length. At an intellectual level, we may be able to appreciate what is being said or taught, but it is not the intellect which gives us the understanding. It is the intuition, manifest as a higher state of consciousness. The intuition functions on a higher level and this must be in resonance with the ones who are teaching what we wish to understand. For the necessary knowledge will pass from Master to Pupil in an unspoken way, as an energy exchange, or unspoken attunement. The pupils who are ready will automatically receive via the Master, an energy imprint of the next stage of the higher realities.

The words in this book are my truth as I stand '*on the ground*' now, in this moment in time. They will always be my truth or realisation, because I have lived them and proved them to be true by my experiences. However, the truth is not static and it must continue to unfold into new realisations or none of us would evolve. When one has had repeated experiences that prove themselves to be true, then one has gathered experiential knowledge. This knowledge always remains truth at that stage of one's evolutionary process. When one moves on to a higher state, these truths will still remain valid, although things might be a little different now and things may be achieved by different means. This does not mean those earlier truths will not work for others. They will. They are a very necessary step on the way. However, the mind and consciousness must forge onwards in order to perceive higher realities. This is always hard work. It is far easier to stay where you are, in the safety of the cocoon of limitation. Again, we must not judge anyone for this. Some people are well aware of their limitations and consciously decide not to go further, at least for the present.

In my own evolution, I often reach a point of saturation, a point where the whole system, but mainly the mind cannot take any more new concepts; cannot do any more work at trying to understand who and what we are and how best to utilise the time in this incarnation, how best to conduct oneself to reach the ultimate goal; how best to help others and encourage them to help themselves. It is easy to repeat the realisations of others, as read in books, but to be at a point where one can live the higher realisations is a very difficult path, whilst trying to function in the material world.

I can only help those gulls who are '*high enough to see*'. This is not a criticism of anyone. It is a spiritual reality, which it is impossible, I repeat *impossible* to understand or see from a point where one is just starting out on one's spiritual aspiration. As one evolves, to a new '*heaven*', it then becomes possible to see both those on the path behind and those on the path in front, for now we have a point of perspective from which to see. Even though I can see those birds on the shore of their heaven ahead of me, I cannot understand or perceive their heaven because my consciousness is not yet operating on their wave length or vibration. But I can understand and appreciate those on the heavenly shore behind me because I have travelled that way.

Try to understand fear. Don't be afraid of it, just see it as another barrier to freedom, which we all must deal with at some level. Know fear and know when it is active within your being, holding you back from embracing freedom, which also means embracing new concepts. If you are not ready to work with new concepts, then don't close them out. Remain neutral but open minded. Say to yourself, "I can't grasp that yet! ... But I'll leave it where it is in case it becomes appropriate for me later". It is like buying a book that you know you may need in the future for reference, perhaps for a project you are thinking of undertaking. You buy the book now, but are not ready to see it's truth until you are truly ready.

A closed mind is held closed by fear. Learn to see it in your daily life and get to know it, so that when it rears its head, you can confront it, gently, acknowledging it with grace and a wary eye. Befriend it and every time it surfaces, know it a little more. It is by seeing it more often that one gets the opportunity to heal it.

I'm not sure, was it the Buddha who said "there are as many ways to God as there are people on the planet trying to get there?" Therefore, follow your own path, pick up anything from anyone which helps you, put aside anything which does not work for you right now. Don't struggle with noble tasks for the sake of work and be true to your own realisations, not somebody else's.

Today, things happen for me that don't make sense and I don't understand, but I have had to learn to accept them for I know them to be true. When working with the earth consciousness I often come across extremely harmful radiations which are causing serious problems within a home environment. When working out what to do about these, I sometimes receive a message which says "just ask". After confirming this message by several different methods, I do as I am bid. I say a little prayer and I ask for the problem energy to be resolved. Low and behold it always is. Now who or what is doing this? There can only be a higher consciousness at work which can take a powerful source of earth radiation and harmonise it within seconds at a mere request. *Ask and you shall be given.* This is an example of working at a higher heaven. At this level it doesn't make sense any longer in terms of the physical laws or the physical reality which most of us are used to experiencing. But through many, many examples, I have proved this to be true to my satisfaction. Therefore, I now have some different tools to work with, but the skill required to use them is Trust. This is something which is not possible to teach others, for they have to arrive at this point by their own labours and experiences. The old saying rears its head again which reminds us, 'the more we know, the more we realise we know very little'.

The essence of God is within every person. One does not go outside looking for God. God is within. All answers come from within, not from without. Spend a few moments each day in trying to rise above your daily consciousness and you will touch the place where answers are found.

Finally, let me invoke some simplicity and direct you to take just three things from this book.

**1.** Be aware of what psychic attack is. Know the symptoms.

**2.** Put the names of two people in your diary who can rescue you in an emergency.

**3.** Don't believe anything. Don't disbelieve anything. Be open to everything, no matter how far-out, ridiculous or bizarre it may seem. Yes, there are crazy people out there, but there are also many people who hold truths which are stranger than fiction. Follow your intuition and develop knowledge and truth from your own experiences. Then you will truly know; then you will truly evolve.

All I can now do, is infuse this work with as much love as I can focus upon it, so that you, the reader may benefit from it at whatever level it will help you most, from the perspective of your present *Heaven*.

*Peace be with you.*

Jesus of Nazareth

# BIBLIOGRAPHY

**Dr. Edmond Bordeaux Szekely,** *The Essene Gospel of Peace, Book One.*
Translated from ancient Aramaic texts.

**C.W. Leadbeater,** *The Chakras.* ISBN 0-835-604-22-5

**Dr. Lori M. Poe,** *Mystic Wisdom for Richer Living.*
Finbarr International, Folkestone, Kent CT20 2QQ, England.
Finbarr Book No. 160.

**Dion Fortune,** *Psychic Self Defence.*
Society of Inner Light, 38 Steeles Road, London, NW3 4RG.
ISBN 0-850-307-66-X

**Richard Bach,** *Jonathan Livingstone Seagull.*
Harper Collins Publishers, 77-85 Fulham Palace Road, London, W6 8JB.
ISBN 0-330-236-47-4

**Dr Gabriel Cousens** MD MD(H) *Spiritual Nutrition and the Rainbow Diet.*
Tree of Life Rejuvenation Center, Patagonia, Arizona, AZ 85624, USA.
ISBN 0-961-587-52-0

**Frank Arjava Petter,** *Reiki, The Legacy of Dr. Usui.*
Lotus Light/Shangri-La, Box 325, Twin Lakes, WI 53181, USA.
ISBN 0-914-955-56-X

# ADDITIONAL READING

Also by Dr. Edmond Bordeaux Szekely there are many, many other works including translations of original manuscripts as well as publications on the Essenes and their biogenic way of life as taught by Jesus.
Highly recommended.

Please contact Norma (Mrs. Edmond) Bordeaux Szekely at the International Biogenic Society. I.B.S. Internacional, P.O Box 849, Nelson, British Columbia, Canada V1L 6A5.

For those interested in Jesus and the Essene way of life, other publications and information can be obtained from:

**The Essene Church of Christ**, P.O. Box 516, Elmira, Oregon 97437, USA. Telephone: (Int. code) 541 895 2190.

*The Sevenfold Peace* by Dr. Gabriel Cousens MD MD(H).
ISBN 0-915-811-28-6

*Reiki Fire* by Frank Arjava Petter.
ISBN 0-914-955-50-0

*The Original Reiki Handbook of Dr. Mikao Usui*
Presented by Frank Arjava Petter.
ISBN 0-914-955-57-8

*Pranic Healing* by Master Choa Kok Sui.
ISBN 0-877-287-13-9

*Wheels of Light* by Rosalyn L. Bruyere.
ISBN 0-671-796-24-0

*Vibrational Medicine* by Richard Gerber MD.
ISBN 0-939-680-46-7

# CONTACT INFORMATION

### David Ashworth
Original Channel of The Emerald Heart Light and Wheel of Light
Spiritual Teaching, Spiritual Evolution, Geomancy

Telephone Consultations:  +44 (0) 161-772 0207
Website: www.davidashworth.com    Email: dave@davidashworth.co.uk


### Denise McAvoy Dip. Nat. Nut.
Diploma in Natural Nutrition
♥ Emerald Heart Practitioner and Mentor
Essence Therapist and Dowsing Healer
Workshops available on Self-development, Dowsing and Essences

Telephone Consultations:  +44 (0) 161-772 0207
Website: www.denisemcavoy.com    Email: denisemcavoy1@aol.com


### Emerald Heart School
David Ashworth is the original channel of The Emerald Heart Light.
The Emerald Heart Light is a light which unlocks your Spiritual Evolution.
The Emerald Heart School teaches advanced spiritual concepts to take your work beyond Healing and into the realms of Spiritual Evolution.
Joint Principals: Denise McAvoy and David Ashworth

Telephone:  +44 (0) 161-772 0207
Website: www.emerald-heart.co.uk    Email: dave@emerald-heart.co.uk


### Anne Betts RGN (Rtd.)
♥ Emerald Heart Practitioner and Mentor
NLP Master Practitioner and Trainer
HK Practitioner, Guided Vibrational Healing, (Reiki Master)

Telephone: 01274 879988          Cell Phone: 07717 223915
                                 Email: anne.betts@onetel.net


### The Devic Essences
A co-creation of David Ashworth and the Devas in nature, these energy signatures cover many aspects of healing and transformation. Categories include; Physical, Mental, Emotional, Spiritual, Auras and Chakras. Also Geomantic Essences which help bring you closer to the consciousness of Nature Spirits for communication and Earth Healing.

Website: www.davidashworth.com


### Wheel of Light Essences
Containing channelled frequencies of extremely high Spiritual Light these essences are powerful aids to Spiritual Evolution.

Website: www.davidashworth,.com

# USEFUL INFORMATION

**BAFEP: British Association of Flower Essence Producers**
Where to find United Kingdom Essence Producers.
Website: www.BAFEP.com          Email: silvercordessences@compuserve.com

**BFVEA: The British Flower and Vibrational Essences Association**
This organisation can help you to locate a flower remedy practitioner.
Tel: 0207 267 4106 / 02920 256554
Website: www.bfvea.com          Email: info@bfvea.com

**Dr. Tim Duerden**
University course leader in Complementary Medicine (BSc).
Dr Tim Duerden also leads workshops and courses in natural philosophy and
meditation. His illustration of The Subtle Bodies in the colour section plus
other illustrations and useful information can be viewed at his website.
Website: www.openmeditation.com     Email: _tim@openmeditation.com_

**Nick Clarke** – Psychic Artist. Commissions undertaken.
Tel: (UK) +44 (0) 1254 396345          Email: njcengage@aol.com

**Pyramids of Light**
The Pyramids of Light are very powerful energy tools made by Pauline Knight.
Tollbar Cottage, 240 Wakefield Road, Stalybridge, Cheshire SK15 3BY.
Telephone: +44 (0) 161 303 7020

**Dinah Arnette** – Author of *Never Alone*.
For a copy of Dinah's book or any feedback to do with the Entity Photo
in the colour section of this book, contact Dinah:
Website: www.DMariepress.com     Email: darnette@aol.com

**Ron Scolastico**
Spiritual Readings in the USA
Telephone: 001 818 224 4488
Website: www.ronscolastico.com     Email: rs@ronscolastico.com

**Gabriel Cousens** MD MD(H)
Author of *Spiritual Nutrition and the Rainbow Diet*.
Tree of Life Rejuvenation Center, P.O. Box 778, Patagonia, AZ 85624, USA.
Tel: (int. code 001) 520 394-2520
Website: www.treeoflife.nu          Email: healing@treeoflife.nu

**British Society of Dowsers**
The BSD has many professional practitioners in many different esoteric fields concerned
with Water Finding, Subtle Energy Work, Geomancy, Geopathic Stress and Healing.
Telephone: +44 (0) 1684 576969
Website: www.britishdowsers.org     Email: info@britishdowsers.org

**Health Kinesiology**
HK is a very powerful way of accessing the many levels of consciousness within the body
for healing and removing blockages to one's evolution.
Website: www.hk4health.com

# THE EMERALD HEART

Dave is the Original Channel of The Emerald Heart Light.

The Emerald Heart Light is a frequency of extremely high Spiritual Light which has been brought to Earth to help with the evolution of humanity and the healing of the planet.

The Emerald Heart is seeded into Earth through Dave by Spirit Guides.

Every aspect of The Emerald Heart is governed by The Guides through The Laws of The Emerald Heart which have been given to teach us how to use this most amazing Light to uplift ourselves, others and the Earth itself.

## Developing The Emerald Heart

Over a period of around three years Dave carried out many experiments with healers, therapists and clients around the world following instructions from The Guides in how to use The Emerald Heart Light. Through this experimentation he discovered the incredible but subtle power of The Emerald Heart to transform lives as he connected it remotely into people as far away as America and Australia. The continued teaching from The Guides eventually lead to a new paradigm in distant healing. Dave's work is now all performed at a distance.

## Training as an Emerald Heart Practitioner

In January 2005, The Guides began to teach Dave the Second Phase of developing The Emerald Heart which is 'Seeding the Light to Others'. They began to teach him new concepts of bringing Light into practitioners so that they can use it to help uplift their own clients too. As a natural consequence of this connection, The Guides and the Light will also begin to unfold, develop and evolve the practitioner as they work to uplift their clients.

When connected to the Emerald Heart in this way, it will begin to:

- ♥ Transform everything in your life.

- ♥ Bring you True Evolution.

- ♥ Bring greater results with your clients.

- ♥ Transform the way you work.

- ♥ Open you into a completely new level of perfection.

- ♥ Continually push your evolution.

When you have a connection to The Emerald Heart Light, you also have access to the same Guides who work through Dave. As you learn to allow them to connect with you, they will further enhance your work by bringing guidance and information based on what you can currently achieve, but always pushing you to achieve more.

## Two Paths into The Emerald Heart

There are two paths by which you can access The Emerald Heart for yourself.

- ♥ You can access it for your own Spiritual Development and Evolution through working with Dave or one of the Emerald Heart Practitioners.

- ♥ It is also here for those of you who are already Healers or Lightworkers who are ready for the challenges of moving into higher light. Working with The Emerald Heart will then allow you to accomplish greater results with your clients.

The Emerald Heart is more than just a Light for Evolution, it is an organisation of many parts serving the evolution of Humanity, the Animals and the Earth.

For more information go to

**www.emerald-heart.co.uk**

# THE WHEEL OF LIGHT

Dave is the Original Channel of The Wheel of Light.

## The Wheel of Light

Through a development period of two years the Wheel of Light reached a point where it was activated fully in May 2004. The Wheel of Light is a unique transmission of new evolutionary energies entering the Earth realm. It is a calling together of the old soul groups who are now ready for the next stage of evolution.

## The Guides Speak

"The children of the Lord who will benefit from this movement of energy we call The Wheel of Light will 'absolutely know' it is part of their pathway. If they are ready, if their evolution is progressing to a point where their vibration is resonating with these energies, there will be no question in their minds. Their consciousness will speak to them and they will just 'know' that they have to be connected to this source. All truth comes through the heart and those with the heart open and ready to see at this level, will feel the truth within them speak. They will feel the truth of The Wheel of Light."

"The Wheel of Light is a gateway which is being opened into Earth, and it's light will call out to the children who are meant to pass through it's doors. Many lessons will unfold for each individual through the connection. One of these lessons will be trust."

"Lack of trust is a great limiting factor in the evolution of human beings. There is great fear of trusting that you are protected; trusting that you are guided; trusting in many things which are of the nature of creation and the process of moving forwards. Trust is learning to open your heart. Without the opening of the heart, evolution cannot take place. Therefore, those who are fearful will not trust The Wheel of Light. Quite simply, this is because their evolution has not reached a point where they can step into the unknown in trust. Those whose evolution is approaching the highest vibrations of spirituality on Earth at this time will hear the call."

"The doors will be opened, but only those who can perceive the pathway will enter. Throughout history there have been those who could see and understand the hidden meanings in the messages of the teachers, and there have been those who just could not understand and would continue to question. The time is now with us where many are opening and understanding."

"If The Wheel of Light calls to you, then you will feel it in your heart. If you feel the call in your heart, then you will not question, you will have no fear of trusting in the process, you will just know."

## Further Information

To read the history of the development of The Wheel of Light and all the current available information, see the website:

www.wheel-of-light.com

# ABOUT THE AUTHOR

Many people know of Dave and his work through television and radio appearances and his book *Dancing with the Devil as You Channel in the Light*. Many others know him by reputation through his highly successful practise or his talks, workshops and lectures on many aspects of Healing and Light Work. Others know him from personal experience of the life-changing energies he channels through his unique gifts and talents.

Yet, Dave is also a low profile person, a very private person, beavering away with the Light and information he receives, learning how to use it, writing about it and sharing his knowledge so that others can benefit from his insights by being uplifted into the knowledge of how to use Spiritual Light successfully for their own evolution.

By working with his Guides, Dave has brought a continuous stream of new concepts to the world of Light Work. Some of the doors which have been opened through Dave, such as The Wheel of Light, are so advanced that there are not many people who are yet ready to connect at this level, but the important thing to note is that the Universe is preparing the space for those who are opening quickly.

## Gifts and Talents

Dave is a Mystic. A Mystic is someone who can, not only see into deep consciousness, but also bring about change to that consciousness through the use of the dynamic forces of Heaven and Earth. The Guides and energies Dave works with give him the ability to repair Energy Systems, bring about extremely deep Earth Healing and facilitate the evolution of the consciousness of people.

Let's now try to put this into perspective. There are Subtle Energy Systems and there is Consciousness. They are both very different.

## Subtle Energy Systems

The Subtle Energy Systems of people are the aura and the chakra system. The Subtle Energy Systems of the Earth are the various forms of energy grids such as the Hartmann Net, the Curry Grid and the flowing energies that we call Ley Energies or Ley Lines. All of these are Subtle Energy Systems, not to be confused with consciousness.

## Consciousness

The ability to see into consciousness is being able to go beyond Energy Systems. For example when one looks into the consciousness of a chakra, you go beyond the colours and shapes, and beyond the bits and pieces of detritus one often sees as heavy energy which can form blockages. When you look into the consciousness, you can see into thousands of different realms or levels of information, going ever deeper until you reach the soul.

When you can go beyond Energy and into Consciousness, you can find the answers from the highest of sources to help bring about healing and evolution to Humanity and the Earth. Dave has the ability to touch many places between the gates of Heaven and the Core of the Earth.

Dave's work today with The Emerald Heart is primarily about unlocking the evolutionary potential and the hidden gifts and talents of Healers and Lightworkers, enabling them to move to ever higher levels of perfection in their work with their own students and clients.

www.davidashworth.com        www.emerald-heart.co.uk